Telling Political Lives

LEXINGTON STUDIES IN POLITICAL COMMUNICATION

Series Editor: Robert E. Denton Jr., Virginia Tech

This series encourages focused work examining the role and function of communication in the realm of politics including campaigns and elections, media, and political institutions.

TITLES IN SERIES:

Governing Codes: Gender, Metaphor, and Political Identity,
By Karrin Vasby Anderson and Kristina Horn Sheeler

Paving the Way for Madam President, By Nichola D. Gutgold

Maryland Politics and Political Communication, 1950-2005,
By Theodore F. Sheckels

Images, Issues, and Attacks: Television Advertising by Incumbents and Challengers in Presidential Elections, By E. D. Dover

Democracy as Discussion: Civic Education and the American Forum Movement, By William Keith

Nuclear Legacies: Communication, Controversy, and the U. S. Nuclear Weapons Complex, Edited by Bryan C. Taylor, William J. Kinsella, Stephen P. Depoe, Maribeth S. Metzler

Picturing China in the American Press: The Visual Portrayal of Sino-American Relations in Time *Magazine, 1949–1973,* By David D. Perlmutter

Post-9/11 American Presidential Rhetoric: A Study of Protofascist Discourse, By Colleen Elizabeth Kelley

Making a Difference: A Comparative View of the Role of the Internet in Election Politics, Edited by Stephen Ward, Diana Owen, Richard Davis, and David Taras

Seen and Heard: The Women of Television News, By Nichola D. Gutgold

Telling Political Lives

The Rhetorical Autobiographies of Women Leaders in the United States

EDITED BY BRENDA DEVORE MARSHALL AND
MOLLY A. MAYHEAD

LEXINGTON BOOKS

A division of
ROWMAN & LITTLEFIELD PUBLISHERS, INC.
Lanham • Boulder • New York • Toronto • Plymouth, UK

LEXINGTON BOOKS

A division of Rowman & Littlefield Publishers, Inc.
A wholly owned subsidary of The Rowman & Littlefield Publishing Group, Inc.
4501 Forbes Boulevard, Suite 200
Lanham, MD 20706

Estover Road
Plymouth PL6 7PY
United Kingdom

British Library Cataloguing in Publication Information Available

Library of Congress Cataloging-in-Publication Data

Telling political lives : the rhetorical autobiographies of women leaders in the United
States / edited by Brenda DeVore Marshall and Molly A. Mayhead.
    p. cm. — (Lexington studies in political communication)
Includes bibliographical references and index.
ISBN-13: 978-0-7391-1947-1 (cloth : alk. paper)
ISBN-10: 0-7391-1947-8 (cloth : alk. paper)
ISBN-13: 978-0-7391-1948-8 (pbk. : alk. paper)
ISBN-10: 0-7391-1948-6 (pbk. : alk. paper)
1. Women politicians—United States—Biography. 2. Autobiography—Women
authors. I. Marshall, Brenda DeVore, 1951– II. Mayhead, Molly A., 1961–
HQ1391.U5T45 2008
973.92092'2—dc22

                                                                2008011175

Printed in the United States of America

♾™ The paper used in this publication meets the minimum requirements of American
National Standard for Information Sciences—Permanence of Paper for Printed Library
Materials, ANSI/NISO Z39.48–1992.

Dedicated to our husbands

Tyrone Marshall
Ed Dover

and to the memory of Alberta Bowyer DeVore
and Glenda DeVore Lakey

Contents

Foreword

On the opening day of the 110th Congress, excitement and hope filled the chamber as incoming freshmen and members were joined by their young children on the floor of the House of Representatives.

Ascending to the Speaker's Chair to take the Oath of Office was a mother of five and grandmother of six, a distinguished legislator with the vision to launch a leadership campaign that would ultimately propel her to the third highest political office in the United States. It is a position to which only fifty-one men in American history have been elected.

"This is an historic moment, for Congress, and for the women of this country. It is a moment for which we have waited more than 200 years," Nancy Pelosi of California declared to a roaring ovation in the filled House chamber. "For our daughters and granddaughters, today we have broken the marble ceiling. To our daughters and our granddaughters, the sky is the limit."

As she invited all the girls and boys in the chamber, including her own grandchildren, to join her up at the Speaker's chair and hold the gavel, Pelosi proclaimed this Congress to be for all of America's children. Her mission was clear: providing a new direction for America and affording the next generation of Americans standing beside her the opportunity and means to create a brighter future for our nation and the world.

The sky is indeed the limit.

In my own lifetime, American women have moved from behind the scenes to the forefront of political power. At each step along the way, we have pursued interests that reflect where we are in life's journey.

I got my start in politics quite literally by accident: my young son tumbled from a public swing set onto the concrete pavement below, hurting his head. It was the 1970s, when playground safety was not even an afterthought of the men who served on public boards and dominated local elective offices. As the primary caretakers of the era, other mothers agreed that a softer surface below the play equipment made more sense. When the local Park Board wasn't responsive to our concerns, I ran for office myself, and we changed the hardtop to bark dust.

That "accident" led to a series of opportunities to serve in continually higher offices, next as a West Linn City Councilor, an Oregon State Representative, a Clackamas County Commissioner and Chair, and ultimately, as a member of Congress from Oregon's 5th district. In each office, I was the first woman to be given the chance to serve my community in that position.

Representing the part of our state that marks the end of the Oregon Trail has always held special meaning for me. The American pioneers set out on an arduous journey that spanned a continent in hopes of establishing a new order in America's Eden. Each man, woman, and child helped to blaze the trail, leading the way for others to follow.

In three decades of public life, I've been fortunate to play a small part in helping other women go where none had gone before—and cleared a few paths of my own along the way. I joined Margaret Carter, Oregon's first African American State Representative, to help our colleague Vera Katz wage a winning campaign to become the first woman Speaker of the Oregon House. As the first woman Clackamas County Commissioner, I was proud to support the election of Oregon's first woman Governor, Barbara Roberts. In the halls of Congress, I've worked under the leadership of America's first woman Speaker, Nancy Pelosi, second in the line of succession to the Presidency. And I've lent a hand to Senator Hillary Clinton's 2008 presidential campaign in her quest of the ultimate political "first" for an American woman.

Like the pioneers, women in politics can look back with pride in how far we've come and then look forward to new territory we have yet to explore.

Telling Political Lives: The Rhetorical Autobiographies of Women Leaders in the United States examines how our personal stories become part of our politics and how political decisions influence our personal lives by analyzing the autobiographical writings of Barbara Jordan, Patricia Schroeder, Geraldine Ferraro, Elizabeth Dole, Wilma Mankiller, Hillary Rodham Clinton, Madeleine Albright, and Christine Todd Whitman. The analysis illustrates that through their personal narratives female political leaders may serve as mentors to inspire, instruct, and empower other women to follow in their footsteps.

It is with great pleasure that I commend to you this latest work of twenty-first-century pioneers in the field of women's political rhetoric, editors and authors Brenda DeVore Marshall of Linfield College, Molly A. Mayhead of Western Oregon University, and their contributors.

Congresswoman Darlene Hooley
Oregon's Fifth District
December 2007

Acknowledgments

We extend our gratitude and debt to the women whose personal stories we examine in the following pages. We thank them for making a difference through their political participation and leadership. Their efforts and accomplishments have reframed the twenty-first century political landscape in the United States and serve as inspiration for those who follow in their footsteps.

Brenda and Molly offer their appreciation to Catherine Dobris, Nichola Gutgold, Emily Plec, Karrin Vasby Anderson, C. Brant Short, and Kristina Horn Sheeler for their contributions to this volume. Their scholarship and astute observations have made this project possible.

Collectively, we thank our students for challenging and inspiring us to continue learning through our teaching and scholarship.

Dialogues with our colleagues, past and present, often find their way into our thinking and writing without our explicit awareness. So, to those of you who have joined our conversations, thank you. We also are grateful for the support of those colleagues with whom we teach and interact on a daily basis.

We extend special appreciation to our families. Thank you for your patience, understanding, and encouragement.

We thank Robert Denton, series editor, for his belief in and advocacy on behalf of this project and for his continued dedication to the scholarship of women's political rhetoric. Our appreciation also goes to Joseph Parry, Paula Smith-Vanderslice, Melissa Wilks, and the staff at Lexington for their contributions to this book. We also thank Congresswoman Darlene Hooley, and her Chief of Staff, Joan Mooney Evans, for providing us with a Foreword that captures the spirit and tone of this volume.

Finally, Molly and Brenda acknowledge that because each contributes equally to their collaborative endeavors, they elect to alternate the order of their names in their co-authored and co-edited publications.

Introduction

During the latter part of the twentieth century and the first decade of the twenty-first, the images of "women as politicians" increasingly have found their place in the iconic portrait albums of the U.S. political landscape. These revised snapshot collections emerge from the fact that in the last forty to fifty years citizens of the United States have witnessed women's increased participation in politics, both formally in elected positions and informally in a variety of public roles. The figures in our political vision even include a female Speaker of the House, positioning, for the first time in the history of the country, a woman second in the line of succession to the presidency. And, early posturing for the 2008 presidential election has inserted an image of a viable female presidential candidate into our collective consciousness.

Publishers' best-seller lists during this same era indicate a proliferation in autobiographical writing by those in the public arena, including women and minorities. Clearly, "more women than ever before have written and are writing their life studies" (Jelinek, *Tradition* 185). Estelle Jelinek, writing in 1986, argues that this phenomenon resulted from a "decade [the 1970s] of feminist activism and consciousness raising, which gave legitimacy and affirmation to women's lives" (185). She contends that women "autobiographers no longer apologize for writing about themselves; if anything it has become commonplace to write an autobiography" (185). This trend continues today. It is not surprising, then, that over the past several decades many key women political leaders, within the United States and around the globe, have crafted their life stories. Like the woman suffragists of the nineteenth century, these women approach "the art of autobiography with their public identities well crafted and their public voices tuned closely to a particular pitch of the cultures they [seek] to influence" (Gordon 111).

Telling Political Lives: The Rhetorical Autobiographies of Women Leaders in the United States and its companion volume, *Telling Political Lives II: The Rhetorical Autobiographies of International Women Leaders*, investigate the autobiographical writings of fourteen of these female leaders. The analysis of each work focuses on the autobiographical text as political discourse and therefore, as an appropriate site for the rhetorical construction of a personal and civic self situated within local, national, and/or international political communities. By writing their autobiographies, these female leaders further legitimize their roles in the public sphere, where, even in the first decade of the twenty-first century, the validity of their participation may be contested. In so doing, they empower others to join them in public engagement and dialogue. Specifically, *Telling Political Lives: The Rhetorical Autobiographies of Women Leaders in the United States* examines the following issues: the intersection between the "politicization of the private and the personalization of the public" (S. Smith, "Autobiographical" 186) evident in the women's narratives; the description of U.S. politics the women provide in their writings; the ways in which the women's personal stories craft arguments about their political ideologies; the strategies these women leaders employ in navigating the gendered double-binds of politics; and, the manner in which the women's discourse serves to encourage, instruct, and empower future women leaders.

This volume explores the autobiographical writings of Barbara Jordan, Patricia Schroeder, Geraldine Ferraro, Elizabeth Dole, Wilma Mankiller, Hillary Rodham Clinton, Madeleine Albright, and Christine Todd Whitman. The difficult decision about whose texts should be incorporated and, by virtue of that inclusion, whose should be excluded in a volume such as this inevitably calls for some justification. These eight women represent the diversity that permeates the cultural backgrounds, life adventures, and ideologies women bring to the political table. From differences in race, class, and geographic location, to variations in personal and family experiences, religious beliefs, and political ideology, these women illustrate many of the divergent standpoints from which women craft their lives in the United States. While each may have attained a version of "the privileged life" at the time they penned their life stories, most did not enter the world from that vantage point. Rather, in her own way, each of these women exemplifies the existence of a feminist American Dream. In addition, these women achieved notable "firsts" in American history. Barbara Jordan was the first African American female elected to public office in Texas (Holmes vii) and the first to deliver a keynote address at a Democratic national convention. Patricia Schroeder became the first woman from Colorado elected to the U.S. House as well as the first woman to serve on the House Armed Services Committee. Geraldine Ferraro made history as the first female to run for the vice presidency on a major party ticket. Serving in President Reagan's Cabinet, Elizabeth Dole became the first female Secretary of Transportation and, in that position, the first woman to serve as the departmental head of a branch of the military, the U.S. Coast Guard. Wilma Mankiller was the first woman principal chief of the Cherokee Nation of Oklahoma and the first woman in modern history to lead a major Native American tribe. When she was elected to the U.S. Senate from the state of New York, Hillary Rodham Clinton became the first First Lady of the United States elected to public office. Madeleine Albright, Secretary of State in the Clinton administration, was the first woman in the country to hold this position of power. And, Christine Todd Whitman served as the first female governor of New Jersey. As these brief snapshots indicate and as the discussions in the following chapters will verify, the contributions these women have made to political dialogue and change in the United States merit their inclusion in this analysis.

The relevance of this investigation lies in the appeal of autobiographies, especially those of notable individuals, to a large audience and to the potential of writers to influence their readers through those texts. "People are interested in other people, in the fortunes of the individual" (Tuchman 134). As Martine Brownley and Allison Kimmich suggest, "reading an autobiography is an act of voyeurism: it allows us to look in on the high and low points of another person's life. At the same time," they continue, "reading an autobiography is an act of self-discovery. Learning how others live, think, and feel can teach us about ourselves" (xi). According to Doris Sommer, autobiography constitutes "a medium of resistance and counter discourse" (111) which "not only challenges, but often subverts the dominant discourse" (Loftus 18). Because political or activist autobiographies, in particular, often "give voice to oppositional or counterhegemonic ways of knowing that repeatedly invite readers to challenge their own assumptions and level of comfort with the status quo" (Perkins xii), these works introduce readers to what Henry Giroux terms a "language of empowerment" (qtd. in Perkins xii). Thus, the self-discovery and sense of agency emerging from the reading of these autobiographies potentially leads readers to identify with the writer and to imagine themselves following in her footsteps.

Chapter One, "Women's Autobiography as Political Discourse," provides an overview of the rhetorical nature of autobiography and its implications for political dialogue. While the discussion necessarily includes a brief examination of the characteristics of autobiography, it does not contribute intentionally to the canonical debates about the general criteria of the autobiographical genre(s). Rather, Jelinek's assertions that "each autobiography . . . is unique and defies a formal definition that subsumes all autobiography" and that the classification includes the "work each autobiographer writes with the intention of its being her life story—whatever form, content, or style it takes" (*Tradition* xii) ground our understanding of this literary mode. Thus, acceptance of pluralistic approaches to writing one's life story creates a natural foundation for the works in this collection. Likewise, multiple methodologies and perspectives frame the rhetorical analyses of the narratives.

Brenda DeVore Marshall explores the political discourse of Barbara Jordan's autobiography in Chapter Two, "Getting from There to Here." Marshall suggests that Jordan's work mirrors issues, themes, and stylistic choices found in African American orality. Jordan's understanding of the power of public discourse, her outstanding talents as an orator, and her ability to integrate her knowledge and skills with political reality allowed her to challenge both racial and gender stereotypes. Written with fellow Texan Shelby Hearon, the book reads as a continuous dialogue between the two, providing insights into how Jordan crafted a life that took her from a humble upbringing in the Lone Star state to the halls of power in Washington, D.C.

In Chapter Three, Molly A. Mayhead and Brenda DeVore Marshall examine two of Patricia Schroeder's political autobiographies, *24 Years of House-*

work . . . and the Place Is Still a Mess and *Champion of the Great American Family*. The authors note the distinct link between Schroeder's personal experiences and her political advocacy. Schroeder observes that her male professors, and later her male congressional colleagues, paid little attention to, and cared even less about, issues and problems facing average Americans, particularly women. Throughout her life, Schroeder both recognized and challenged gendered barriers in education, health care, and politics, and her autobiographical works provide ample examples demonstrating the tenacity with which she worked to eliminate inequality.

Catherine Dobris' essay, "The 'Feisty' Feminist from Queens," provides an analysis of Geraldine Ferraro's two autobiographical works, both written several years after the senator's historic candidacy for vice president. According to Dobris, Ferraro's two works demonstrate that she recognized the significance of gendered roles in politics and enjoyed great success in challenging them. In addition, Dobris points out the senator's ability to skillfully morph the public and private spheres, most notably in Ferraro's discussion of abortion rights, and in her ability to have a family life and simultaneously run for the nation's second-highest office. At the conclusion of Chapter Four, Dobris notes that Ferraro's refutation of traditional stereotypes served to liberate women from traditional gendered binds and made it possible for any woman to run for office.

In Chapter Five, "Just Like 'Azaleas in the Spring': Elizabeth Dole as a Daughter of the South," Nichola Gutgold details the uniquely "southern" communication style of Ms. Dole. Her autobiography, written in partnership with her husband, Bob Dole, reflects a penchant for amusing and insightful anecdotes from decades in politics. Dole recounts in her autobiography that her work ethic, her Southern roots, and her religious upbringing serve to underpin her success in politics. According to Gutgold, Dole uses these qualities to her advantage, cleverly blending personal stories with political ideology. All of these attributes contributed to her lengthy career in public life, whether it was chairing the Red Cross, winning a U.S. Senate seat, or even making a failed bid for the presidency.

Emily Plec demonstrates the complexities and significance of Native American rhetoric in her Chapter Six study of Chief Wilma Mankiller's autobiographical works. In this analysis, Plec posits that Mankiller's writings explicate the inextricable link between her life and the life of the Cherokee people. Specifically, using her life story of triumphs and tragedies, Mankiller provides a clear "vision of feminist ecology and Indian sovereignty" that allows her to articulate an activist agenda to improve humanity's relationships among people and with nature.

In Chapter Seven, Karrin Vasby Anderson examines Hillary Rodham Clinton's book, *Living History*. Anderson's investigation reveals Rodham Clinton's skilled blending of the personal and the political, noting in particular the "kitchen table issues" on which she focused. In looking at the work through a feminist lens, Anderson notes that Rodham Clinton used personal stories to present key themes of human welfare, especially that of women and children, demonstrating the blurred boundaries between human rights and women's rights. Perhaps more importantly, though, this autobiography interrogates the duality and paradox of women's political voices, challenging the artificial limits of the public and private spheres.

Chapter Eight explores Madeleine Albright's rich autobiography, *Madame Secretary*. In this analysis, C. Brant Short argues that Albright's story of her rise to serve as the first female Secretary of State reflects her savvy understanding of gender, status, and power in politics. Her autobiography presents her evolution from an immigrant outsider to a powerful political operative in the Clinton administration. Short demonstrates that, always mindful of the impact her advancing career would have on her family, Albright's narrative illustrates the inevitable intersection of public and private events. Her life story, he concludes, proffers a key "case study of gender, power, and collective memory."

Christine Todd Whitman's critique of the Republican Party focuses the discussion in Chapter Nine. In her analysis of Whitman's *It's My Party Too*, Kristina Horn Sheeler posits that this autobiography functions as an activist argument to change the party from within. Sheeler discovers that Whitman uses personal stories of her political experiences to illustrate her commitment to unity and consensus within the party. Further, Sheeler notes that Whitman emphasizes the importance of bringing more women into the political arena. Perhaps more than any other autobiography studied in this collection, *It's My Party Too* serves as rallying cry, encouragement, and inspiration for other women to become politically active.

In 1999, Martha Watson published *Lives of Their Own: Rhetorical Dimensions in Autobiographies of Women Activists*. Her book provides a rhetorical analysis of the autobiographies of nineteenth-century activists Frances Willard, Emma Goldman, Elizabeth Cady Stanton, Anna Howard Shaw, and Mary Church Terrell. Scholarship on women's autobiographies as rhetorical discourse remains an area worthy of further development. Watson concludes her book with "an invitation to [her] colleagues for further conversation" (119). *Telling Political Lives* presents an RSVP to that challenge.

Chapter One

Women's Autobiography as Political Discourse

Brenda DeVore Marshall and Molly A. Mayhead

I'm not as concerned with telling my personal life as I am with explaining what made me the public person that people know.

One other reason why I chose to write a political autobiography is that in the life of my generation, politics determined our lives. And in my personal life, the choices I was able to make depended entirely on the politics of the world in which I lived.

—Gerda Lerner

The telling of one's life story exemplifies the human desire to connect with others, provide insight into one's personal and public choices, give advice to those who may wish to follow in one's footsteps, contest others' representations of self, and leave a legacy validating one's existence. Concomitantly, autobiography "appeals to readers, who seek in it some 'truth' about another human life" (Watson 7). These functions, "like those used for coping with the multiple threads of identity involved in the autobiographical act, are many, and each is equally legitimate" (Bruss 12). While the proliferation of autobiographical narratives in the last fifty years may suggest the genre appeared rather recently, the impetus to create a personal narrative transcends generations and cultures. Although scholars disagree about the essential nature of the autobiography and thus, about its origins, James Olney argues that "wherever and on whatever grounds we may wish to assign priority and to whatever books we may be willing to grant the title the practice of autobiography has been with us for a long time, and it is with us in generous supply today" (*Autobiography* 7). Traditional Western definitions of autobiography, according to Georges Gusdorf, one of the earliest twentieth-century scholars of this literary form, have granted the purview of the genre primarily to the individual whose actions in the public sphere warranted societal respect and acclaim. Gusdorf declares that "the concern . . . to

7

turn back on one's own past, to recollect one's life in order to narrate it, is not at all universal. It asserts itself only in recent centuries and only on a small part of the map of the world" (29). Other scholars, such as Adetayo Alabi, disagree with Gusdorf, contending that one may speak one's life tale and that oral autobiographical texts have been "a long-established and popular communication medium" in African and other oral cultures for centuries (6). Despite early critical works about autobiography that identified only Western male writers, Mary Mason asserts that "though it is not generally recognized" in 1432 Margery Kempe wrote "what is actually the first full autobiography in English by anyone, male or female—*The Book of Margery Kempe*" (209). Mason describes Kempe as "a determined woman, in no way more than in this very determination to get her story told and to get it told right" (221).

Robert Sayre describes U.S. American autobiography as "the preeminent kind of American expression" ("Autobiography" 147) and "the special form in which some of the builders [of the country] have compiled their own records of their work . . . their own character" (149). He expands the discussion, noting that "autobiography has been a way for the builder to pass on his work and his lessons to later generations, to 'my posterity,' as Benjamin Franklin called it" (156). Historically relegated to the private sphere, most women did not receive recognition for their contributions to the building of the country. Consequently, they did not find themselves in a position to create public documents like autobiographies. They also understood that to do so would violate social norms in ways that ultimately would reinforce their literal and figurative roles as objects. For those women who challenged the male domain and achieved some degree of public notoriety, "to justify an unorthodox life by writing about it . . . [was] to *reinscribe* the original violation, to reviolate masculine turf" (N. Miller, *Subject* 52) and "to intensify [her] sense of transgression" (L. Anderson 85). Living in "a symbolic order that equate[d] the idea(l) of the author with a phallic pen transmitted from father to son," the very act of writing "place[d] the female writer in contradiction to the dominant definition of woman and [cast] her as the usurper of male prerogatives" (Stanton 13). Although women penned their life stories in various formats, these works seldom found a readership beyond the author, especially during her lifetime. In addition, critics "assumed that 'autobiographer' was a synonym for 'man'" and that women were not "'real' autobiographers, especially if [they] wrote life stories that diverged from the textual models established by their male counterparts" (Brownley and Kimmich xii). In spite of these constraints, many women "imagine[d] new ways to write autobiographies that reflect[ed] their experiences" (1). The literary conventions they employed and the texture of the work they created were "ultimately determined by the ways in which meaning can be signified in a particular discursive context, an (ideo)logical boundary that always already confines the speaking subject" (Stanton 9). Sidonie Smith notes that "there have always been women who cross the line between private and public utterance, unmasking their desire for the empowering self-interpretation of autobiography as they unmasked in their life the desire for publicity. Such women approach the autobiographical territory from their position as speakers at the margins of discourse" (*Poetics* 44). Without question, the pioneering women who "broke the rules" as they told their life stories paved the way for contemporary female autobiographers.

Taking a cue from Sidonie Smith, this study proceeds from a theoretical vantage point which suggests that "since all gesture and rhetoric is revealing of the subject, autobiography can be defined as any written or verbal communication that takes the speaking 'I' as the subject of the narrative, rendering the 'I' both subject and object" (*Poetics* 19). Today, therefore, if a woman possesses language or a symbol system, she can tell her own story.[1] She may write letters or poetry, keep a journal or diary, and she may re-read, revise, and disclose her story if and whenever she chooses. With the means to record her story through writing, dictation, or oral narrative she can share her story with a wider audience. As an Internet savvy rhetor in the twenty-first century, she can write a blog, launch a website, and reach countless audiences with her version of her personal narrative. And if she has visibility, marketability, and sustainability as a public persona, the interest of a suitable publisher will help catapult her story into the literate world of major booksellers.

The story the rhetor tells is *her* story. She tells it through her own lens of bias, prejudice, existential angst, and lived experience. She chooses to tell the truth, to embellish, or to lie in every line she creates. She tells the stories of others—the dead, the major and minor characters, and those who will write their own autobiographies juxtaposed with hers—stories that may or may not be read by her own readership. The author may designate heroes and villains in a logical narrative form that represents her version of reality so as to set the record "straight." Or, she may write her life the way she thought it was or the way she wishes it had been. In the end, her story is entered into the literary canon of nonfiction, a genre of self-styled "truth" and "reality," a form of history.

Elaborating on the relationship between history and autobiography, Olney contends that:

> If autobiography is in one sense history, then one can turn that around and say that history is also autobiography, and in a double sense: the makers of history, or those through whom history is made, could find in their autobiographies the destiny of their time achieved in action and speech; and the writers of history organize the events of which they write according to, and out of, their own private necessities and the state of their own selves. Historians impose, and quite properly, their own metaphors on the human past. History, as almost everyone acknowledges, is not an objective collection of facts but one historian's point of view on the facts: a point of view that, taken as a sum of what he has experienced and understands, reveals to us the historian. (Olney, *Metaphors* 36)

Martha Watson labels autobiography "personal history, a retrospective on a life that tells one of many possible stories about the individual's experiences" (7). Despite such arguments for understanding the inherent nature of personal perspective in historical scholarship as well as in other disciplines, literary scholars have long argued the essentially fictive nature of autobiography. Until recently critics regarded autobiography as "a kind of flawed biography at worst, and at best a historiographical document capable of capturing the essence of a nation or the spirit of an age" (S. Smith, *Poetics* 3). As Sidonie Smith and Julia Watson suggest, the autobiographer's "'experience' and the 'memory' through which it is routed are already interpreted phenomena and thus at least once removed from any pure facticity. After all," they continue, "autobiographers sometimes take liberty" with elementary facts and "memory is selective and untrustworthy" (Introduction 4–5). Smith posits that:

> Memory leaves only a trace of an earlier experience that we adjust into story; experience itself is mediated by the ways we describe and interpret it to others and ourselves; cultural tropes and metaphors which structure autobiographical narrative are themselves fictive; and narrative is driven by its own fictive conventions about beginnings, middles, and ends. Even more fundamentally, the language we use to "capture" memory and experience can never "fix" the "real" experience but only approximate it yielding up its own surplus of meaning or revealing its own artificial closures. (S. Smith, "Construing Truth" 34–35)

Consequently, while "it can be read as a history of the writing/speaking subject . . . life narrative cannot be reduced to or understood only as historical record" (Smith and Watson, *Reading* 10). Autobiography presents a truth "derive[d] not from the *facts* of a life truly remembered . . . but from the *meanings* the autobiographer assigns to and extracts from the representation of her life" (Smith and Watson, Introduction 5). It is "a form of symbolic memory, a confluence of culture and consciousness" (Braxton 208). In other words, the autobiographer "reads meaningful reality into her life and we read her reading. Because of the interpretive nature of any autobiographical act, then the distinction between autobiographical narrative and fiction remains elusive. Autobiography is always a story in time interweaving historical fact and fiction" (Smith and Watson, Introduction 5). Although "autobiographical narratives may contain 'facts,' they are not factual history about a particular time, person, or event. Rather they offer subjective 'truth' rather than 'fact'" (Smith and Watson, *Reading* 10). Jill Ker Conway describes this uneasy relationship between "truth" and "fiction" in the following passage:

> Autobiographical narratives are fictions, in the sense that the narrator imposes her or his order on the ebb and flow of experience and gives us a false sense of certainty and finality about causation in life. Yet they are not fictions but accounts of real lives, lived in a specific time and place, windows on the past, chances to enter and inhabit the real world of another person, chances to try on another identity and so broaden our own. (*Written* vii)

Adding another thread to the discussion, Leigh Gilmore suggests that the "distinction between self-representation as a political discourse and self-representation as an artistic practice is less important than their simultaneity of function in a particular culture and for specific audiences" (xiv). Autobiographical truth, then, becomes "an intersubjective exchange between narrator and reader aimed at producing a shared understanding of the meaning of a life" (Smith and Watson, *Reading* 13). Situated between history and literature, the genre of autobiography occupies the interstitial regions between public and private spheres. Such works, then, are well-suited to women's political discourse, which itself creates an in-between space where the politicization of the private and the personalization of the public coalesce (Mayhead and Marshall 12–18).

Smith and Watson maintain that "each specific autobiographical subject speaks not from a single location within the community but simultaneously, from multiple locations determined by gender, race, class, nationality, ethnicity, religion, and sexuality among other makers of identity" (Introduction 5). Furthermore, "from her specific location within a complex experiential history, [a woman] may quietly contest, critically adjust, or actively resist normative autobiographical meanings" (5). Written from these multifaceted standpoints, women's political autobiographies provide fertile ground for rhetorical analysis since they constitute "a dimension of public rhetorical discourse" (Watson 1). Margo Perkins extends this argument, suggesting that "as a site of both ideology and pedagogy, [autobiographical] literature is always inextricably bound to past or present political struggle. . . . It becomes important that we study [autobiographical] literature not just as a repository of culture, but also as a pedagogical resource in the work of *transforming* culture" (25). Arlyn Diamond claims that "the nuts and bolts of politics may not be what we look to autobiography for, but these are instructive texts for women working for change" (231). Women autobiographers may "simply recount how they have lived and what they feel life has taught them, how they pulled themselves out of the various beds of quicksand life scattered across their paths, with the tacit assumption that this knowledge will somehow be of use" to others (Ingram 142). Often, these political or "oratorical autobiographies focus more closely on the author's life work, particularly its importance and its meaning, than do other personal life stories" (Solomon 354). As former U.S. Secretary of State Madeleine Albright attests, these narratives "combine the personal with policy and describe not just what happened but also why and how events were influenced by human relationships" (xi). They also illustrate the "close relationship of the autobiographical genre to the political and historical moment" (Braxton 142). Therefore, autobiographical discourses contribute valuable insights into why and how political events take place, "provide evidence of the impact of the [author's] ideology on [her] life" (Watson 3), bring "readers to a fuller understanding of important social issues" (114), and "urge the readers' appreciation of [the author's] commitment" (3). In addition, Martha Solomon argues that autobiographies "serve as an inspirational model. . . . Within these works," she continues, "the author not only will recount the details of a life but also may suggest the roots of his or her commitment to the cause and the value of dedicating one's life to working for the advancement of the ideal" (355). Thus, they encourage and guide future women leaders into a life of public service.

Autobiographies are not simply stories; they are "rhetorical acts" (Smith and Watson, *Reading* 10). Solomon argues that these personal narratives produce two distinct rhetorical strategies: "the potential to depict the emergence of [the authors'] beliefs and commitments from experiences in the world and the ability to demonstrate the feasibility and desirability of enacting the tenets of their doctrine" (355). Additionally, she claims, "the nature of autobiographies as texts enhances the persuasive force of this depiction and enactment for the receptive reader" (355). To the extent that they ask readers to accept and become part of an author's experiences and viewpoint, autobiographies rhetorically "supplement and complement formal arguments" (Watson 79) through the inclusion of "sustained, personal examples of a particular ideology enacted in a real life" (Solomon 355). As Watson suggests, the "narrative structure [of the autobiography] permits the author to utilize what might be called refutation through demonstration" (79) through the presentation of her own life as a case study. Thus, the "narrator's experience is the primary kind of evidence asserted in autobiographical acts, the basis on which readers are invited to consider the narrator a uniquely qualified authority" (Smith and Watson, *Reading* 27). For public figures, the author's name alone "assures the reader of the authority of the writer to tell his or her story and promises that the public will find the story a credible disclosure" (Smith and Watson, *Reading* 27–28).

Smith and Watson note that "the impact of [the author's] autobiographical mediation depends on the narrative adjustments she makes as she pursues her narrative act, her audience, the models available to her, and her social context and historical circumstances" (Introduction 5). As Jeremy Popkin suggests, when autobiographers "decide to write for publication, [they] have to decide where the boundary between public and private should be. . . . [T]o publish one's life story is to make it public property and to invite scrutiny and criticism" ("Historians" 726). By choosing which events to emphasize, which to omit, and even which ones to include, the authors craft a particular worldview about their culture and about their politics. Thus, the women ask readers "to agree with them about the imperfections in the social order they [seek] to correct" (Watson 114). Smith argues that autobiographical manifestos "help us to hope by insisting on the possibility of self-conscious breakages in the old repetitions" ("Autobiographical" 210). Ronald Carpenter notes that "discourse approached, read, and accepted by most people as historical writing embodies certain elements that allow it to shape attitudes and actions" (1). Ultimately, he succinctly posits, "history can persuade" (1). Carpenter continues, arguing that historical accounts such as autobiographies acquire "the status of being among the most persuasive discourse to influence attitudes and actions for the future" (1). Specifically, "as readers we go to history . . . to autobiography . . . to learn more not about other people and the past but about ourselves and the present" (Olney, *Metaphors* 36–37). Popkin contradicts Olney, suggesting that in addition to learning more about ourselves, "the aspiration to know what other people are like and what they have experienced is itself important" ("Historians" 748). Thus, we "read history for its lessons about life" (Carpenter 1), hoping, according to Watson, "to find in the narrative guidelines for [our] own behaviors and beliefs" (7).

As discussed previously, like other mediums of political discourse, autobiographical narratives are "neither static nor uniform" (Smith and Watson, Introduction 5). Furthermore, given the diversity of women who pen their life stories, one cannot assume a single mold for all. Gilmore offers a perspective on this notion:

> For all the instability and incoherence in the category of "women," as well as the category of autobiography, both generate a remarkable negative capability: both categories hold together disparate and contradictory interpretations of identity and history and collect an irreconcilable variety of experience and representation under a single name. The names of "women" and "autobiography," then, come to represent diversity as a natural and stable identity. (xiv)

This discussion of the inherent pluralistic nature of the collective work labeled "women's autobiography" provides a theoretical perspective for this project. While recognizing the specificity of definition literary and cultural critics bring to terms such as autobiography, narrative, personal narrative, memoir, life story, and life writing, the authors in this volume use these terms interchangeably throughout the essays to describe the act of writing one's personal story without reference to definitive political or disciplinary ideologies.

Illustrating one aspect of this diversity, some of the women whose autobiographies provide the cases for analysis in this book act as the sole author of their narratives; others have collaborated with another writer to communicate the story of their lives. This is not a new phenomenon, nor is it limited to women autobiographers. According to Michiko Kakutani, a ghostwriter's job is to "communicate his [the subject's] emotions, his voice, his words" ("It Pays" 94). Albert Stone believes the successful collaborator must have "the ability to submerge himself in another's life without losing critical perspective on that life and personality" (*Autobiographical* 263). Whether the two or more authors physically pen the text together or the ghostwriter(s) work from taped interviews and written notes, in most cases the objective of the collaboration is to present a seamless, single-voiced telling of a life. As Chris Chase, ghostwriter for Betty Ford's autobiography suggests, "if you do your job well . . . they don't notice you" (qtd. in Kakutani, "It Pays" 94). This literary "rule" provides the approach in most of the works discussed in this volume. However, in some cases, the nature of the authorial relationship remains cloudy. As Emily Plec notes in her investigation of Wilma Mankiller's autobiography, "the dynamics of Mankiller and Wallis' coauthorship is unclear from the book itself." Further, in her examination of *Barbara Jordan: A Self-Portrait*, Brenda DeVore Marshall details Barbara Jordan and Shelby Hearon's deliberate inclusion of two distinct voices throughout the text. Despite an acknowledgement of the potential complexities coauthorship may foster in terms of the presentation of an authentic voice, the authors regard the collaborative autobiographies in this volume as genuine reflections of the subjects' lives and thoughts.

Writing about U.S. suffragists Abigail Scot Duniway and Elizabeth Cady Stanton, Ann Gordon remarks that "their own lives had, in real time, continually exhibited new possibilities emergent from nineteenth-century politics and female experience. Thus," she continues, "autobiography should reflect life by insisting that the categories be altered" (125). The women whose autobiographies provide the basis for discussion in the following chapters have contributed to the ongoing alteration of those typologies.

Notes

1. Catherine Dobris contributed both ideas and language to the discussion in this and the following paragraph.

Chapter Two

Getting from There to Here: Political Rhetoric and African American Orality in *Barbara Jordan: A Self-Portrait*

Brenda DeVore Marshall

Anyone who talks of Barbara Jordan starts with The Voice. Those great, deep, booming tones filled your soul like a Bach cantata thundering from a cathedral organ. If you were so lucky as to hear Jordan electrify a Democratic convention, you were struck by the same cliché: "That's what God must sound like."
—Sandy Grady (3B)

Barbara Charline Jordan, one of the most recognized political voices and admired women in the United States in the last decades of the twentieth century, enjoyed a career marked by distinctive accomplishments. She began her political journey as the first African American woman elected to the Texas Senate (1966) and the first to preside as Texas Governor for a Day (1972). Her election to the House of Representatives in 1972 sent the first African American woman from a Southern state to the U.S. Congress, where she became the first Black female to serve on the House Judiciary Committee. Her keynote address at the Democratic National Convention in 1976 and her commencement address at Harvard in 1977 also marked firsts for African American women (Burgchardt 217; Holmes xi–xii). Even in death she continued to break new ground, becoming the first African American to claim a final resting place in the Texas State Cemetery in Austin (Rogers 356; Ivins 17). Born poor, Black, and female in a state steeped in the realities of Jim Crow, Barbara Jordan "was raised at a time and in a place where basic rights of citizenship were routinely denied to African-Americans" (*Fresno* B4). Despite these seemingly insurmountable obstacles, Jordan believed in the American Dream and fought "peacefully, intelligently to secure and protect those rights for herself and her fellow Americans" (B4). Although "she sounded like the Lord God Almighty" (Ivins 17), people noticed more than the

15

voice. "Her implacable legal logic caught the attention of the entire nation" (17). As Jordan biographer Mary Beth Rogers argues:

> Barbara Jordan was the first African American *elected* official to become an American hero. She broke through previously impenetrable barriers to become an "inside" political player who was taken very seriously by the white politicians in power. What made her unique, however, was her "outside" following, a national audience of admirers who looked to her for guidance and inspiration. In late-twentieth-century America, the combination was a rarity—for either whites or blacks. (xi)

Jordan begins her autobiography, *Barbara Jordan: A Self-Portrait*, with the following epigraph:

> People always want you to be born where you are. They want you to have leaped from the womb a public figure. It just doesn't go that way. I am the composite of my experience and all the people who had something to do with it. And I'm going to try to lay that out. (Jordan and Hearon ix)

In her familiar direct style, Jordan makes clear her intent to present a view of her own life within the context of the family, community, and society from whom she garnered support, faced rejection, and learned life lessons. In doing so she follows a tradition in which African American women's writing features "an expression of self, of society, and of self in society" (Royster, *Traces* 5). Barbara Holmes notes that "family, church, and community influences effectively keep her [Jordan] in touch with the reality that she is not a self-made woman" (11). Situating an individual life within the context of society in recognition of the inherent tensions between collectivist and individualist views and with an understanding of the inevitable connection between the self and one's community has long been a hallmark of women's autobiography, particularly African American women's life writings. As Susan Stanford Friedman suggests, "the story of a black woman's selfhood is inseparable from her sense of community" (78).

Published in 1979, just as Jordan bid farewell to electoral politics, *Barbara Jordan: A Self-Portrait* chronicles her life from her birth in February 1936, through her commencement address at Harvard in June 1977. Written by Jordan and Shelby Hearon, "a white novelist and a fellow Texan" (Hunter-Gault 43), the narrative has invoked mixed reviews. William Schenck, writing for the *Library Journal*, characterizes the work as another volume in the "notoriously unsatisfactory genre" of campaign biographies and seemingly finds fault with Jordan's emphasis "on her family and other people who have influenced her life" (178). Echoing this theme, Kate Waters contends that "Jordan relates anecdotes about her life and career but offers no insights into the considerations which go into her decisions" (166). Alton Hornsby argues that a "simplistic approach, unfortunately, characterizes much of the work and greatly reduces its value to the scholar" (138). Taking a different perspective, a *New York Times* reviewer refers to the autobiography as a "personal, intellectual history" (North-cott BR3). Kaye Northcott suggests that the "book fills out a picture of the woman [she] had already glimpsed during her triumphal march across the Texas political battlefield" (BR3). Rogers summarizes reactions to the autobiography:

> While Jordan's stories about her upbringing are indeed fascinating, the book glosses over her public life, particularly the years in Congress. And the off-handed and pithy dismissal of important events had the effect of making Jordan come across as a woman who glided across the surface of her life, driven only by her own ambition; her accomplishments and attributes seem almost com-monplace. Her political insights, her biblical sense of justice and judgment, her understanding of the nature of power, her personal relationships, and her disap-pointments are downplayed, if not completely hidden. Her growing physical in-capacity is barely mentioned. (304–305)

Although the narrative has been "politely received and reviewed," Rogers con-cludes that "political insiders who hoped for some insight into Barbara Jordan and her career were plainly disappointed" (305).

In addition to their dissatisfaction with the content of the autobiography, some reviewers have found the collaborative style disconcerting. The narrative features the two coauthors telling "essentially the same stories in different voices in alternating sections" (Rogers 304) by dividing the text "between the first-person narrative by Jordan and third-person insertions by Shelby Hearon" (Brignano 45). Schenck argues that the "book suffers from a confusing duality of first-and third-person writing" (178). Hunter-Gault agrees, suggesting that "the technique of weaving Hearon's insights and interpretations into Jordan's words just confuses the portrait" (43). Noting the intermingling of "the third-person narration of Shelby Hearon" with "Barbara Jordan's eloquent first-person reminiscences," Northcott offers an alternative view of the text: "this rather awkward format could have been disastrous, but it works thanks to Mrs. Hearon's delicate and empathetic touch. Together they have written a good deal about how Miss Jordan got from there to here, how she thinks and what she's learned about living with herself and other people" (BR3). As was her penchant throughout her public career, Barbara Jordan wanted to "control the flow of in-formation about her life" by telling "her story the way she wanted it told" (Rogers 304). Thus, as Elspeth Rostow, Dean of the Lyndon B. Johnson School of Public Affairs at the University of Texas–Austin, suggests in a 1979 press conference, the autobiography "is a straightforward account of the life of Bar-bara Jordan" (qtd. in Rogers 304).

This chapter examines *Barbara Jordan: A Self-Portrait* as political dis-course—as an exemplar of Barbara Jordan's public dialogue with her fellow citizens. Contemporary scholarship often posits the need to examine the rhetoric and life writings of individuals in the context of the cultures from which they emerge and within which they function as individual members of a community. For example, Molefi Kete Asante argues that the interrogation of any aspect of the lives of African Americans should not only acknowledge their African an-

cestry, but also that the unique characteristics of the resulting worldview must
frame the analysis. He names this perspective, Afrocentricity, "which means,
literally, placing African ideals at the center of any analysis that involves African culture and behavior" (*Afrocentric Idea* 2). Asante concludes that:

> Afrocentric analysis reestablishes the centrality of the ancient Kemetic (Egyp-
> tian) civilization and the Nile Valley cultural complex as points of reference for
> an African perspective in much the same way that Greece and Rome serve as
> reference points for the European world. . . . Without the Afrocentric perspec-
> tive, the imposition of the European line as universal hinders cultural under-
> standing and demeans humanity. (11)

Echoing Asante's argument, Ronald Jackson contends that "an afrocentric
model of communication must act as the foundation for any critique of African
American discourse. It is through these elements that one properly analyzes
rhetoric from the perspective of a community of African descendants" ("Toward
an Afrocentric Methodology" 154). Thus, situating Jordan's narrative within the
tradition of African American women's autobiographical writing and within the
context of African American rhetorical conventions, while acknowledging an
Afrocentric frame for both, promotes an investigation of the text based on the
forms inherent in its composition. The resulting analysis focuses on the following questions: first, how does the autobiography illustrate the ways in which
Jordan navigates the politics of the private, the personal, and the public as well
as the multiple-binds imposed by her race and gender? Second, what view of
U.S. society and politics emerges from the glimpses Jordan and Hearon provide
in the narrative? Third, what political ideologies does Jordan espouse? And,
finally, does Jordan's telling of her political life encourage and empower future
women leaders?

African American Women's Autobiographical Traditions

A discussion of African American women's autobiography requires acknowledgement of a "tradition within a tradition" (Braxton 5). That is, in the creation
of a unique category within autobiographical literature, these narratives employ
the conventions of both African American and women's autobiography. While
drawing from the traditions discussed in Chapter One and elsewhere in this
book, these African American female writers also create their own narrative
forms and practices illustrative of their unique experiences. The variety of
standpoints informing the lives of African American women finds a synergistic
voice in their life writings, exemplifying that they "live [their] lives within a
magic circle, a realm of shared language, reference, and allusion within the veil
of [their] blackness and [their] femaleness" (1). The African American woman
"is neither a woman who is also African American nor an African American
who is also a woman, but [she] must be viewed as 'an African American

woman'—the issues of gender, race, culture, and class in her case interlocked" (Stover 16). Suggesting "participation in the autobiographical tradition is a declaration of selfhood," Regina Blackburn argues that "African American women autobiographical writers," by virtue of their narratives, take "a positive step toward bonding the black and female self in America" (148). The following brief examination of African American autobiography and, in particular, African American women's life stories provides both a context and an analytical frame for investigating Jordan's self-portrait.

Both male and female slaves and freeborn Blacks who committed their life stories to print, either independently or with the assistance of others, as well the men and women who penned conversion and captivity narratives beginning almost fifty years earlier (Andrews, Introduction, *Sisters* 1–2) created the foundation for an African American literary tradition in the United States. "Autobiography holds a position of priority, indeed many would say preeminence, among the narrative traditions of black America" (Andrews, Introduction, *African American* 1). Speaking of Richard Wright's *Black Boy*, Albert Stone argues that "since at least 1945, autobiography is among black Americans one of the richest, most varied, and most revealing modes of personal expression" (*Autobiographical* 231). Vincent Franklin, writing more than a decade later, contends that the influence of African American personal narrative began a century earlier, positing that since the publication of Frederick Douglass's personal narrative in 1845 "the autobiography has been the most important literary genre in the African-American intellectual tradition in the United States" (11). The effectiveness of the Black autobiography and its ability to attract a wide readership from all races, both historically and contemporarily, makes it an important vehicle in African Americans' search for identity. "From their earliest writings in the West, autobiography was sufficiently central to African Americans that they made it the genre of preference in the development of black literary culture. . . . Since then the life story (or portions of it) has been the most effective forum for defining black selfhood in a racially oppressive world" (McKay 96).

Scholars of African American autobiography trace the origins of the genre to the oral narratives of the African continent. "The popularity of autobiography as a genre in contemporary Black cultures can in part be accounted for by its prevalence in traditional African societies" (Alabi 2). According to Adetayo Alabi, autobiography "is a long-established and popular communication medium in Africa" (6). Contrary to theories advanced in seminal studies of the genre focused on European and U.S. models, "the process of analyzing the history of the self has been going on in African cultures, as in other cultures, since time immemorial" (5). Through their texts, the "autobiographers literally write or speak themselves and their societies into prominence" (140). Many African autobiographical texts are oral, handed down from generation to generation and used by "members of various gender, political, and socioeconomic groups" to communicate "their sense of self, contest their representations by others, and teach their histories to younger generations" (6). Additionally, the autobiographical stories provide members of the community with an understanding of "social control, morals, and responsibility" (7).

The view of the individual in relationship to the community foregrounds one of the significant differences between life stories in Africa and those typically found in the West. Generally collectivist in nature, African societies do not perceive the individual apart from the community in which she lives, as exemplified in the Sonjo proverb, "I am because we are, and since we are, therefore I am" (qtd. in Alabi 145). Autobiographies from these cultures generally are more "autophylographical" (Olney, "Value of Autobiography" 216–218); that is, they are more "concerned with the tribal self" (Andrews, "African-American" 209) rather than the individualized self. "For the life portrait that the African autobiographer executes is not the portrait of 'moi, moi seul,' but rather "a portrait of 'nous, nous ensemble'" (Olney, "Value of Autobiography" 218). Alabi explains this concept in more detail:

> In African contexts . . . even when an autobiography is the story of an individual, it is characteristically the representation of the individual in the service of community. . . . Since individual achievements are determined and enabled by the community, individuals normally recognize the community's role in their success and respect it. The life of an individual, as recorded in African autobiographies, ultimately becomes a way of discussing the community, especially the relationship between the individual and the community. (5)

It is not surprising, then, that these writers often use their life stories for the "upliftment of Black people" (Alabi 2). Their works "function not just as a record of individual activities in the various Black communities, but as a record of the struggle for survival and equality with other groups by the various communities themselves" (2). Thus, the autobiographies serve not only as the histories of the writers' societies but also as persuasive messages intended to influence both thought and action within those same communities.

Transplanted to the United States as slaves, members of these African communities brought their traditions with them even as they found themselves in a "veritable seething cauldron of cross-cultural contact" that gave birth to a "dynamic of exchange and revision among numerous previously isolated Black African cultures on a scale unprecedented in African history" (Gates, *Signifying* 4). As strangers in a new land who often faced a horrific life, they depended on one another for survival. "Inadvertently, African slavery in the New World satisfied the preconditions for the emergence of a new African culture, a truly Pan-African culture. . . . What survived this fascinating process was the most useful and the most compelling of the fragments at hand" (4), including the conventional use of autobiographical stories to record history and effect change.

Ultimately, slave narratives, first oral and then written, "functioned as an early form of protest literature," exposing "the nature of the slave system" and providing "moral instruction through the vehicle of autobiography" (S. Smith, *Where I'm Bound* 8). William Andrews argues that slavery created a rhetorical situation that necessitated a discursive response:

Faced with the exigencies of slavery and a mass refusal to see blacks as fully human or hear them as truth-tellers, black autobiographers naturally realized that theirs was a rhetorical situation. They could not think of their task simply as the objective reconstruction of an individual's past or a public demonstration of the qualities of selfhood or a private meditation on the meaning of a life struggle. The writing of autobiography became an attempt to open an intercourse with the white world. (*To Tell* 17)

These texts, which often depict the travesties of slavery in graphic detail while simultaneously creating a humane face for its victims, form effective persuasive messages because they "[personalize] the argument, rendering the experience immediate and concrete rather than abstract and general" (S. Smith, *Where I'm Bound* 8). Thus, the life stories of the slaves respond to "the felt need for a rhetorical mode that would conduct the battle against racism and slavery on grounds other than those already occupied by pro- and antislavery polemics" (Andrews, *To Tell* 5) and serve as "powerful political weapons for converting people to the abolitionist cause" (S. Smith, *Where I'm Bound* 7).

Since the genesis of slave narratives in the eighteenth century, "African American autobiography has testified to the ceaseless commitment of people of color to realize the promise of their American birthright and to articulate their achievements as individuals and as persons of African descent" (Andrews, Introduction, *African American* 1). Andrews asserts that "more than any other literary form in black American letters, autobiography has been recognized and celebrated since its inception as a powerful means of addressing and altering sociopolitical as well as cultural realities in the United States" (1). Moving from the slave narratives to more contemporary works, Franklin suggests African Americans write "their autobiographies with the political and social circumstances for African Americans in mind . . . [using] their personal experiences as a mirror to reflect the larger social context for Afro-America." They employ this literary form "to examine ideological issues and to situate their personal preferences within that larger political context" (11). Thus, African American autobiography began as a site for resistance and continues as "an arena of *struggle*" (Harlow 2). For Black women, "active resistance to oppression of all kinds has been at the center of the history of [their] lives in this country from slavery to the present time" (McKay 105). Their life writings consistently include "social, political, and economic problems and interests as focal points," in which they interrogate matters ranging "from issues of their own agency as capable and intelligent human beings to the impacts and consequences of various conditions of life for African Americans and others, to the implications of economic and political power, to the importance of peace, justice, and equity" (Royster, *Traces* 104). As McKay claims, "their narratives are as politically significant as more overt modes of protest" (105).

Like their African predecessors, African American narratives emerge from and advocate for the communities that offer support to their authors. In addition, the texts exhibit an increasingly complex understanding of a New World individualized expression and the fluctuating relationship between the self and the

community. Using Olney's nomenclature, the texts gradually have included a
worldview that moves from the autophylographical to the autobiographical.
Such a move becomes relative, however, for even contemporary African American autobiographers remain firmly rooted in the communities to which they belong. Thus, one finds contradictory elements within the narratives regarding a
binary conceptualization of individuality and community, resulting in a more
synergistic understanding of the continuum of relationships between these two
modes of "being" in the world. "The practice of self-contextualization, that is,
does not prevent people from speaking their own idiosyncratic selves into textual existence" (Goldman 288). African American autobiographers do not "participate in an ideology of self that separate[s] the self from the black community
and the roots of its culture" (McKay 96). In particular, "black women's autobiography" provides "an occasion for viewing the individual in relation to those
others with whom she shares emotional, philosophical, and spiritual affinities, as
well as political realities" (Braxton 9) and "incorporates communal values into
the performance of the autobiographical act, sometimes rising to function as the
'point of consciousness' of her people" (5).

Freedom emerges as another major motif in historical and contemporary
African American autobiography. Since "the struggle for freedom is a core value
in the collective experiences of African Americans," it comes as no surprise that
the autobiographical genre offers writers an opportunity to express "a personal
account of what freedom mean[s] and how it [can] be achieved" (Franklin 11).
Roger Rosenblatt suggests that the concept of freedom, conveyed as an "expressed desire to live as one would choose, as far as possible," and an "explicit
criticism" of the "external national conditions that . . . work to ensure that one's
freedom of choice is delimited or non-existent" form the major "arguments" of
African American autobiography (170). In these life writings, a journey toward
liberty evolves as a significant element in the theme of freedom. This metaphor
finds expression in the prototypal patterns of slave narratives as "the story of his
[the slave's] radical break *away from* an enslaving community that forbade him
authentic selfhood by foisting a false identity upon him" to "his successful break
into a community that allowed authentic self-expression and fulfillment in a
social role: his achievement of a 'place' within society" (S. Smith, *Where I'm
Bound* ix). The very act of writing suggests movement toward this goal, as the
attainment of literacy becomes not only a hallmark of freedom but a rationale
for the granting of independence as well. "To be able to write, to develop a public voice, and to assert a literary self [represent] significant aspects of freedom"
(Braxton 15) for those excluded from the basic rights of citizenship. As Jacqueline Royster observes, for African American women "the quest for literacy [is] a
symbolic manifestation of their desire for agency and autonomy—as human
beings and as citizens who should have rights and privileges" (*Traces* 109).
Through the journeys depicted in their autobiographies, which represent one
avenue for this pursuit, "they also [accept] personal responsibility for securing
their own rights and [perceive] their opportunities to learn" as an obligation "to
use the benefits of those opportunities for *good* and *righteous* work in solving an

array of problems, not only for themselves but for the race as a whole" (109–10). Thus, "the impulse and imperative" of African American autobiography has been "to 'tell a free story'—to be politically free and to achieve narrative freedom within a given text" (Braxton 15).

As African American women use life stories to construct their selfhood within the context of community, most reject a "black victim status in favor of a self-empowered black female self at the center of their identity" (McKay 100). While racism and sexism may constrain facets of their lives, these women write of their resolution to live life beyond the boundaries imposed on them by the double binds their very existence creates. Describing singer Marian Anderson's autobiography, *My Lord, What a Morning*, McKay contends Anderson "reject[s] the black victim self and [does] not postulate race and class . . . as obstacles that have the ultimate power to determine the destiny of black people who [work] hard and [will] themselves to succeed" (102). Similarly, Zora Neale Hurston does not "perceive race or gender as insurmountable barriers to how" she elected "to live in the world" (103). Obviously, not all Black women share the successful pioneering status of these two icons, but, in general, throughout history African American women autobiographers have expressed "a shared definition of personhood, one that portrays black women as shapers of their own identities and destinies, and as individuals who need not meet the standards of whites and males to achieve their own personhood" (Doriani 202–3). Through her personal narrative, an African American woman unearths a sense of agency, which "frees her public voice . . . and the discovery that she has a public voice gives her agency" (Stover 200). These discoveries engender "a challenge to existing patriarchal structures. And no matter how powerful and repressive those patriarchal structures might be, they have great difficulty in suppressing a black woman who has assumed agency" (200).

African American women's autobiographies embody the characteristics described above. Since language operates as "a place of struggle" (hooks 16), these writings function as sites of resistance and empowerment, not only for the writers, but also for the readers of the narratives. Empowerment for the author emerges, in part, from the very act of writing her life story. "The freedom to write" and to have that text published remain "firmly connected with power politics," so "African American women autobiographers" must "become political," they must "find ways to fool the system, or at least manipulate it to their advantage" (Stover 82). Situated within community while simultaneously expressing the individuality of self, these life writings often make "the importance of the 'self' dependent on a relationship with a larger, communal body" (Stover 30). Whether fleeing from the literal chains of bondage or the restraints imposed by a sexist, racist, and class-conscious society, Black female autobiographers include the telling of their journey to freedom within their narratives, affirming their personhood and self-worth along the way. The autobiographies of African American women "bear witness to the continuity and vitality of black women asserting images of self in many and varied forms" (Braxton 16).

In addition, these narratives employ what Johnnie Stover calls an "African American mother tongue," which "defies the sociopolitical, historical, and literary constraints inherent in the limiting legacies of race, gender, and class" (200). Identified in female slave narratives, the mother tongue invokes "a singular blending of oral and written literary genres and rhetorical techniques that allows African American women writers to speak in voices unique to their experiences" (74). These writers, according to Stover,

> embody the European linguistic stylings of texts written according to Germanic and Romantic language structures, the African stylizing that represented the emerging literary tradition found in the slave narrative, as well as the everyday linguistic stylings—the vernacular—found within the black community. African American women autobiographers merged and subverted the literary tools that were available to them (or stolen by them) and introduced a unique and distinctive voice into the American literary tradition. (202–3)

Stover argues that "these communicative techniques and characteristics continue to shape the works" of African American women autobiographers in the twentieth century (3) and, we may assume, in the twenty-first century as well. The writers combine "the oral and written to produce literature in which race and gender (and often class and sexuality) inform narratives so that readers simultaneously read and hear the 'sounds of Blackness'" (Fulton 7). "By taking control of language and molding it—shaping it with her mother tongue—and by locating other creative nonlinguistic ways to communicate," African American women autobiographers claim "sociopolitical and literary agency," and create "a new literary form—talking back to the traditional autobiography" (Stover 19). These narratives embody the concept of the "speakerly text," which represents "the black speaking voice in writing" (Gates, *Signifying* xxv). According to Henry Louis Gates, Jr., in the speakerly text "the narrative strategy signals attention to its own importance, an importance which would seem to be the privileging of oral speech and its inherent linguistic features" (181). Further, the writers orient a speakerly text "toward imitating one of the numerous forms of oral narration . . . found in classical Afro-American vernacular literature" (181). To better understand the role orality plays in the life writings of Black women, we turn to a brief discussion of rhetorical conventions in African American discourse.

African American Rhetorical Traditions

Since African Americans first arrived in the United States, "oratory has been an essential element" in their "self-expression, community life, and negotiation with whites" (Foner and Branham 2). They have regarded "the development and use of oratorical skills as a means . . . to achieve both social reform and individual advancement" (2). Like African American autobiography, the rhetoric of Black Americans finds its ancestral roots in the societies of Africa as "formal oratory and debate have occupied central roles in many African cultures and continue to do so" (1). Elaine Richardson and Ronald Jackson describe African American rhetoric as "culturally and discursively developed knowledge-forms, communicative practices and persuasive strategies rooted in freedom struggles by people of African ancestry in America" (xiii). Jackson also explains that the concept represents "the manifestation of culture, which seeks to celebrate, sustain, develop, and introduce itself to history and humanity" ("Toward an Afrocentric Methodology" 153). Similarly, Asante defines rhetoric, "in an Afrocentric sense," as "the productive thrust of language into the unknown in an attempt to create harmony and balance in the midst of disharmony and indecision" (*Afrocentric Idea* 46) in order to arrive at truth. As the preceding discussion of African and African American autobiography attests, in both historical and contemporary contexts, orality becomes the primary rhetorical vehicle through which self and community are called into existence and through which harmony, a principal social value, is created collaboratively. According to Asante, "in the whole of Africa and the African world, both past and present, a vocal-expressive modality dominates all communication culture" (71). Charles Hamilton observes that "black culture is characterized by an oral tradition" and that "knowledge, attitudes, ideas, notions are traditionally transmitted orally, not through the written word." He concludes that "it is not unusual, then, that the natural leader among black people would be one with exceptional oratorical skills" (28). In this context, "it is important to remember that orality is not simply a synonym for speech." Rather, "a more accurate view defines orality as a coherent system of cultural values for language use—a symbol system that relies on the spoken voice and face to face discourse, but that also includes bodily gestures, strong appeal to the senses, oral memory, and acoustic elements, especially music" (Middleton 246). DoVeanna Fulton differentiates oral discourse, "an interchange of ideas, thoughts, and actions," from orality, a "speech act that resists or subverts oppression" (13). She claims that "the major distinction between oral discourse and orality is the political nature of orality found not only in resistance to domination and dehumanization, but in its validation of African American culture and communities as significant to the development of self-determined, self-defined subjects" (13). Asante also acknowledges this facet of orality or orature, "the comprehensive body of oral discourse on every subject and in every genre of expression produced by a people" (*Afrocentric Idea* 96):

> With an African heritage steeped in orature . . . the African American developed a consummate skill in using language to produce communication patterns alternative to those employed in the Euro-American situation. These channels remained rhetorical, even as they consciously or subconsciously utilized linguistic changes for communicative effectiveness. During slavery, communication between different ethnic and linguistic groups was difficult, but the almost universal African regard for the power of the spoken word contributed to the development of alternative communication patterns. . . . It is precisely the power of the word, whether in music or speeches, that authentically speaks of an African heritage. (96)

The "power of the word" in African philosophy and culture emerges from a conception of the *word* as "productive and imperative"; it calls forth and commands (A. Smith, "Markings" 369). As Janheinz Jahn explains:

> If there were no word, all forces would be frozen, there would be no procreation, no change, no life. "There is nothing that there is not; whatever we have a name for, that is"; so speaks the wisdom of the Yoruba priests. The proverb signifies that the naming, the enunciation produces what it names. Naming is an incantation, a creative act. What we cannot conceive of is unreal; it does not exist. But every human thought, once expressed, becomes reality. . . . And since the word has this power, every word is an effective word, every word is binding. (133)

This understanding of the word finds its genesis in the concept of Nommo, "the embodiment of Afri-Symbols—the Word pregnant with value-meanings drawn from the African experience which, when uttered, gives birth to unifying images that bind people together in an atmosphere of harmony and power" (Knowles-Borishade 495). Nommo "creates and is created by 'word warriors,' preachers, griots, and rhetoricians who become 'technicians' of verbosity" (K. Williams 96). Functioning as "the generative, life-sustaining force of the word," Nommo mediates between the speaker and her audience (Jackson, "Toward an Afrocentric Methodology" 154). Through Nommo "spiritual and material relationships between speaker and audience become one voice, literally performing a collective experience central to the balanced and harmonious maintenance of communal existence" (Harrison and Harrison 164). Consequently, the speaker's communion with the audience emerges as a primary goal in African American rhetoric, regardless of the topic of the discourse. Success "means that the rhetor has fundamentally achieved harmony with the spiritual, intellectual, and physical essence of the audience" (151). Nommo reveals the subject matter of a rhetorical endeavor and makes possible the communion between speaker and audience.

Jackson postulates four major facets of an afrocentric rhetorical method: rhetorical condition, rhetorical structure, rhetorical function, and ethical standard ("Toward an Afrocentric Methodology" 151). Rhetorical condition "relates to the political constraints placed on" the event through a "hierarchal or structural power source which impacts a rhetorical situation" (151). Asante argues that the "rhetorical condition is the structure and power pattern a society assumes or imposes during a rhetorical situation" (*Afrocentric Idea* 28). Further, he suggests, "different rhetorical situations produce different conditions because the inherent power relationships change from situation to situation" (29). Therefore, the selection of a specific rhetorical form, informative, persuasive, or ceremonial, for example, "is itself the initial commitment to a certain outcome, because the rhetorical condition is established as soon as the form is chosen" (30). In addition, a rhetor or rhetorical critic must consider "the inherent power relationships" within the communicative interaction (151) since they affect both form and content of a discursive act.

Rhetorical structure "attempts to decipher the underlying meanings in words" and "ties in with the internal structure of discourse" (Jackson, "Toward an Afrocentric Methodology" 151). Within the African American tradition, the structure includes the components of styling—the "manipulation of language or mannerisms"; rhythm—the charismatic use of multiple rhythmic elements; lyrical code—inventiveness and creativity in use of language; Nommo—"the generative power of the word"; improvisation—the impromptu delivery of all or parts of a speech; and coherence—"the fluency with which a message is constructed" (151–52). A speaker may or may not include all of these elements in a specific presentation, and she may employ them in various combinations. According to Jackson, these "structural aspects" function as "the internal guides of discourse. The speaker employs them to heighten the message, and achieve intended outcomes" (152).

The third major facet of African American rhetoric, rhetorical function, attempts to determine the purpose of the discourse (Jackson, "Toward an Afrocentric Methodology" 151). Jackson argues that "from an Afrocentric stance, all rhetoric persuades one to act," contending that "a change of attitude is not enough." Thus, the discourse critic faces the "challenge of indicating motive, intention, and generalizability of the message" (151). Obviously, rhetorical condition and function inform and influence each other.

The final element of Jackson's schema, ethical standard, provides "the axiological component of the analysis" (151). It resides "at the core of the afrocentric enterprise, since it places emphasis on the political, economic, and social good for a given community" (151). The ethical standard focuses on harmony, the "supraordinate objective of African speech events" (Knowles-Borishade 498). Intertwined with rhetorical condition and function, "the attainment of Harmony is anticipated from the outset by all participants when the community is called together for a common cause" (498). Adetokunbo Knowles-Borishade theorizes that harmony comes into existence through the interaction of the caller, the chorus, spiritual entities, Nommo, and responders.

In African and African American discourse, the caller serves as the "primary creative element" in the rhetorical event since she "bears the responsibility of presenting solutions to the social and political problems of the people" (Knowles-Borishade 490). Recognizing the unique relationship between the self and the community, "the individual desires of the Caller are subsumed as s/he becomes a conduit who speaks on behalf of the group" (490). In the African belief system, the moral character of the speaker cannot be separated from the rhetorical event. Thus, "the word (Nommo) gains in power and effectiveness in direct proportion with the moral character, strength of commitment, and vision of the Caller, as well as the skill s/he exhibits" (490). The caller does not bear all of the responsibility in initiating the word, however. "S/he is flanked by a Chorus whose role is to validate, to bear witness to the truth of the Word" (494). The caller's "utterance is accompanied by the echoes of the Chorus" (494). This "concept symbolizes and perpetuates the ultimacy of the collective, whereby decisions are made and actions are taken by consensus rather than by solitary decree" (494).

Spiritual entities permeate rhetorical activities in the African tradition. According to Knowles-Borishade, "there is no line of demarcation between the spiritual and the secular in African oratorical events" (492). She observes that "Africans inject spiritual elements into their oratorical events, and thus seek and expect to reach a higher consciousness during such events" (492). Through Nommo at the beginning of her speech, the caller assumes responsibility for invoking the spiritual entities, which "include the creator God" and ancestors, among others (492, 495).

The audience or responders contribute another element to the African and African American rhetorical tradition. The "responders are the community who come to participate in the speech event. They are secondary creators in the event, containing among them a vital part of the message" for they "either sanction or reject the message" presented by the Caller (497). This does not mean that the Caller has not prepared for the event. Rather, the idea suggests that "a vital portion of the prepared message is not available to the Caller and must be provided by the responders spontaneously during the speech act. . . . As a process, call-and-response promotes levels of perfected social interaction through these verbal checks and balances as the event progresses" (498). The "strong sense of community and the group unity and cooperation it engenders" emerges as "the hallmark of call-response" interaction (Harrison and Harrison 166).

The quest for harmony, sense of community, and agency draws Black women autobiographers to intertwine oral and written linguistic features in their life writings. "Reconfiguring or constructing the past in contexts that recognize and make use of oral traditions permits narrators and writers to control representations of Black women and their experiences" (Fulton 6–7). The authors "blur the lines between the oral and the written, treating all language as a continuum. They play with language and merge the interests of Western prose with the voices and values of their own cultural orality" (Middleton 247–48). In doing so, they also "remind us that the rhetorical power and ability to speak, to tell one's story . . . is a highly prized human attribute that continues to characterize our cultural and political histories, experiences, and relationships" (248). Through the use of their mother tongue to create speakerly texts, African American women autobiographers engage in testifying that "challenges racist assumptions and provides examples others can identify with and emulate" (Fulton xi).

The Intersection of African American Women's Autobiography and Orality in *Barbara Jordan: A Self-Portrait*

The synergy created by the interplay of the conventions found within African American women's autobiography and African American rhetoric contributes to the uniqueness of structure and content in Jordan and Hearon's *Barbara Jordan: A Self-Portrait*. The following discussion interrogates these interwoven traditions to illustrate the ways in which Jordan's personal narrative provides a glimpse of how an intensely private woman, whose gender, race and class created seemingly unconquerable barriers to life beyond Houston's Fifth Ward, negotiated the politics of the era to become an influential, national public persona. The autobiography employs the medium of the written word as it takes its place within the Western literary canon, but its spirit retains the qualities of African American orality. Emphasizing the oral, storytelling nature of the text, Rogers refers to *A Self-Portrait* as "a dialogue" (292) and "the most complete set of interviews Barbara Jordan ever gave" (387).

Although little published evidence exists to detail the rhetorical condition or exigence that led to the writing of *Barbara Jordan: A Self-Portrait*, a brief statement in Hearon's Preface for the book suggests that Jordan's friends and close associates encouraged her to tell her life story at what many thought was the midpoint of an increasingly distinguished political career. Jordan also wanted to "set the record straight," believing that stories about her that appeared in the press were inaccurate, especially those about her personal life (Rogers 291). Jordan did not like to write and "knew she would need a collaborator when it came to putting the details of her life on paper" (291). In describing her first meeting with Jordan, Hearon notes that "in March of 1977 mutual friends introduced me to Barbara Jordan in the hope of our working together on a book" (Jordan and Hearon vii). After engaging in small talk about family, Jordan "got to the point" stating, "'we are supposed to talk about a book.' 'So I understand,'" responded Hearon (vii). From this rather inauspicious beginning, Jordan and Hearon developed both a friendship and working relationship that culminated in the publication of the autobiography. In December of 1977, Jordan made the decision to end her career in electoral politics, announcing that she would not run for a fourth Congressional term (Mendelsohn 164). So, rather than paving the way for a transition in her political endeavors, the personal narrative signaled a major turning point in Jordan's life journey. She did not see herself as a token woman or African American in state and national politics and refused to be the poster woman for social causes. But, Jordan's keen awareness of the political and societal barriers she had scaled and the legacy she would leave, not only for women and Blacks but also for all those who feel disenfranchised, must have played a role in her decision to agree to the autobiographical project. As noted earlier, to the extent possible Jordan also wanted to manage her public image and to tell the story of her life her own way. The publication of the personal narrative guaranteed her an opportunity to do that.

Jordan and Hearon elected to take a novel approach to the rhetorical structure of the narrative as detailed in the previous discussion of critical reactions to the book. Unlike a traditional ghostwriting arrangement in which writers and readers measure the success of the ghostwriter by her ability to go unnoticed in the account of the life she helps present, Jordan and Hearon intentionally created a text in which their distinctive voices compose a contrapuntal telling of Barbara Jordan's life. They "conceived the book as a dialogue between the two of them, a collaboration through conversation" (Rogers 292). In the Preface, Hearon recounts the succinct discussion she and Jordan engaged in as they auditioned each other for this cooperative venture:

> But we both hesitated. . . .
> "I have nothing to say," she stated.
> "I have nothing to ask," I responded.
> We sat awhile in silence. . . .
> "Well, if you did a book," she asked at last, "how would you see it?"
> "Well, if I did a book," I told her slowly, "I see it as how you got from There to Here. Everyone gets from there to here. So everyone can relate to that."
> "Where do you think here is?" Suddenly it was the Jordan voice, conveying a lifetime of chips on the shoulder, the expectation of misunderstanding.
> I met her dark gaze. "I think here is on the road to Barbara Jordan."
> I said *on the* road because for Barbara wheels are the symbol of freedom. The vehicle, as metaphor and fact, is her means of exit and entrance.
> I said *here* because Barbara exists and reacts only and always where she is at the moment. . . .
> "Do you think I'll ever get there?" she asked.
> "No, but I think you'll die trying."
> "I want you to do the book." (Jordan and Hearon vii–viii)

Hearon describes the book as "a continuation of our initial dialogue" (viii). Assuming this statement represents an accurate depiction of the process the two authors engaged, their interaction finds its grounding in the call-response nature of African American orality. While Jordan initiates the message, as indicated in the preceding passage, Hearon responds and encourages Jordan, the caller and "primary creative element in the interaction" (Knowles-Borishade 490), to expand and reframe the discussion. This brief conversation illustrates the degree to which the caller and responder interact collectively in the construction of the discourses that ultimately form the autobiographical narrative.

Additionally, in its use of both first- and third-person narrative, the published text resulting from the call-and-response process also embodies characteristics of that style. As noted earlier, in African American rhetoric the caller does not necessarily carry the entire burden for the genesis of the message; rather, an additional entity, the chorus, also contributes to the dialogue to approbate the message presented by the caller. Throughout the autobiography, Barbara Jordan fulfills the role of caller, or initiator of the conversation, while Hearon acts as the chorus, providing both context for and commentary on Jordan's reflections. For example, in the opening chapter of the narrative titled "Grandpa Patten," Jordan describes spending Sunday afternoons with her favorite grandfather and the special interactions that characterized their relationship, an "attachment . . . formed at the beginning" of her life (Jordan and Hearon 3). She notes that "he felt himself quite different, just a little cut above the ordinary man, black or white." She elaborates, adding that this idea "was continually driven into me in those years: Look, this man can make it, my grandfather. He can put together whatever combination of things necessary and just kind of make it. And that had an impact on me" (8). Following the almost nine pages of Jordan's storytelling, Hearon provides thirteen pages of commentary in which she offers a glimpse of John Ed Patten and the social conditions in which he grew up and lived. Having endured the often violent horrors and injustices of the racist South, Patten became a rather eccentric gentleman, not always understood or appreciated by other members of his family or community. But, as Hearon notes, in his granddaughter he found "someone at last to whom he could give all the lessons he had learned" (22). She continues: "he talked to her as a teacher to a student, as a guide to a traveler, as an aging man to what had become the idol of his life—allowing him to become the foundation, the cornerstone, of hers" (23). Neither of the singular images constructed by Jordan and Hearon forms a complete picture of Grandpa Patten, of Jordan's interaction with him, or of their relationship. The combination of the two discourses, however, provides the reader with a comprehensive understanding of the era, Patten's background, the special bond created between Jordan and her grandfather, and the influence he had on her life. This format continues throughout the narrative, enhancing the telling of Jordan's life story.

The use of the caller and chorus convention allows what some would consider the best features of both autobiography and biography to emerge in the text. That is, the first-person narrative allows the reader to experience the author's life as she recalls it and to validate that experience through the lens of a more objective third-person observer and researcher, creating a synergy between personal memory and public history. Within the Afrocentric tradition, the verification of the caller's (Jordan's) message through the contributions of the chorus (Hearon) in a "checks and balances" interaction calls into being Nommo, the word, that exhibits enhanced power and reliability because of its association with the character of the speaker as positively intensified by the witnessing of the chorus. The interaction between caller and chorus also contributes to a unified or harmonious message that details both individual and societal enterprises. Thus, this combination of voices represents the collective understanding of the events of Jordan's life within community, creating a unity indicative of the ethical standard in African American rhetoric identified by Jackson. From this perspective, the structure of the narrative doesn't confuse the text but rather clarifies the story for the reader. As Hearon notes, "her [Jordan's] voice, as she told the story, remains hers; mine, as I have reconstructed the world's perceptions and conceptions of her, remains mine. We feel this view of a singular life, representative of each of us in its complexities and its longings, rings true both in its facts and in its underlying meaning" (Jordan and Hearon viii).

Making the decision to commit her story to print and to work with another individual to accomplish that goal could not have been easy for Jordan. By all accounts, she valued her privacy. At the same time, she also recognized the "public nature of political life" (Holmes 22), stating that "we cannot have it both ways. If we choose to be public officials, we must accept being in the public eye—and we must be willing to accept public scrutiny" (qtd. in Holmes 22). Holmes argues that:

Jordan's interest in privacy can be attributed, in part, to her choice to be a fa-
cilitator and not the subject of discourse. Although she is willing to be scrutinized in her public life, she is unwilling to relinquish her privacy. In fact, she
would have considered such an intrusion a hindrance to her public goals. For
Jordan considers herself a provocateur of the national conscience, a sounding
board and proponent of public values. Jordan wants those ideas to be considered on their own merits without reference to personal issues. (22–23)

Rogers also comments on Jordan's penchant for privacy:

Jordan had the audacity to believe her life was nobody's business. Deeply stoic,
she never talked about her troubles or let anyone know when she felt pain or
discomfort. Her strong personal boundaries, shielding and protecting her, were
impenetrable for groupies, politicians, the press, or colleagues. Her circle of intimate friends was small, and even they were never sure whether they knew
everything that was going on behind those boundaries. Many people who considered themselves close friends never knew the details of her upbringing and
had no idea that her mother was a maid or that her father was a Teamsters union steward as well as a Baptist preacher. Still others never had a conversation
with her about her illness, multiple sclerosis, even after she was confined to a
wheelchair. . . .
    Jordan's notion of integrity was grounded in her idea of privacy, and one
did not violate it. She would not allow it. She believed that neither public officials nor private citizens should parcel out bits and pieces of their lives for en-
tertainment or titillation, and she refused to do so. (xiv–xv)

Certainly, through her speeches, Jordan had allowed the public momentary
glimpses of her background. For example, in her now famous 1974 testimony
before the Watergate committee, Jordan states:

Earlier today, we heard the beginning of the Preamble of the Constitution of the
United States. "We, the people." It is a very eloquent beginning. But when that
document was completed on the 17th of September in 1787, I was not included
in that "We, the people." I felt somehow for many years that George Washington and Alexander Hamilton just left me out by mistake. But through the process of amendment, interpretation, and court decision, I have finally been included in "We, the people." ("Testimony" 105)

Presenting the keynote address for a student leadership conference at the University of Texas, Jordan shares the following story with her audience:

I graduated from high school before most of you here were even an idea. I then
enrolled in Texas Southern University. I was sixteen. There was a student body
election about to get under way. I located the campaign office, picked up the
necessary forms, and filed for president. I had made the decision to lead. Of
course, I was later informed by the dean of women that a freshman could not be
president. But I had made a choice: to lead. ("Ethical" 89)

These examples illustrate the types of personal information Jordan felt comfortable revealing to her audiences, including the readers of her autobiography. The distinction between private and personal proves significant in discussing Jordan's discourse. She felt no need to include in her speeches or in her life story the intimate or "private" details of her life or the specifics of the process she engaged in when making legislative decisions. She "refuse[d] to allow the mirror of her personhood to reflect anything other than her public persona" (Holmes 23). In fact, Rogers' statement about Jordan's negative reaction to those who expose private matters to the public aptly describes her hostility toward such disclosure. Despite her preference to guard her personal privacy, however, Jordan did not "want to be ignored; she wanted to be politically influential" (Mendelsohn 12). To accomplish this goal, Jordan knew it was important to generate common ground with her audiences and for them to find points of identification with her. She had learned these lessons within the framework of African American orality as it emerged in Black communities in general and church services in particular, as well as from the study of the Western rhetorical practices she encountered in collegiate debate. Therefore, she included "personal" but not "private" information in her public communication. Even then, she was most comfortable when the personal stories reflected her relationship to others and her place within the communities to which she belonged. We should not be surprised that, faced with the need to provide information about herself and the historic roles she had played in U.S. politics, she chose as the focus of her autobiography the "laying out" of her experience and "those who had something to do with it" (Jordan and Hearon ix).

Jordan's comments also suggest she decided a commitment to a public life in politics precluded the traditional personal life expected by and for her contemporaries. Following her second loss for a seat in the Texas House, Jordan contemplated the role of women in U.S. society in the 1960s and her own future, including whether or not she should stay in politics:

> The public believed that a woman had to have, over and above and beyond other aspirations, a home and family. That was what every normal woman was supposed to want. And any woman who didn't want that was considered something a little abnormal. People didn't expect a woman to make rough decisions. She was the ward of her man; she was always to be available at her husband's side no matter where he had to go or what he had to do. She must always be prepared to turn and kiss his puckered lips.
>
> Now, I thought it unfortunate that the public perceived such a neat little box for us, and that in most cases we felt that the box was right. I thought: The question you have to decide, Barbara Jordan, is whether you're going to fly in the face of what everybody expects out there because you've got your eye someplace else, or whether you can bring the public along to understand that there are some women for whom other expectations are possible. (Jordan and Hearon 118)

"Meanwhile," she acknowledges, "my family and my friends out there started in on the refrain that if I was not going to be winning, I ought to want to get married" (117). She continues:

> I realized that my friends out there thought that marriage was the most important thing there was, and that they all wanted to guarantee that they got the right man and the right home. I ticked them off in my head, all the people I went to school with . . . and I thought: "Now they've already done that and they expect me to do that." My mother wanted me to be married, and my father wanted me to be married, and so did everybody else. But they also wanted me to be successful. I decided I would tell them: "Down the road a piece." In those years I always said: "Down the road a piece. Just let me get it all organized, and then we'll see."
>
> But I made the decision, and it was a fairly conscious one, that I couldn't have it both ways. And that politics was the most important thing to me. I reasoned that this political thing was so total in terms of focus that, if I formed an attachment over here, this total commitment would become less than total. And I didn't want that. I did not want anything to take away from the singleness of my focus at that time. (118–19)

Although she resolved to forgo marriage and family and focused almost exclusively on her public life, Jordan always maintained a close relationship with her parents and sisters. She also recognized the need for some relief from work as she indicates in the following passage: "one of the things I learned at Boston was that you can't work all the time. You can't maintain a public face all the time. You need friends you can be with who don't care what your title is . . . but who would come just because you're a person they want to be with" (Jordan and Hearon 142). She developed a close circle of friends in Austin, friendships that continued throughout the rest of her life. She enjoyed a good party and found she could relax and feel safe around these confidants who expected nothing from her in return for their authentic friendship. In Washington, D.C., Hearon notes:

> Barbara's only real privacy . . . was in her muted black-and-tan, high-rise apartment, which had a view of the Capitol but was far enough from it for escape. There . . . she could be alone and catch her breath. Or, on the rare occasions when close friends visited, [she] talked over barbeque and scotch about whatever came to mind, whatever was personal and apart from legislation. (252)

As Hearon writes throughout the autobiography, Barbara Jordan lived in the "present tense" (viii). Most of the time living in the moment meant focusing only on her work. "Barbara in Congress was wholly in Congress. Which meant that all her time not spent on the floor . . . shepherding her legislation and reacting to that of others, was spent reading reams of related material, in order to gain the perspective she felt others must somehow have" (203). For Barbara Jordan, there was little negotiation between a public and a personal life during her political career. While there were brief respites, her public, political work became her life.

Like other African American women autobiographers, Barbara Jordan tells her life story from the perspective of her connections to the "worlds" she inhabited. The tripartite macro organization of the book, which includes sections titled, "Black World," "White World," and "World," not only exemplifies Jordan's view of herself within community, it also illustrates the structure of the U.S. society she encountered and endeavored to change. Jordan and Hearon place the first three chapters of the book, "Grandpa Patten," "The Jordans," and "Phillis Wheatley High School," in the "Black World" category. These stories trace Jordan's ancestry, her childhood, and her education through high school in the African American neighborhoods of Houston's Fourth and Fifth Wards. By the time she attended Wheatley, Jordan had developed a fatalistic view of life in a "Black" world, a life with little promise of equality. She describes her thoughts:

> I did not think it right for blacks to be in one place and whites in another place and never shall the two meet. There was just something about that that didn't feel right to me. And I wanted that to change, but I also had those feelings that it was going to be this way for a long, long time, and that nobody was going to be able to do anything to change it. It was a fatalistic kind of acceptance of what was, and we had that at that time.
>
> I felt nobody could change it because it just seemed so big that it was everywhere. I had no quarter of experience which I could relate to to say: "But it's different there." So it was massive and I felt that no one would be able to change it because it was something bigger than anyone I knew. And it wasn't only the school system, it was everywhere. The church, the city. (Jordan and Hearon 63)

Moving from a general description of the atmosphere in which she and other African Americans lived, Jordan characterizes some of the specifics of that existence. She continues:

> We would ride on the back of the bus and there was a sign on the bus with a little colored bar, and you had to walk back there to sit.
>
> We would go to Weiengarten's to shop, and there were drinking fountains, one of which said *White* and one said *Colored*; and you couldn't go to the bathroom because most of the time there was none for blacks, and if there was, it was separated from the main rooms for men and women, in the back of the building with an outside entrance. We would go downtown and there were people sitting and eating and enjoying themselves—and it was all a totally white world. There was nothing you saw to indicate that a black person and a white person could be together on a friendly basis. . . . And looking at how widespread this was, my feeling was, well, this is just it. I guess it's always going to be this way. (63–64)

In the second grouping, "White World," the authors present the story of Jordan's encounters in a world in which she comes face-to-face with the myth of "separate but equal" and finds ways to survive in the "White" world. The chapters titled "Boston," "Houston," and "Austin" tell Jordan's story from her college days at Texas Southern University to law school at Boston University, to her return to Houston where she attempts to establish a career and eventually enters politics, and finally to the Texas Senate in Austin. For Jordan, "going to Boston" was her "first departure from the womb" (Jordan and Hearon 83). She notes, "I'd been living at home, being the chief of my own tiny little world, and here I was going farther away than anybody in my family had ever been" (83). As Hearon notes, Jordan discovered that white society "turned out to be a harder world than she could have conceived" (83). Jordan acknowledges that as she began to interact in the white world she "realized that the best training available in an all-black, instant university was not equal to the best training one developed as a white university student. Separate was not equal; it just wasn't. No matter what kind of face you put on it or how many frills you attached to it, separate was not equal" (93). She encountered numerous illustrations of this notion during her first semester at Boston University. For example, she found the language of law school foreign, remarking:

> Everything was so different to me. *Contracts, property, torts* were strange words to me. Words I had not dealt with. And there I was. It appeared that everybody else's father was a lawyer. . . . Can you understand how strange this was to my ears? This was a language that I had not heard before. How could I hear it? From anybody? To them it was so familiar, it was just like mother's milk. (87–88)

Jordan concedes that she knew she "could not catch up" (90):

> It would take a lifetime. I'd have to be born again and just come from another mother's womb and have a totally different kind of upbringing. My whole life would have to be different. It was not a matter of trying to catch up. You couldn't. What you wanted to do was slot in right where you were and deal with that, and you knew that you had to work extraordinarily hard to function right there, where you were.
>
> So I was at Boston University in this new and strange and different world, and it occurred to me that if I was going to succeed at this strange new adventure, I would have to read longer and more thoroughly than my colleagues at law school had to read. I felt that in order to compensate for what I had missed in earlier years, I would have to work harder and study longer, than anybody else. (90–91)

Barbara Jordan also learned that the law school world she had entered was not just racist; she found that being female also meant there were additional obstacles to overcome in this white, male bastion. She describes one of those barriers:

I was always delighted when I would get called upon to recite in class. But the professors did not call on the "ladies" very much. There were certain favored people who always got called on, and then on some rare occasions a professor would come in and announce: "We're going to have Ladies Day today." And he would call on the ladies. We were just tolerated. We weren't considered really top drawer when it came to the study of the law. (91–92)

The "white men's only club" described the world of Texas politics at the time as well. However, in 1965, court decisions led to the reapportionment of legislative districts in Harris County, and Jordan "found herself in the newly created Eleventh State Senatorial District, an area including the Fifth Ward, composed of 38 percent blacks, a large block of Chicanos, and white laborers affiliated with the AFL-CIO" (129). Knowing she had won most of these precincts in her two failed bids for the Texas House, Jordan decided to give electoral politics one more try and in 1966, ran for the state Senate. She won the election. "The law had allowed Barbara, at last, to enter the all-white world of the Good Old Boys" (136).

In the final chapter of this category, Jordan discusses the need for friends and the difficulty of determining who one's friends are in the white world. She offers her observations on this issue:

But out here in the white world it took a long time to decide the criteria for whom you could trust, and it was a judgment call every time. I would not be able to write down the rules for judging people, but it was just there in my head. Some people fit, and some people didn't, and you learned over the passage of time which ones would and which ones wouldn't. (143)

Indeed, Barbara Jordan had discovered how to survive in the "white worlds" of Boston and Texas. Yet, some of her greatest challenges were still to come.

The final section of the autobiography, "World," depicts Jordan's life as a member of the U.S. Congress in chapters labeled "Entrance," "Entrenchment," and "Exit." In Chapter Seven, the first chapter included in this classification, Jordan recounts her "entrance" into the world of national politics in the shadow of the Watergate scandal. Almost immediately she observes the challenges the representatives face in making a difference in Congress:

There were so many members of Congress. And I was coming from a 31-member state senate into that 435-member House of Representatives. It became obvious to me that it was going to be difficult to make any impact on anybody with all of these people also trying to make an impact, in order to create the impression back home among their constituents that they were outstanding.

The first thing was, I would have to get in good with my colleagues from Texas. I would be the unique new kid on the block to them and I wanted to work comfortably with them. For instance, I knew that women had never been allowed to attend the Texas Democratic Delegation luncheon that had been meeting at twelve-thirty on Wednesdays since the early tenure of Sam Rayburn, and I intended to change that. Which I did. (180).

Of course, that was not the only effect she had on the House of Representatives or the nation. Jordan's "entrance" into Congress officially concluded with her testimony before the House Judiciary Committee on Watergate in July 1974. Hearon describes the impact the speech created:

> Her audience was stunned. It was the first time she had reached them with no one in between. The first time they had seen and heard her with their own eyes and ears. The first time she was a primary source to them.
>
> Before that, she had long since been stereotyped by a press used to summing up secondary sources. . . .
>
> The night of the impeachment hearings, Barbara broke through her interpreters. Thereafter, to her audience, she would be a myth of their own creating, an institution, a legend accountable to their prejudgment. Thereafter she would be public property, would be a folk-hero. But on that single evening she reached America one to one. (192–93)

The discussion in "Entrenchment" outlines Jordan's major legislative involvement during her three terms in office. Even though she had earned the respect of many in Congress and continued to garner their esteem, the doubts Jordan experienced at Boston University still haunted her, leading her to believe that "she must work harder than the rest to make up for what she did not know" (203). For Jordan this meant learning all that she could about any topic relevant to congressional debates. She admits:

> If there is an issue on the floor of the Congress, a big one, then I am interested in the historical background of that issue because that helps me to understand where we are now. I send over to the Library of Congress to get the simplest things. I want to be steeped in what we are discussing. I think that there are people who already know that information, but I don't. So I'm doing background for legislation all the time. (203)

In describing Jordan's congressional efforts Hearon contends, "inevitably, her primary concern—minority legislation—reflected her present conviction that where she was she owed to the law" (204–5). She continues stating Jordan's belief "that no amount of confidence and determination could win elections without redistricting and reapportionment; that discriminatory voting practices and segregated public accommodations could close doors that only the law could open" (205). Always mindful of her own experiences of segregation and sexism, Jordan devoted many of her congressional efforts to civil rights legislation, including the extension of the Voting Rights Act, and to women's rights issues such as federal aid for abortion and the Equal Rights Amendment. From the beginning of her first term, Jordan gained astute knowledge of the inner workings of Congress. In addition to understanding the issues of the specific bills she fought for on the House floor, she knew that "Congress was also always politics" (220). Hearon acknowledges that "Barbara had done her apprenticeship in the Texas Senate" and that "she had no difficulty handling the same covert maneuvers on a national level" (220).

On July 12, 1976, Barbara Jordan delivered one of the keynote speeches for the National Democratic Party Convention. As she took her place on the platform, Jordan noted the inattentiveness of the delegates and was told "not to worry, that the people in the hall were going to be walking around and talking and not paying attention" (229). According to Hearon, who offers a description of the event, "Barbara knew better" (230):

> At the first sounds of her rising inflections, her sonorous repetitions, the hall grew silent as a church. "I looked up," [Jordan] recalled, "and people were not milling around. All milling stopped. Now, really, the response was startling, as startling to me as that first standing ovation I got from the Harris County Democrats. Everything had been dullsville at the convention up to then, and I just thought: 'This is the way it will be.'" (230)

In the now famous speech, Jordan began by talking about the significance of her presence at the convention. She states:

> "But there is something different about tonight. There is something special about tonight. What is different? What is special? I, Barbara Jordan, am a keynote speaker.
>   A lot of years passed since 1832, and during that time it would have been most unusual for any national political party to ask that a Barbara Jordan deliver a keynote address . . . but tonight here I am. And I feel, notwithstanding the past, that my presence here is one additional bit of evidence that the American Dream need not forever be deferred." (qtd. in Jordan and Hearon 230)

By all accounts, the crowd went wild after the speech, "chanting 'WE WANT BARBARA'" (231). The delegates "surrounded her, making over the new darling of the party. 'They were all kissing my ass, that's all I can say about that time,'" Jordan remarks (232). The morning following the convention began with a "full-fledged drive" to place her on the democratic ticket as the vice presidential candidate (234). The pragmatic Jordan knew this was not a possibility, so she suggested that Carter's team call a press conference to "stop the groundswell" (234). In a prepared statement, she announced: "'It is improbable that Carter would take the bold, daring, unconventional, and un-southern move of naming a black or a woman as his running mate. Certainly not both at once. . . . It is not my turn. . . . When it's my turn, you'll know it'" (234). Although she realized that some doors still were not open to her, Barbara Jordan understood that she had gained acceptance as a member of a large political community.

In the final chapter, "Exit," Jordan reflects upon her recognition that she had become a national political figure, that she had collapsed, at least to some extent, the boundaries between the "Black World" and the "White World" to enter a seemingly more tolerant and accepting "World." After the convention, Jordan campaigned for Carter. Inevitably, in the discussion sessions following her campaign speeches, members of the audience would ask about what position she might hold in a Carter cabinet. "What no one seemed to understand," she reminisces, "was that it had not occurred to me that I would be anything in a

Carter cabinet" (244). After reading the speculations in the press, Jordan began to think: "'well, what would I do if I were asked?'" (244). She and her friends finally concluded that she would be willing to accept the position of Attorney General. Jordan elaborates:

> Look, [they decided], you're a lawyer and if you do anything it ought to be in your field, and you ought to be head of it. What we came to then was that if the position of Attorney General was offered, I would consider that. But nothing else. And that's where we stood, although I knew that making that decision was like saying I was not going to be a member of the Carter cabinet. (244)

Following his election, Carter met with Jordan to discuss possible positions within his administration. She made it clear to him that she "wouldn't consider anything else but Attorney General" (245). And that "was how [she] was not in the Carter cabinet" (246). Instead, she began another term in Congress.

Jordan and Hearon end the autobiography with a description of Jordan's commencement address at Harvard. At Texas Southern University, Jordan had announced that she wanted to attend Harvard Law School. "I want to go to the best," she declared, "and Harvard is the best" (82). When her debate coach told her she would not be able to get into Harvard, Jordan decided to apply to Boston University. Despite her many successes, she always regretted not attending Harvard. So, when the university voted to give her an honorary doctoral degree, she accepted. "Harvard was a pinnacle for Jordan. It was perhaps the last remaining institution in which she sought to be accepted, to be 'let in'" (Rogers 292). She also accepted Harvard's invitation to give the commencement address. Jordan began that speech with the following words:

> Mr. President, were I to begin what I am going to say this afternoon by starting out, "I am very pleased to have been invited to speak to the Harvard community," you would probably discount that as a trite beginning. But if you did that, you would be in error. I have always held Harvard in high regard. I have always viewed a Harvard education as an unexcelled badge of intellectual achievement—if not superiority. I've always felt that way.
>
> My appearance here this afternoon may not honor you very much, but it certainly honors me.
>
> You know, the truth of the matter is, that one of the reasons I attended Boston University Law School was because I wanted to be close to Harvard. (qtd. in Jordan and Hearon 260)

Following the ceremony, Hearon describes the audience's reaction:

> Hesitantly, the crowd came forward to her. It was as if no one else but Barbara Jordan had spoken. Young and old, black and white, academically gowned and top-hatted, barefooted, gray-suited, they all stood in orderly rings around her until there were hundreds pressing forward, all wanting the same things, to touch her, to speak to her, to get her scrawled "BJ" on their program. (266–67)

Hearon continues her depiction of the event:

> What they [the audience] had been interested in were her words. Earlier she had
> said that the trouble with President Carter was that he couldn't speak, that he
> didn't know how to project the passion and compassion which let you bring
> your audience into where you were. But she had done that; she had taken them
> back to the southern Negro college of her early days and led them to where
> they sat that day. She had led them from her past to their present. (267)

After the speech, Jordan also reflects on the day:

> "I had them, didn't I?" . . . .
> "Sometimes I just stare in the mirror and look at myself and I say: 'Bar-
> bara, by golly you've done okay. It wasn't easy but you've done okay.' Tom
> Freeman told me I'd never get into Harvard, not to apply. But here I am. I did
> get in. Right now here I am. I'm in." (268)

Through Jordan and Hearon's storytelling within the configurations of "Black
World," "White World," and "World," we become acquainted with the societies
with which Jordan interacted, the challenges she faced as she sought inclusion in
worlds most considered beyond her grasp, and her responses to the principal,
often hegemonic, ideologies expressed within those broad-based communities.

In addition to the various segments of the national communities to which
she belonged, Jordan grounds her autobiography in the family and neighborhood
groups that guided and taught her life's lessons as a child. Particularly in the
early chapters of the book, Jordan invokes the spiritual entities, both religious
and ancestral, found within her community and family. Stories of her religious
upbringing and spiritual inclinations permeate much of the narrative. "The thing
of super importance in our life at my Grandfather Jordan's house, where we
lived," Jordan remembers, "was the Good Hope Missionary Baptist Church.
Sunday morning was a time of much activity in that household because everybody had to get ready and we had to be at Sunday school; and there was never
any discussion about whether you would go, you just always had to go" (25).
She describes her baptism and her decision to join the church, a conclusion
reached because she "got tired of being a sinner" (27) in a childhood game in
which the sinners were separated from the Christians. She could not become a
member of the Christians because she had not joined the church. She states: "I
decided to bring that to a halt" (27). Although much of her early life revolved
around the church, Jordan was not always a fan of the teachings of organized
religion, as she explains:

> I do not recall joy related to my experience of these years at church. What I got
> from them was a charter, a single plan offered to you that you must fulfill be-
> cause that was the only acceptable way. . . .
> How to die; we got that. But we were missing how to live. I do not recall
> any message of joy or love or happiness generated out of this experience. It was
> a confining, restricting mandate. I did not feel free to do anything other than

what was being presented to me as the way one must proceed; that whatever
you do in this life has to be in preparation for that other life. So, on balance, my
church relationship was, without doubt, a very imprisoning kind of experience.
(43–44)

One should not interpret this statement as Jordan's abandonment of Christianity, however. She "was so steeped in the Baptist biblical tradition . . . that she
could not escape the prophetic call of the Old Testament book of Daniel, in
which the prophet pointedly demands that the successful exiles in the land of the
enemy take responsibility for the less fortunate" (Rogers 128). Jordan's life and
the telling of that life in her autobiography illustrate her sense of obligation to
create opportunities and solve problems not only for herself but for her race as
well. Her "religious upbringing" constantly reminded "her that because she was
the successful exception, the glowing symbol of progress to her community, she
had a definite responsibility to 'the rest'" (128). According to Jordan in a 1981
speech to the Women's Committee at the Metropolitan AME Zion Church in
Hartford: "we live in this world in order to contribute to the growth, the development, the spirit, and the life of the community of humankind. . . . Christ, for
me, is love, caring, sharing, peace, hope" (qtd. in Rogers 128). She continues,
telling her audience that upon entering politics, she questioned her ability "to
perform in a political capacity and remain true to my Christian heritage" (qtd. in
Rogers 128). She recalls that she "consulted scripture, as well as my innermost
feelings and quickly recognized that . . . politics does not represent a divorce-
ment from Christianity. . . . It is the basis for my acting out my commitment to
myself and to all humankind" (qtd. in Rogers 128). Thus, the autobiography
exemplifies Jordan's pursuit of Jackson's ethical standard in African American
rhetoric.

As noted previously, Jordan's narrative begins with a discussion of her
Grandpa Patten followed by details about her Grandfather Jordan and her immediate family. In the role of caller, she invokes the spirit of Patten in the beginning of the discourse; this spirit then permeates her autobiography just as it did
her life. Jordan credits Grandpa Patten with teaching her the real lessons of life
during the Sunday evenings they spent together at his house in the Fourth Ward,
an even poorer section of Houston than the Fifth Ward. She recounts the experiences: "in those early years it was certainly the case that he was the only one
who talked to me—because mostly what adults do to children is to give them
catechism in some form or another. But in terms of instructions about how to
live, that is missing" (Jordan and Hearon 9). Part of the education Grandpa Patten dispensed involved the Bible. Jordan speaks about the lessons they shared:

So then we would read about the life of Christ. And I could understand Jesus
and God better from my grandfather talking than from the church, and that was
because he communicated in a language I could understand. He taught me that
if I followed his standards, and did what he said, and just followed the plan of
action that he set out for me, I would be moving in the path of following Christ.
And His Path was an overwhelming degree of self-sufficiency—that's a pre-

sent-day term, but that's the way I perceived it at that point. Grandpa was saying that the message of Jesus is: Don't get sidetracked and be like everybody
else. Do what you're going to do on the basis of your own ingenuity. He was
also saying that you couldn't trust the world out there. You couldn't trust them,
so you had to figure things out for yourself. But you had to love humanity, even
if you couldn't trust it. That's what he said the message of Jesus is. (10)

Grandpa Patten reinforced his lesson about autonomy in other ways as well. For
example, Jordan notes that "Grandpa didn't want me to be like the other kids.
That came through loud and clear. He would say this very directly" (7). His
words rang in Jordan's ears throughout her life: "You don't have to be like those
others. . . . You just trot your own horse and don't get into the same ruts as everyone else" (7). In fact, she had always known she was different. Upon her birth,
her father exclaimed, "Why is she so dark?" (qtd. in Jordan and Hearon 22).
Jordan indicates that as a child she had learned that "the world had decided that
we were all Negro" and that "some of us were more Negro than others. . . . The
whole system at the time was saying to us that you achieved more, you went
further, you had a better chance, you got the awards, if you were not black-black
with kinky hair" (62). Even within the African American community, some
shunned her because of "her excessive blackness" (61). In high school when
almost everyone she knew proclaimed they would become teachers, Jordan "began to announce that [she] was going to be a lawyer" although she "had no fixed
notion of what that was" (64). She concludes that "at the time when I decided
that I was not going to be like the rest, my point of reference was other black
people. It seemed an impossibility to make any transition to that larger world out
there" (64). Clearly, Jordan could not escape Grandpa Patten's advice. He left
his indelible imprint not only on her private life but also on the public policy for
which she advocated on behalf of "the rest."

Barbara Jordan calls forth another important spiritual entity in her narrative—her mother. As a young girl, Arlyne Patten had begun "to make a name for
herself as an orator in the Baptist Church" (21). Hearon notes that "as she
[Arlyne] grew up [Grandpa Patten] encouraged her, built up her command of
English, shaped her flare and fire with his inflections and intonations" (21).
People described her as an "eloquent, articulate person" who "if she'd been a
man . . . would have been a preacher" and "the speaker de luxe" [sic] (29). Patten hoped his eldest daughter would craft a better life for herself than he had
been able to fashion for his family. But, "eschewing her considerable gifts, she
chose instead to secure the middle-class respectable family life. . . . She married
the catch of the church, handsome Tuskegee student Ben Jordan, and put her
past, good and bad, out of her life" (21). With that decision "her talent for oratory was submerged into mothering, ambition transferred, remaining only as a
golden voice talking to babies" (30). Despite the fact that she endured a subser-
vient role in her marriage, Arlyne Patten Jordan attempted to maintain some
independence. For example, when her youngest daughter was just a toddler, she
"took the bus to town . . . and got herself fitted for a diaphragm at the Planned
Parenthood Center." She had decided "that three children born in four years

were enough to raise" (36). Jordan, who describes their relationship as "close," loved her mother and recognized the oratorical talent and sense of independence she inherited from her. These examples illustrate Jordan's sense of connection and responsibility to the immediate community to which she belonged as well as her passionate desire to become something more than she saw all around her. From her mother and especially from her Grandpa Patten, she gained a conception of empowerment and agency that ultimately led her to a life in politics.

The combination of the topical organizational approach found in the three major sections of the narrative and the chronological structure presented in its chapters frames Jordan's quest for liberty and the journey she describes in her life story. As Hearon promises in the Preface, the autobiography depicts how she got "from There to Here" (viii). Like her ancestors, Jordan details her movement toward freedom, away from a world of oppression to an entrance into a national community that allowed a measure of "authentic self-expression and fulfillment in a social role" (S. Smith, *Where I'm Bound* ix) as she engaged her work in the U.S. Congress. For example, observing her mother spending her days washing, ironing, cooking, and cleaning, Jordan knew she wanted something more, that she wanted her life's journey to explore new territory, as she indicates:

> I don't know that I ever thought: "How can I get out of this?" I just know that there were some things that I did not want to be a part of my life, but I had no alternatives in mind at that point. Since I didn't see movies, and we didn't have television, and I didn't go anyplace with anybody else, how could I know anything else to consider?
>
> So I was as accepting of life then as I could manage, because I did not have a choice. It would have been fun to rebel at some point, but I didn't. You just didn't. I had to be where I was because at that point in time I had to be taken care of by my parents. I knew there were some things that I wanted to be different for me at some later date, but most of the time I went along with the way things were. (48–49)

Jordan eventually discovered education would help her find a different path. During her first years in high school, she felt compelled to fit in, to engage in the activities other teenage girls and boys enjoyed. She was not a serious student. As she suggests, "it was all very fun at that time" (61). Ultimately, she recognized she did have some "ability." She was smart and she had inherited striking oratorical skills from her mother and her father. Jordan decided that she would rather stand out from the others than blend in with them (61). She describes this revelation: "So I started to think maybe I should take school more seriously. It also pleased me when I had discovered I was brighter than a lot of the kids in my class. . . . It makes it a more rewarding experience to go to school if you feel, as in my instance, that you're a little brighter than your classmates" (62). After graduating, Jordan attended Texas Southern University, which at first "seemed an extension of Phillis Wheatley High School: a continuation of the black strip of Houston, of riding around in cars with Bennie [her sister] and the crowd, of feuding with her father" (75). Still wanting to distinguish herself, however, she joined the debate team where, through her travels throughout the South, the

Midwest, and the East, she encountered the meaning of segregation in the white world outside the oppressed, but somewhat safe, confines of Houston and Prairie View, Texas. She also discovered what it meant to be able to enter restaurants through the front door (79), as she found herself encountering many new paths.

In 1954, during Jordan's junior year at Texas Southern, the Supreme Court declared in *Brown v. The Board of Education* that "separate" could never be "equal." She was thrilled with the decision. She recalls thinking that "finally . . . those kids in elementary and high schools are going to be able to go to school with white kids, and that's going to be good. I wish it had happened a few years earlier so I could have been with those white kids myself, because I would have loved it. But they sure have something to look forward to" (Jordan and Hearon 80). But Jordan's elation was short-lived. Despite the Court's decision, little was happening to move integration forward. She describes her impatience: "I woke to the necessity that someone had to push integration along in a private way if it were ever going to come. That was on my mind continually at that period—that some black people could make it in this white man's world, and that those who could had to do it. They had to move" (81). And so, Jordan resolved to become one of those who would work to deconstruct segregation; she decided to attend law school.

In her first year at Boston University, Jordan continually feared she would not make the grades, but she also refused to accept the possibility of failure as she notes: "I had to make law school. I just didn't have any alternatives. I could not afford to flunk out. That would have been an unmitigated disaster." (92). As she explains, she also found a new level of education in law school:

> Finally I felt I was really learning things, really going to school. I felt that I was getting educated, whatever that was. I became familiar with the process of thinking. I learned to think things out and reach conclusions and defend what I said.
>
> In the past I had got along by spouting off. Whether you talked about debates or oratory, you dealt with speechifying. Even in debate it was pretty much canned because you had, in your little three-by-five box, a response for whatever issue might be raised by the opposition. The format was structured so that there was no opportunity for independent thinking. (I really had not had my ideas challenged ever.) But I could no longer orate and let that pass for reasoning. Because there was not any demand for an orator in Boston University Law School. You had to think and read and understand and reason. I had learned at twenty-one that you couldn't just say a thing is so because it might not be so, and somebody brighter, smarter, and more thoughtful would come out and tell you it wasn't so. Then, if you still thought it was, you had to prove it. Well, that was a new thing for me. I cannot, I really cannot describe what that did to my insides and to my head. I thought: I'm being educated finally. (92–93)

Despite the lack of confidence she experienced throughout the three years of law school, Jordan did not flunk out. But, she refused to allow her family to plan the trip to Boston to attend her commencement until she was certain she would graduate. "When I went by the office and got the computation that said that I

was a law school graduate, when it was definite I was going to make it," she
admits, "I called home, and my father just couldn't wait. . . . They all loaded up
to come: my mother and father and Bennie and Rose Mary" (98). She continues,
describing her reactions to the ceremony:

> But it turned out the law school graduates got to walk across the stage to get
> their degrees. I couldn't wait to get that scroll, tied with a little red ribbon, back
> to my room, and open it to make sure that it was really a law degree from Bos-
> ton University. But that's what it was. And I sat down and cried. I thought:
> Well, you've done it. You've really done it.
>   Then we all went out and had a celebration—and we were a long way
> from the low ceiling on [Houston's] Campbell Street. (98)

Jordan's journey after law school brought her back to Houston, where she
passed the Texas bar and asked herself, "What next?" (109). Still living with her
parents, she had business cards printed that said "BARBARA JORDAN, Attorney at Law" (109), and began distributing them to friends, family, church members and anyone else who would take one. This strategy worked. She notes that
"then people did start asking me to do things for them as an attorney, so that I
was working out of the dining room at Campbell Street and driving the little
Simca to the courthouse" (109). Finding herself with more time than business,
Jordan wondered, "What does one do after work with one's free time?" (110).
She found the answer in volunteering for John F. Kennedy's campaign for the
presidency. Eventually, she became a speaker for the Harris County Democrats.
She describes her speaking activities: "I spoke primarily to black groups, political groups, civic organizations, clubs, and churches. Any group could call who
needed a speaker, and I would go. I was not restricted to black groups, but of
course all of the white groups were of a liberal bent" (111). After the election,
Jordan acknowledges that she "had really been bitten by the political bug" (111).
She elaborates: "my interest, which had been latent, was sparked. I think it had
always been there, but that I did not focus on it before because there were certain things I had to get out of the way before I could concentrate on any political
effort. . . . Now that I was thinking in terms of myself, I couldn't turn politics
loose" (111).
     Encouraged by a friend, Jordan entered a new phase in her political adven-
tures when she announced her candidacy for the Texas House of Representatives
in the 1962 election. In the primary election she failed to gain sufficient votes
from the largely white electorate even though many of them had appeared to
support her (113–16). Despite the disappointment of losing, Jordan continued to
actively participate in the local political scene. Two years later she decided to
run once again for the Texas House, and once again, she lost (117). Jordan describes her reaction to the second loss:

> When I saw that the second race was an extension of the first [in 1962] . . . I
> didn't go to the campaign headquarters. Instead, I just got in my car and drove
> around most of election night. The question was: "Is a seat in the state legisla-

ture worth continuing to try for?" . . . . Am I just butting my head against something that's absolutely impossible to pull off?" . . . .

I had to decide by myself whether I was going to stick it out a little longer, and thinking that if I did I certainly couldn't do it in concert with anybody else. I couldn't let anyone else get in my head and make my decision any more. . . .

The first order of business was to decide: is politics worth staying in for me? (117).

Ultimately, Jordan's response to her own question was "yes." As discussed previously, the 1964 Supreme Court's decisions that led to reapportionment of legislative districts in order to uphold the principle of "one person, one vote" "put into effect the machinery which would change the voting outcomes in Harris County" (128). Following the loss in her second race for the Texas House, Jordan continued to ask herself: "'How many more times are you going to run, Barbara?' Now with the redistricting of Harris County, the answer was simple: 'One more time'" (130). In a speech crafted to win the backing of the Executive Committee of the Harris County Democrats for her bid for a Texas Senate seat, Jordan declares: "I ran a race in 1962. You endorsed me and I lost. I ran a race in 1964. You endorsed me and I lost. I want you to know I have no intention of being a three-time loser" (132). Hearon notes that "the campaign was on, and this time Barbara was not going to go around talking about retrenchment and reform. . . . She knew that you didn't do that in Texas. You just sold yourself; so she would sell Barbara Jordan" (132). She set up her campaign headquarters "down the street from her office, in the Fifth Ward where her constituents lived" (132), not in downtown Houston. She "set up her own appointments" with journalists rather than relying on others to do this for her (132). Directing "her own block work . . . she sent out sample ballots to all the thirty-five thousand black voters in her district, showing how to vote for her" (132). This approach to personal interaction with voters and the media proved a successful strategy. She beat her opponent "two to one—making nationwide news as the first black woman in the Texas Legislature" (134). Jordan reflects on her victory, "this [is] the way it ought to be. I am going to stay in the Senate as long as I want to stay there. Nobody can stop me now" (134). As indicated previously, Hearon describes the victory, noting that "the law had allowed Barbara, at last, to enter the all-white world of the Good Old Boys" (136).

Jordan began her tenure in Austin as "an exception to every rule" (138). Hearon offers the following description of those early days in the state capitol:

To reporters who ganged around to see how this black female from Fifth Ward in Houston was fitting into this closed world, she answered tartly: "As it turned out, the Capitol stayed on its foundations and the star didn't fall off the top."

It stayed in place, and the Senate gradually relaxed, because Barbara remained an exception. She made it clear there would be no need to rewrite the rules.

She took her own advice (delivered to the Lincoln, Nebraska, NAACP in a speech): "Throw away your crutches and quit complaining because you are black. Don't belch, choke, smoke, and wish for something to go away. Because when you are finished belching, choking, smoking, and wishing, society will still be here."

Her still-increasing bulk worked for her. She was massive, commanding, safe. She didn't look like their dear old mother, and she didn't look like their beauteous young girlfriend, so none of the old patterns needed to operate. Here was someone cut from a different mold, who, being outside their standard frame of reference, would not disrupt it. (138–39)

As she had done during the campaign, Jordan relied on personal interactions with her senatorial colleagues to forge professional relationships that would allow her to function effectively in the Senate. So, among other strategies, she attended various social gatherings. "I wanted them to see me firsthand and not just read about this great thing that had happened in Houston. I wanted them to know I was coming to be a senator," she continues, "and I wasn't coming to lead any charge. . . . I was coming to work and I wanted to get that message communicated personally" (140). Her strategies worked, eventually earning her an invitation "to bring her guitar along and join Senator Charles Wilson's annual quail hunt, hitherto an all-male junket" (140). She also knew that she needed to carefully gauge when to weigh in on issues. "You don't get in there having a drink quickly," she notes. "You work and you learn the rules and you keep your mouth shut until it is time to open it" (145). As she quietly and quickly learned the ropes of conducting business and passing legislation in the Senate, Jordan earned the respect and trust of colleagues on both sides of the aisle. "By the time she presented her first bill," Hearon notes, "she had learned to take advantage of this mutual trust" (148). Jordan also ascertained that her "outsider" position as both a woman and an African American generated considerable credibility on some issues. "I am a member of two groups long discriminated against in Texas politics," Jordan proclaims. "But I discovered that the weight of those factors that are a part of whatever I am, will sometimes cause people to vote for an issue I am in favor of rather than against it" (148). By the end of her first term, Jordan had gained "the knowledge that she could get things done behind the scenes in the Texas Senate, that she knew the rules that were not in the book and how to apply them" (151). Hearon describes Jordan's journey during those first two years:

> She and the Senate club had come a long way in her first term. Far enough that she could say to her colleagues when they elected her Outstanding Freshman Senator: "When I first got here we approached one another with suspicion, fear, and apprehension. But now I can call each one of you singularly *friend*." And they could feel safe, and good, to hear that. (152)

In 1968, Jordan was elected to a second term of four years, during which she was appointed to a number of major Senate committees and given the responsibility for overseeing important legislation, including a "workman's compensation reform package" and "legislation on unemployment compensation" (153). Her work and speeches in the Senate gained the attention not only of the citizens of Texas, but members of the National Democratic Party and President Lyndon B. Johnson as well.

Sensing the time was right, Barbara Jordan decided in 1971 to seek a newly established U.S. congressional seat representing the Houston area. In October, she organized a "gala fund-raising event" in downtown Houston to raise money for her campaign (157). She invited President Johnson to speak on her behalf and he agreed to attend the event. Hearon provides the following account of his speech in support of Jordan's candidacy for the U.S. House of Representatives:

> Turning to the radiant candidate on the platform, he told them whom they had come to honor. "Barbara Jordan proved to us that black is beautiful before we knew what that meant," he said. "She is a woman of keen intellect and unusual legislative ability, a symbol proving that We Can Overcome. Wherever she goes she is going to be at the top. Wherever she goes all of us are going to be behind her. . . . Those with hurting consciences because they have discriminated against blacks and women can vote for Barbara Jordan and feel good." (159).

Jordan won the election. Before she departed the Texas Senate, her colleagues elected Jordan president pro tem of a special session, putting her third in command should the governor or lieutenant governor both travel out of the state at the same time. Thus, on June 10, 1972, Barbara Jordan served as Governor for a Day, "the first black woman governor of any state" as reported in the *New York Times* (qtd. in Jordan and Hearon 172).

Jordan's political journey now took her to the nation's capitol. Both literally and metaphorically, Washington, D.C., was a world away from the Black neighborhoods of Houston, Texas. Her experience in the Texas Senate, however, proved valuable as she learned her way around the House. One of the first items of business new representatives attended to included making requests for committee assignments. With guidance from President Johnson, Jordan requested the Judiciary Committee and, with his assistance, she received the appointment. Service on that committee catapulted her into the midst of the Watergate hearings and national history. Jordan recalls reactions to her testimony before the committee:

> Well, when I walked out the front door, they broke into this big cheer—screaming, "Right on!" and waving fists in the air. And someone said: "I knew that when you talked you were going to base whatever you were going to say on the law, if you had to go back to Moses." And that was the first reaction I had to my speech.
>
> I think they liked it that I didn't present a harangue, but that I was very serious about what I was doing. I felt that was what I was communicating. That here was a person who had really thought this through and had reached a decision, a considered, sincere, and sensible decision. (199–200)

Jordan maintained that seriousness and focus throughout her tenure in the House. A 1975 article in the *Wall Street Journal* concluded that "Rep. Jordan has achieved, in one congressional term, more honors and perhaps more power than most members of Congress can look forward to in a lifetime" (qtd. in Jordan and Hearon 220). As she began a new congressional term in 1977, Jordan recalls that she "felt [herself] in a different kind of role in that third term" (246). She states:

> By that time I could read that I was a national figure and not flinch, because I was a national figure, and people had heard about me all over the country. So what had to be considered was: What does one do now? Well, I had a real sense that ultimately a woman or a black would be the President or the Vice President, but not now. So I was not thinking in those terms.
>
> Although I was still very junior in the congress, I had begun to feel very senior. I felt that I had been in the Congress many more years than I had been. What started to creep into my thinking was the question: How many times do you repeat these performances? How many times do you keep presenting a bill and getting it passed and getting the President to sign it? How many pens do you want? (246–47)

Feeling the constraints imposed by constituent expectations and the more mundane congressional routines, Jordan began to ponder the possibility of moving beyond Congress in order to exercise more influence on national issues. She remembers feeling "more of a responsibility to the country as a whole" than to the "people in the Eighteenth Congressional District" (247). She comments, "I thought that my role now was to be one of the voices in the country defining where we were, where we were going, what the policies were that were being pursued, and where the holes in those policies were" (247). Believing staunchly that the government of the United States was a government of the people and that she could help generate the requisite citizen participation necessary for the successful workings of the democracy, Jordan concluded that "being an elected public official took time away from the time [she] would otherwise have to think about other problems and address specific problems" (249). She expands this idea, noting:

> I was now convinced that I had reached a point where my words were going to be heard and attended to, whether I prefaced my name with Representative, Congresswoman, Senator, or whatever. And If I had reached that point, then I didn't have to be a part of those political institutions which demand so much of your time in a routine way. I believed that in order to free myself to move fully in a new direction, I would of necessity have to leave elected politics and pursue the platform wherever I could find it. And I was thinking at that point . . . that the platform would be presented to me, that it wouldn't be difficult to find.
>
> So the thing to do, I told myself, was not to run for reelection for a fourth term, but rather to free my time in such a way that it could be structured by the country's needs as I perceived them. I decided to move in a new direction. (249–50)

Following her commencement address at Harvard, Jordan comments on her decision to leave politics, offering the following insights about the next phase of her journey. She concludes her personal narrative with these words:

> "I don't know here this afternoon what will be next for me," she said. "I won't know what the next step is until I get there. I know that when I went to Boston, and Austin, and Washington, I took with me everything I had learned before. And that's what I will do this time. That's the point of it, isn't it? To bring all you have with you wherever you go." (269)

Conclusion

Upon her retirement from electoral politics in 1979, Barbara Jordan began teaching public policy at the Lyndon B. Johnson School of Public Affairs at the University of Texas in Austin. Rogers contends that "Jordan was intrigued with the idea of becoming a professor. It would be a role compatible with her desire to speak out on national issues. . . . She would be able to read and think and further develop her ideas about the Constitution, the national community, and the role of government" (296). She also remained involved in state and national politics and maintained an active lecture schedule. In 1988, she seconded the nomination of Lloyd Bentsen at the Democratic National Convention. Texas Governor Ann Richards appointed her Special Counsel for Ethics in 1991. She delivered a second keynote address at the 1992 Democratic National Convention. In 1993, President Bill Clinton appointed her Chair of the U.S. Commission on Immigration Reform. She died on January 17, 1996.

Barbara Jordan fiercely protected her privacy and independence, yet she wanted a public dialogue with the nation in order to contribute to the realization of a government, of a country, that she could both respect and honor. She understood the power of the word, of Nommo. Jordan knew she had exceptional oratorical skills and that she could use them to her advantage—both for personal advancement and for the upliftment of women and the African American community. When she retired from the House of Representatives, Jordan responded to a question from a reporter for the Houston *Forward Times* when he asked "what she thought her greatest accomplishment as a member of Congress had been." She replied:

> Do you want to know what I *really* think? At this point in time, my single greatest accomplishment is, and I mean this quite sincerely, . . . it is representing hundreds, thousands, of heretofore nameless, faceless, voiceless people. . . . The letters I enjoy most are those who write and say, "For the first time I feel there is somebody talking for me." If I've done anything, I have tried to represent them, and I've done that to the best of my ability. I consider that as the best accomplishment. (qtd. in Rogers 297)

Using the autobiographical format, Jordan and Hearon delineate numerous examples of the ways in which Jordan navigated the multiple-binds imposed by her race and gender. Clearly, at the beginning of her political career, Jordan made a conscious choice to limit her private life in order to focus on her public work. She chose not to marry and become a mother. That is not a decision other women included in this volume made. Jordan, however, did not feel she could meet the demands of the traditional feminine role and succeed in politics. Hers was a singular vision. As various stories throughout the narrative attest, Jordan employed personal contact and genuine interpersonal communication as rhetorical strategies to overcome the prejudices of others created by both her race and her gender. And, there was the voice. One cannot overlook the power of her oratorical prowess to influence both detractors and supporters. Indeed, she developed a variety of tactics to succeed in what was literally a white male political world.

Throughout the narrative, the authors provide detailed glimpses of U.S. society and the effects hegemonic political policies have on the lives of individuals within marginalized groups. The images depicting Jordan's early life present particularly vivid accounts of the plight of African Americans in the South prior to the civil rights legislation of the 1960s and provide the foundation for Jordan's legislative agenda. In many ways, Barbara Jordan's life journey embodies the search for civic justice and equality in twentieth-century U.S. culture.

Ideologically, Jordan had "faith in the Constitution" (Jordan and Hearon 187) and believed laws created by a government of the people had the power to uphold the humanity of all. In her youth, she learned that "separate was not equal" (73) and that it was not "right for blacks to be in one place and whites in another place and never shall the two meet" (63). These lessons formed the basis of her political agenda. She concluded that minorities could gain equality "only through legal changes" (213). A staunch individualist, Jordan never forgot her Grandpa Patten's advice: "don't get sidetracked and be like everybody else" and "you [have] to love humanity, even if you [can't] trust it" (10). She embraced the idea that "we live in this world in order to contribute to the growth, the development, the spirit, and the life of the community of humankind" (Jordan qtd. in Rogers 128). "Jordan's intent was to translate abstract discussions about the common good into the nitty-gritty work of actually creating a better society" (Holmes vii). These themes, woven together, create the fabric from which Jordan fashioned her life and the telling of her story.

By virtue of the political life she lived and her ability to write and publish her autobiography, Barbara Jordan embodies the very notion of personal empowerment. Through example she proves that women, and in particular African American women, can shape their own destinies, despite the challenges they may encounter. Jordan's narrative stands as a testimonial to female personhood, self-worth, and agency. Her personal story encourages and empowers women to embrace equality and seek leadership opportunities, as the following passage exemplifies:

The problem remains, my friends who are assembled here, the problem remains that we [women] have difficulty defining ourselves. The problem remains that we fail to define ourselves in terms of whole human beings, full human beings. We reduce the definition of our lives just a little bit because somewhere in the back of our minds is the thought that we really are not quite equal. . . . So what are women going to do about it? What are we going to do about it? How are we going to change all that? How are we going to reverse the trend that has women at the bottom of whatever profession we are talking about? . . . . It is going to take long, hard, slow, tedious work. And we begin with ourselves. We begin with our own self-concept. We begin to try to internalize how we really feel about ourselves and proceed to actualize the thinking that we finally evolve from the look inward and the projection outward. . . . The women of this world . . . must exercise a leadership quality, a dedication, a concern, and a commitment which is not going to be shattered by inanities and ignorance and idiots, who would view our cause as one which is violative of the American dream of equal rights for everyone. . . . We only want, we only ask, that when we stand up and talk about one nation under God, liberty, justice for everybody, we only want to be able to look at the flag, put our right hand over our hearts, repeat these words, and know that they are true. (Jordan qtd. in Jordan and Hearon 218–20)

Barbara Jordan's "Voice" still inspires women in the twenty-first century as they continue the long journey toward equality.

Notes

The author offers her appreciation to Barbara Seidman, Professor of English and Vice President for Academic Affairs/Dean of Faculty at Linfield College, and Susan Whyte, Director of the Linfield College Library, for their continued encouragement and support of her professional endeavors and to her departmental colleagues, Janet Gupton, Tyrone Marshall, Jackson Miller, and Vicky Ragsdale for always "being there."

Chapter Three

From Housework to House Work: The Political Autobiographies of Patricia Schroeder

Molly A. Mayhead and Brenda DeVore Marshall

Patricia Schroeder launched her political journey in 1972 from campaign head-quarters located around her kitchen table in what appeared a most improbable bid for a seat from Colorado's First Congressional District. A mother, wife, lawyer, feminist, and community activist, Schroeder did not envision herself as a politician. She admits that she had only "approached politics from the safe perch and vantage point of a classroom, teaching political science and constitutional law first at the University of Colorado, then at Regis College" (*24 Years* 3). Her husband encouraged her to run, saying that if she "didn't get into the race and articulate the issues, they will not be discussed. You think the government's policies on Viet Nam and the environment are wrongheaded, and you're always urging your students to get involved. It is an opportunity that may not come again" (6). These were not her only issues, however. She did not run "only to champion women's rights and the American family" (*Champion* 24). She thought of herself as "one of the many men and women across the country who were working together to improve the quality of life on many fronts" (24). To her own astonishment, as well as that of the pundits who didn't give her a chance of winning the election, Schroeder became the first woman to win a U.S. congressional seat in the state of Colorado. She joined four other new female representatives, including Barbara Jordan, in the House chambers on January 3, 1973. In a Dorothy-like whirlwind, Patricia Schroeder found herself propelled from a life of housework on behalf of her family to one of House work on behalf of her constituents. Although seventy-one women had served as congresswomen prior to the election of these five individuals, the U.S. House of Representatives in the early 1970s remained a male bastion that challenged political acumen and leadership from its female members.

It comes as no surprise, then, that from the beginning of her political career, Patricia Schroeder faced discrimination from many of her congressional colleagues and learned firsthand the degree to which the issues labeled "women's" and "family" concerns received little or no serious consideration in political debates and legislation. Always somewhat an outspoken activist, Schroeder reveals that "during her first day on Capitol Hill, a male colleague asked how she could be a mother of two small children and a member of Congress at the same time. She responded, "I have a uterus and a brain and they both work" (Schroeder, *Champion* 28; Mayhead and Marshall 42; "Schroeder"). Early in her congressional tenure, Schroeder successfully lobbied for a seat on the Armed Services Committee, whose control epitomized male political power (*Champion* 25). Fueled by her general sense of social injustice and her own personal experiences as a female, Schroeder championed the causes of women, families, and community throughout her political career.

In this chapter, an analysis of Patricia Schroeder's autobiographies, framed within the perspectives of feminist standpoint theory, examines the relationship between her personal lived experiences and the public political causes she advocated and in so doing reaffirms the existence of intersections between the "politicization of the private and the personalization of the public" (S. Smith, Autobiographical" 186). Knowing that many women viewed her position as a congresswoman as an opportunity to have their voices heard, Schroeder understood the importance of her role as a woman and a politician. As she explains:

> From my earliest days in Congress I noticed that many women, visiting Washington, would stop to see the representative of their home district and then come by to see me, their "congresswoman." These meetings, and the letters I got, all began the same way—with a short apology, because the woman was not from my district, and then the explanation that she didn't know where else to go. The letters and visits had a common complaint: the people who made laws were out of touch. (*Champion* 26)

The following investigation mines Schroeder's narratives to elucidate the rhetorical strategies she engaged during her twenty-four years in office to successfully stay in touch with the electorate, challenge the status quo, and effect public policy decisions on behalf of those whose voices are marginalized.

Feminist Standpoint Theory and the Politics of the Marginalized

In her personal narratives, *24 Years of Housework . . . and the Place is Still a Mess* and *Champion of the Great American Family: A Personal and Political Book*, Patricia Schroeder describes her political career from the vantage point of an outsider-within, "a person who is inside a particular social group through daily interaction and activities but is also excluded from that group because she is defined as not 'one of them'" (Wood, *Communication* 209). That is, while Schroeder operates as a member of the male-dominated U.S. Congress, she does so from the social location or standpoint of a woman, an outcast or "other" in the eyes of many of her congressional colleagues. "Standpoint in this context refers to a specific societal position, the result of one's field of experience, which serves as a subjective vantage point from which persons interact with them-selves and the world" (Orbe 26). However, as Nancy Hartsock argues, the social location in and of itself does not constitute a standpoint. "A standpoint is not simply an interested position (interpreted as bias) but is interested in the sense of being engaged" ("Feminist Standpoint: Developing" 107) within a particular context of experience (Orbe 26). Julia Wood comments on this point as well:

> But social location is not standpoint. A standpoint is achieved—earned through critical reflection on power relations and through engaging in the struggle re-quired to construct an oppositional stance. Being a woman does not necessarily confer a feminist standpoint. . . . A feminist standpoint grows out of (that is, it is shaped by, rather than essentially given) the social location of women's lives. ("Feminist Standpoint Theory" 61)

Furthermore, the concept of standpoint "refers to historically shared, *group-*based experiences" (Collins, "Comment" 375). Patricia Hill Collins elaborates on this idea, concluding that "the notion of standpoint refers to groups having shared histories based on their shared location in relations of power—standpoints arise neither from crowds of individuals nor from groups analyti-cally created by scholars or bureaucrats" (376). Thus, it is not one's individual-ized marginalization that creates one's standpoint, but rather one's experience of oppression as a member of a specific group or groups. Scholars have used standpoint theory as a "feminist theoretical framework to explore the lived expe-riences of women as they participate in and oppose their own subordination" (Orbe 25; Hartsock, "Feminist Standpoint: Developing" 126). These descrip-tions suggest that through the invention of an "oppositional stance," an active resistance to the dominant worldview, the creation of a standpoint necessarily entails the political.

Mark Orbe asserts that "the first principle of standpoint theory is the con-viction that research must begin from one's concrete lived experiences rather than abstract concepts" (26–27). Thus, standpoint theory challenges traditional notions of epistemology as it acknowledges multiple approaches to the creation of knowledge. "The concept of a standpoint depends on the assumption that epistemology grows in a complex and contradictory way from material life" (Hartsock, "Feminist Standpoint: Developing" 108). Feminist standpoint theory, then, "asks what we know if we start from women's lives" (Wood, "Feminist Standpoint Theory" 62). Consequently, feminist standpoint theory provides an effective lens for interrogating women's political autobiographies.

Julia Wood articulates five key arguments found in feminist standpoint theory. First, "society is structured by power relations, which result in unequal social locations for women and men" ("Feminist Standpoint Theory" 62). Typically, men have formed the dominant or privileged groups while women have been relegated to the subordinated and marginalized. Second, "subordinate social locations are more likely than privileged social locations to generate knowledge that is 'more accurate' or 'less false'" (62). Because those in positions of power benefit from "not seeing oppression and inequity" (62), their vision becomes "both partial and perverse" (Hartsock, "Feminist Standpoint: Developing" 107). On the other hand, some scholars argue that those who are oppressed understand their own circumstances as well as the positions of privilege that ultimately create the domination they experience and are more likely to investigate the sources of that oppression (Wood, "Feminist Standpoint Theory" 62). Third, standpoint theory posits the existence of the "outsider-within," and suggests it "is a privileged epistemological position because it entails double consciousness, being at once outside of the dominant group and intimately within that group in ways that allow observation and understanding of that group" (62). Fourth, as noted earlier, "standpoint refers not simply to location or experience, but to a critical understanding of location and experience as part of—and shaped by—larger social and political contexts and, specifically, discourses" (62). And, fifth, individuals with multiple group memberships, including but not limited to those "defined by sex, race, ethnicity, sexual orientation, and economic class" may achieve multiple standpoints (62).

From a rhetorical perspective, feminist standpoint theory supports the concept that discourse both shapes our communities and is itself molded by our experiences in those same groups. Susan Hekman argues that "feminist standpoint theory is part of an emerging paradigm of knowledge and knowledge production that constitutes an epistemological break with modernism," and suggests that it "defines knowledge as particular rather than universal; . . . it defines subjects as constructed by relational forces rather than as transcendent" (356). She continues:

> Under this new paradigm, politics is defined as a local and situated activity undertaken by discursively constituted subjects. Political resistance, furthermore, is defined as challenging the hegemonic discourse that writes a particular script for a certain category of subjects. Resistance is effected by employing other discursive formations to oppose that script, not by appealing to universal subjectivity or absolute principles. (357)

Given Schroeder's personal experiences as a member of a marginalized group, her actions within the Congress, and the manner in which she both reflects upon and explicates her political life within her personal narratives, feminist standpoint theory provides a viable lens through which to examine those discourses.

Housework and House Work

Patricia Scott was born in Portland, Oregon, but moved a great deal. Her father, a private pilot, flew along the West coast, asked by the government to "report anything he saw" during World War II (*24 Years* 98). The family lived in several different cities before settling down in Des Moines, Iowa, after the war. Schroeder reports that her mother went to work as a school teacher while her father found employment in aviation insurance (98). Her mother, she recalls, "believed it was better to read a book than to dust it, and housekeeping was considered an equal-employment opportunity in [their] home. Mother," Schroeder posits, "had it right" (98). Following in her father's footsteps, she earned her pilot's license, and to pay for college she flew to crash sites to assess aviation losses (100). She made so much money her first year that she not only paid her tuition but bought a Lincoln, "a bright pastel aqua," and she fondly recalls that "it looked like an Easter egg on wheels" (101).

In her two books, Schroeder spends little time discussing her early years, choosing instead to begin a detailed description of her life within the framework of her education. She recalls the gendered boundaries in her undergraduate career, noting that she had wanted to study "aerodynamic engineering," but a guidance counselor screamed at her that she would "just be wasting" her parents' money (101). So, as she puts it, she "caved and launched into a history major" (101). After graduating in three years Schroeder began considering a stint in law school. "It seemed," she recalls, "not too narrowing as a profession, with lots of options and possibilities" (102).

Schroeder's decision to go to law school dismayed her parents. They thought no one would want to marry her if she had a law degree and worried that they would never be grandparents (*24 Years* 102; *Champion* 23). Her mother found Schroeder's choice so traumatic that when friends asked where her daughter was and what her daughter was doing, she replied vaguely, "'Oh, back East. On some project'" (*Champion* 23). As Schroeder reveals in an aside remark, though, "of course I fooled [them] by marrying another law student" (23).

Schroeder enrolled in Harvard Law School and recalls that she had an "absolutely miserable time" (*24 Years* 95). In 1961 the class there consisted of fifteen women and 500 men who "acted as if [the women] constituted estrogen contamination" (93). Male professors and male classmates resented the presence of women. Schroeder recounts her experience with one of the professors, Erwin Griswold, who "invited the freshman women to his home" and informed them "that he was opposed to women attending law school but that the board had outvoted him" (94). He added that the admissions committee admitted additional men to that year's class, certain that the "women would never use their degrees and the world might otherwise be deprived of enough Harvard lawyers" (94). Griswold then ordered the women to sit on folding chairs and articulate why they were "wasting such sacred space" (94).

Harvard's male students echoed Griswold's disdain for women. Schroeder reports that on her first day, one of her male classmates "refused to take his assigned seat when he saw that he had been placed next to a woman," next to Schroeder (*Champion* 23). "He let me know," she continues, "that he had never gone to school with a girl before and he didn't think he should have to start now. Before he stomped off to have his seat changed," she muses, "he also sniped that I should be ashamed of myself for taking up a spot in the class that should have gone to a man" (23). Although she found herself "submerged in sexism," Schroeder still considered Harvard useful. Not only did she find her husband, Jim (*24 Years* 95), but she later recognizes that "the best preparation for infiltrating the boys' club of Congress was the boys' club of Harvard" (93).

After graduation, Schroeder and her husband moved to Denver. They wanted to start a family early in their marriage but waited until they both had earned their degrees. In 1966, Schroeder became pregnant with the couple's first child, Scott. Two years later, she experienced a very difficult pregnancy. Two weeks before her due date she knew something was terribly wrong, went to the hospital, and then waited for twelve hours while the staff tried to locate her obstetrician (107). Schroeder wanted another doctor to look at her, but a nurse kept telling her to "calm down" (107). Schroeder was actually hemorrhaging (108). She learned for the first time that she had been carrying twins and that one had died earlier in the pregnancy and that the other had suffered a brain hemorrhage and couldn't be saved.

"This second pregnancy," writes Schroeder, "had been an intense, draining, and humiliating nightmare. I was angry at the doctor for refusing to listen to me, but I was angry at myself for putting up with it. Here I was," she continues, "letting a doctor convince me I had no right to question his judgment about my pregnancy and my baby. He intimidated me and made me feel powerless," she continues. "The staff," she concludes, "put me in a position of surrendering all control. I vowed never again" (109). She changed doctors, and her next pregnancy, in 1970, "was a pleasant, uneventful nine months" (109). Unexpected hemorrhaging two days after leaving the hospital shattered the illusion of a safe and uneventful delivery, however. Schroeder spent her thirtieth birthday in intensive care, convinced she was going to die (*Champion* 32).

In recalling the difficulty of her pregnancies, Schroeder reveals that "these experiences certainly reinforced [her] belief that a woman has a right to decide what happens to her own body. That is a basic right, and it should not be curtailed by the government or anyone else" (33). She elaborates:

> Pregnancy is not like a nine-month cruise; it can be life threatening. I also understand that other women may have compelling reasons to avoid a pregnancy that could wreak havoc with their lives and the lives of their children. For this reason, I was active on reproductive health issues long before I became politically active. I have always been amazed that a fetus is assigned a personality immediately upon conception—girls have hair ribbons and are holding dolls in the womb, boys are playing with trucks—but the woman is rarely mentioned by conservatives in debates on reproduction. She is just an impersonal receptor. She has no right to decide what is best for herself or any children she might have. This kind of thinking seems illogical to me. (33)

Except for the difficult pregnancies, Schroeder and her husband found life in Denver enjoyable. Jim Schroeder worked for a small law firm and Schroeder practiced law with the National Labor Relations Board (*24 Years* 3). When her first child was born in 1966, Schroeder "had the luxury of giving up full-time employment and taking on, mostly at home, only projects that sang" to her such as pro bono work for Planned Parenthood and the Denver Fair Housing Group (3). Actively involved in local politics, her husband came home one night from a democratic committee meeting and informed Schroeder that her name had come up as a candidate to challenge the incumbent Congressman. She describes the attitude of her husband and the other committee members: "'you'll never win, but you know you really ought to carry the flag; somebody ought to discuss the issues.' I think they thought it would hurt me the least to do it because I didn't have some big job. I had part-time jobs at that time because we had two little kids" ("Patricia Schroeder" 217). After some "sleep" and "some arm-twisting," she agreed to run (*24 Years* 6).

Schroeder thus entered the rough-and-tumble, sometimes perplexing, and often frustrating world of politics. Friends in advertising came up with the slo- gan, "She wins, We win" (10), and they designed posters addressing what Schroeder thought were "the three most important issues of the campaign" (11). Her one trip to Washington seeking financial assistance proved disastrous, as the "professionals" there looked at her posters aghast. "Surely these haven't hit the street yet," they said (12). They informed her that "a real candidate would 'dis- cuss' issues, but not boldly take sides" (12). Schroeder recalls that as a "neo- phyte in politics" she "didn't understand that ducking the issues was the goal of most campaigns." She thought she was "supposed to deal with them" (12).

While campaigning, Schroeder sought help from organizations she believed supported her candidacy. One of her "greatest disappointments," the National Women's Political Caucus that she helped establish in 1970, didn't back her because "the people running it thought it was too early for a woman to run for Congress" (14). While she counted on women's support, she recognized early in her congressional experience that "the community support received by other minority representatives was much stronger than the support that [she] got in the women's community" (193). Certain that her "female colleagues would be eager to join the advocacy" for women's issues, Schroeder was surprised when they "often argued that [she] was moving too fast and pushing too hard" (193). Schroeder thought she would have the support of "certain issue-focused groups but they could not get past [her] gender" (14). For example, the National Labor Relations Board for whom she had worked sent her "a whopping $50 check" (14). Ultimately, Schroeder decided that rejection from the "establishment" helped her, for she listened to her friends' instincts, rather than the "advice of high-paid pros" (14). Gathering with her friends, she called her campaign "kitchen-table" media and believes that the voters "responded to [her] direct- ness" for "it seemed to penetrate the normal clutter and noise of politics" (14– 15).

Schroeder won the primary with 55 percent of the vote and began to campaign seriously in the general election. She recalls that in the campaign she discovered early that she "enjoyed talking to people one-on-one and did a lot of it" (*Champion* 14). Since the Republican Party believed she had no chance to win, they kept her opponent in Washington until the very last month. Schroeder believes their dismissal of her candidacy gave her a head start (14). She suggests that her greatest asset in this campaign turned out to be her opponent, James D. "Mike" McKevitt, who referred to her as "Little Patsy" (*24 Years* 15). He hired a group of young women to wear plaid skirts and to bubble about what a "great guy" he was (15). "They looked liked real period pieces and were decimated in the press" (15). Early polls showed Schroeder leading, but she felt there was some mistake. However, when the votes were finally counted on election day in November 1972, she won with 52 percent of the vote (15). Schroeder had promised her children a vacation, win or lose, and so the day after the election they left for Disneyland. "What better place to regroup and plan ahead than Tomorrowland?" she asks (15).

Arriving in Congress, Schroeder quickly discovered that sexism pervaded the hallowed halls, much as it had at Harvard. She hadn't realized that "women officeholders were considered such aberrations. The House of Representatives," she continues, "was not representative of the population" (*Champion* 18). "I felt like I had broken into a private club," she fumes (*24 Years* 19). She recalls that "most of her new colleagues considered [her] a mascot or novelty, as if the Denver voters had mistakenly thought 'Pat' meant 'Patrick,' or else they assumed [her husband] was the congressman" (19). Few of her colleagues bothered to mask their hostility, as one said, "'politics is about thousand-dollar bills, Chivas Regal, Learjets and beautiful women. So what are you doing here?' I gave the dumbest possible answer, way beyond his ken," Schroeder replies. "'Because I care about the issues.' He looked at me as if I were mad" (20).

As noted previously, four other women began their congressional careers when Schroeder arrived in Washington; two others joined later, assuming the offices of their newly deceased husbands (21–22). Schroeder recalls that "the women in Congress had to wage virtually every battle alone, whether we were fighting for female pages (there were none) or a place where we could pee" (31). She notes that when she arrived in Congress, "there were no women working as . . . Capitol police, doorkeepers, or parliamentarians" (155). "Congress," Schroeder continues, "had passed laws about sex discrimination but conveniently exempted itself" (155). She recounts her early months in Congress when much of her time was "spent trying to master the rules and procedures of the House. It often seemed so stilted and obtuse," she observes. "But I also spent a lot of time learning about other sets of rules, the unwritten ones of the guy gulag. Those were even harder to ascertain" (37). Schroeder found one of these unwritten "rules" particularly rankling: "many of [her] colleagues liked Washington as a female-free zone" (38).

As a freshman member of Congress, Schroeder expected to be assigned to a low ranking committee like "Merchant Marines and Fisheries" (40). However, she fought to earn a seat on the Armed Services Committee, recalling that she "wanted to be part of a committee that controlled approximately sixty-five cents out of every dollar allocated to Congress" (40). She got the appointment but was denied a "seat." The Chair of the committee, F. Edward Hébert, objected to Schroeder's appointment and that of Ron Dellums, an African American. Hébert announced that while he couldn't "'control the make-up of the committee, he could damn well control the number of chairs in his hearing room,' where he was enthroned on a carpet of stairs, surrounded by military flags. He said," Schroeder remembers, "that women and blacks were worth only half of one 'regular' member, so he added only one seat to the committee room and made Ron and me share it" (41).

Colleagues, the press, and the public found Schroeder particularly unique. While only a handful of women occupied seats in the House (and none at the time in the Senate), Schroeder was an even "bigger novelty" because she was the only congresswoman with young children (*Champion* 18). "During those first years," she recalls, "reporter after reporter wanted pictures and stories of the congresswoman with toddlers. They all seemed to be convinced that our family somehow wasn't normal. In a way," she suggests, "they were right. I was the only member of Congress to come to the House floor with diapers in a handbag. Few members kept a bowl of crayons on the office coffee table," she continues, "or had birthday parties for their children . . . in the members' dining room" (18). Even Bella Abzug, the congresswoman from New York and America's "premier feminist" told Schroeder that with small children she "[wouldn't] be able to do this job" (*24 Years* 22). Shirley Chisholm also told her that she didn't "think [she] could do this" ("Patricia Schroeder" 223). The job of working mom required significant juggling from everyone in the Schroeder family. In the first year of her congressional tenure, Schroeder used to tell reporters that what her family "desperately needed was a wife" (*Champion* 17). "Our house was never a page out of *House Beautiful*, but after my election I had a great excuse for the way it looked," she jokes. "I was doing House work elsewhere" (*24 Years* 131). More seriously, Schroeder notes that at the time "only 27 percent of mothers who" like her "had at least one child under the age of three were in the workforce" (*Champion* 18). "I was one of the fortunate ones," she concludes, "that could afford a full time housekeeper. Even for families with resources, housekeepers and child care were difficult to find; for most families and single mothers, the tighter financial bind made such help almost impossible" (18).

Schroeder intimates that she did not go to Washington as a one-agenda politician, that is, to focus only on matters of concern to women. She "knew that there were many areas of American life the government had neglected, not only the so-called women's issues" (*Champion* 24). While she notes that her "congressional issues were broad," she also believed it important to push for "women's equality" (25). She found, however, that the gendered barriers of the legislative branch extended to the executive branch, determining what topics could be discussed and by whom. She says little about Presidents Gerald Ford and Jimmy Carter, but heaps criticism on Richard Nixon, Ronald Reagan, and George Bush for their antipathy to problems faced by women and families.

Nixon vetoed a large day care bill soon after Schroeder arrived in Congress (*24 Years* 142). The supporters could not get enough votes to override the veto. She recalls being shocked, for she "thought any reasonable person would under-stand that subsidizing a parent's day care was more cost-effective than subsidiz-ing a non-working welfare family. Yet Nixon couldn't figure that out" (142). One of the problems, Schroeder suggests, is that most elected officials have "traditional families with those 'good wives' held up as paragons in [her] fifties home ec course. But only about ten percent of America's families share the so-cioeconomic lifestyle of members of congress. When someone says 'day care,' the men in Congress hear 'baby-sitting.' They don't understand," she concludes, "that day care is not a luxury for working people" (143). Schroeder adds that "today's young mothers have a much tougher time than [she] did when [she] had [her] family twenty-five years ago" (*Champion* 65). She elaborates:

> Although I valued my career, I had no second thoughts about quitting work to stay home with my young children. In that economy, we could live on one sal-ary without fearing that the house would be repossessed. I could find part-time work, something that is so hard to come by today. There was less competition for good child care than there is now, and part-time child care was much easier to find. (63)

"One reason changes in the workplace have been slow in coming is that our society is still, to an overwhelming degree," Schroeder posits, "governed by older upper-middle-class white men who know little of the family balancing act because their wives have insulated them from it" (67). Her observations regard-ing her work on the House Armed Services Committee validate her concerns about the misperceptions surrounding childcare. She recalls that she would "talk to generals who tell [her] privately that their number-one personnel problem is inadequate child care for the families of service people in their command" (67). "Family issues" become one of the greatest factors men and women use to de-termine if they will reenlist, Schroeder argues, and they "also affect the readi-ness of our armed forces" (67). But the commanders would say nothing publicly about these concerns in committee hearings, for they feared "being labeled soft if they push family issues" (67). "We must make it okay for men to deal with family issues," she asserts, "if we are to speed up progress" (67).

The Reagan presidency, Schroeder argues, "was a devastating period for se-rious policy-making about issues of concern to women. The new women's is-sues were: Where is your diamond insured? and Who is your decorator? The Equal Rights Amendment died" (*24 Years* 72). The Reagan administration did not like controversy, she recalls, and the message from it was, "'we don't deal with women who demonstrate, so lower your voices and put on some pearls'" (72). When Reagan did deign to meet with women leaders, the occasion served as little more than a "meet and greet" where the president "told stories about his movie career" (73). Even when Nancy Reagan agreed to meet with the Congressional Women's Caucus the terms of her appearance were explicit: "no substantive issues were to be discussed" (74). The result: "no elected female leaders in either party got to discuss women's equity with the president or the First Lady for eight years" (74).

Schroeder recalls that when George Bush took office Democrats held hope that things would be different. He had promised a "kinder, gentler America" and Schroeder thought he meant it (77). She remembers that his wife, Barbara, "was certainly more approachable than Nancy Reagan and had supported wonderful projects concerning disadvantaged women and literacy" (77). Schroeder believes, however, that Bush somehow lost the will to enact positive change for women (77). At best, she suggests, "both Reagan and Bush seemed terrified of women's issues. They appointed some women to Cabinet positions and deflected questions about women's legislation by pointing to them" (77). Schroeder recalls with particular disdain Bush's veto of the Women's Health Equity Act (77). This act mandated that the National Institutes of Health establish an office of women's health to review every study congress funded, for science and doctors did not know enough about women's health as every study was based on male subjects (78–80). Schroeder recounts that the Congresswoman's Caucus "made the act the centerpiece of its legislative agenda, educating [their] colleagues one by one" (81). Bush's veto of the bill aroused women's anger, so to deflect ill will, the president appointed a woman to head the National Institutes of Health, "hiding behind her skirt when asked about the veto" (81). Schroeder suggests that "one of the major creators of the gender gap in the 1992 election was Bush's veto of the Family Leave and Women's Health Equity acts. Women were furious about Bush's action," she concludes, "and voted for Bill Clinton in big numbers" (82).

It didn't take long for the newly-elected president, Bill Clinton, to meet with the Women's Caucus, Schroeder writes (82). The members were thrilled when he talked with them for over two hours (82). "He told us to start passing our bills again. We did—what a joy," she exclaims. "He signed the Women's Health Equity Act and Family Medical Leave, lifted the outrageous restrictions on RU-486 and the gag rule prohibiting medical caregivers from discussing reproductive choices with women. It was wonderful," Schroeder concludes (83).

In 1992, the same year the country elected Clinton, a new crop of congresswomen arrived. "Suddenly," Schroeder exclaims, "10 percent of Congress was female" (121). But, not everyone found the change in Congress positive, as Schroeder recounts: "on swearing-in day in January 1993, as I was beaming at all my new colleagues in skirts one of the old bulls said to me, 'look at what you've done. The place looks like a shopping center'" (122). She notes that although the women enjoyed success, many of her female colleagues lost their election in 1994 due to what she terms a "male backlash" (122). Unfortunately, she concludes, "polls later showed that many women who had voted in 1992 didn't bother to vote in 1994, no longer feeling threatened. Never forget that politics and democracy need constant maintenance" (122).

Throughout her career as a congresswoman, Schroeder continued to press for reforms in a variety of areas, including family leave, reproductive rights, workplace equality, and child care. She recalls that some of her most vociferous opponents happened to be women:

> It was depressing that while I was pushing hard for women's rights, the first to criticize my agenda were often other women. Opportunity for all women has been a hard sell. Women in government who have power to come on board often refuse to lend their support unless the issue strikes a personal chord. When we wanted to open the military academy doors to women, some women responded, "Who wants to go to a military academy?" When I was working on breast cancer legislation, I'd hear, "My sister has lupus, and I want funding for that." Other minority communities are much better at rallying politically around generic betterment for all. They understand that more opportunity is good for everyone, even if it's seemingly irrelevant to their own personal lives. (168)

Apparently, issues can only be political if they are personal.

In the spring of 1987, Schroeder was "cochairing the presidential campaign of fellow Coloradan Gary Hart" (173). She recalls, in a somewhat perplexed fashion, that Hart kept saying she was his "good friend," and mused, "*if I am his good friend, he has no good friends*" (174). She states she felt comfortable with Gary, but never close. "There was always a wall" (174). Schroeder remembers that for years there had been rumors of his sexual proclivities. Hart's presidential bid collapsed after he challenged the press to find evidence of his affairs. They accepted his dare to "go ahead and follow" him. *Miami Herald* reporters photographed Hart on board a yacht with a blonde woman, Donna Rice (176). He subsequently withdrew from the race. Schroeder reflects on her disappointment when Hart, and other male power brokers, hurt themselves politically because of private affairs. She says of Hart: "I felt we'd all been let down by him. I felt he used me because having a woman at the head of his campaign might deflect these issues" (177). Part of her disappointment regarding Hart stemmed from her belief that he "was in so many ways a feminist. . . . On every women's issue raised in Congress, he was instinctively there" (177). As an aside, Schroeder notes that Oregon Senator Bob Packwood, forced to resign after charges of sexual harassment, "was every Democratic woman's dream—on the issues" (177). She adds, "I'm not sure why I have these different standards, but I keep hoping people will act as they vote, that their private lives will match their public personae. If they have a lousy voting record on women's issues," she bluntly states, "I don't expect much" (177).

After Hart dropped out, Schroeder's friends, supporters, and family members urged her to "take a look" at entering the presidential race herself (178). In June, someone leaked to the press that Schroeder was considering a presidential bid. Upon her return to the Denver airport after a trip, she found "the world was there. [She] never had to call a press conference" (178). As she recalls, "the essential question" she "was looking at was, 'is America man enough to back a woman'" (178). The pressure to be a successful candidate was significant. "Instantly," Schroeder ruminates, "I was seen as Everywoman, advancing the female struggle for a stronger voice in government. Like it or not," she continues, "my potential candidacy for the highest elected office in our country was going to be a hook for political pundits to appraise the progress of women" (179).

Schroeder took her presidential potential seriously, and she demanded that others do the same. She decided that she would "not make this a symbolic campaign. I would only run," she states "if I had a good chance to win. The press had categorized me as a 'women's candidate' (180). I didn't want to deny my gender, but I also did not want my gender to block my message" (*24 Years* 180; *Champion* 6). She planned to assess her chances at the end of summer to determine if her candidacy was viable. She did "not want to go into debt," and if at the end of summer she "didn't have enough campaign money to be competitive," she said she "would pull the plug" (*24 Years* 180–81). David Brinkley on his weekly television show reduced this to the phrase, "no dough, no go" (*24 Years* 181; *Champion* 7). Schroeder had to keep reminding herself that "common sense" and not ego had to be the driving force of her campaign (*Champion* 7). She recognizes that task would be formidable. "Almost overnight," she muses, "I had to explore publicly the questions other candidates had considered much earlier" regarding money, organization, staffing, and message (*24 Years* 179). She also believes that her appearance constructed another barrier, for "women still don't 'look presidential' to many voters. At least I didn't" (*Champion* 6). Despite the difficulties associated with mounting a presidential bid, Schroeder learned a valuable lesson during that summer of campaigning:

> Traveling across the country, I found that men and women, from college students to senior citizens, wanted politicians who understand what is going on in their lives and government policies that reflect that understanding. Audiences asked questions about my personal life, to make sure I wasn't just spouting rhetoric. "How do you work and have a family?" and "What did you do about child care?" were questions that made it clear Americans were desperate for someone to help them juggle all the roles and chores modern life has laid upon them. (*24 Years* 181)

After assessing her situation early in the fall, Schroeder decided she "didn't have the pieces in place for the professional campaign she wanted to run" (*Champion* 6). She gave a speech to supporters in Denver, trying to make it clear, she states, "that I had learned that the presidency was not necessarily out of my grasp, but that to win would take a lot more preparation and time and money than I had" (7). As she got to the part of her speech stating that she would not continue her bid, the crowd groaned, and then began to chant, "'Run, Pat, Run'" (*24 Years* 185). She then burst into tears, observing that while she went on with her speech, it was her tears and not her words that made the headlines (*Champion* 8; *24 Years* 185). She wryly notes that the one good result from showing emotion was that "crying came out of the closet" (*Champion* 8; *24 Years* 186). She postulates that a gendered double standard exists around the act of crying. She received letters from a variety of politicians and power brokers recounting times they cried. "What do Mikhail Gorbachev, Norman Schwartz-kopf, Ronald Reagan, Margaret Thatcher, Chile's General Pinochet, John Sununu, Governor Jim Thompson, Oliver North, George Bush, minority leader Bob Michael, California Speaker Willie Brown and almost every famous American athlete and Pat Schroeder have in common?" she asks ironically. "We are all in the weep-stakes. Now crying is almost a ritual that male politicians must do to prove they are compassionate, but women are supposed to wear iron britches" (*24 Years* 187).

Schroeder continued serving in congress after she ended her presidential bid. She retired from the House in 1996 having performed twenty-four years of House work. However, she warns readers of her political autobiographies, "I can't imagine not working on behalf of causes that will improve the family, the nation, the world, the planet. In my dotage," she predicts, "I will probably be faxing or e-mailing or communicating by whatever twenty-first century method I cannot even fathom about social wrongs that need to be righted" (*24 Years* 240). Noting that the work to improve society is never done, she issues a clarion call for collective action at the end of *24 Years*: "I have no time for a lot of [hand] wringing but a lot of time for shirtsleeve-rolling. It can get lonely. Con-sider this a postcard from the front. Wish you were here. Roll 'em up" (241).

Good Housekeeping: Personal Standpoints, Political Action

Patricia Schroeder's autobiographies recount her life in politics. They detail the attitudes she encountered and the battles she fought in twenty-four years of House work. She enjoyed success and suffered failure, and her writings reveal the lessons learned in the gendered worlds of law school and Congress. Wood's articulation of the five key arguments of feminist standpoint theory provides a framework with which to assess Schroeder's work as important political argu-ment.

A child of the 1940s, Patricia Schroeder certainly knew first hand the ine-qualities society's institutionalized power relations created for women. Even as early as high school, Schroeder was told that men could do things that women couldn't. The male professors and classmates at law school reinforced that no-tion by protesting the presence of Schroeder and the other female students. Her first campaign and early years in Congress extended the gendered barriers even further. She had to discover and then learn to navigate the impenetrable rules of the male bastion. Told that she couldn't have a career and family at the same time, Schroeder proved the critics wrong. But doing so always remained a strug-gle. Whether it was actually gaining a physical seat on the Armed Forces Com-mittee or ensuring women access to medical care, Schroeder continually had to fight the preconceived and gendered notions of her male counterparts. Through-out both of her autobiographical texts, Schroeder details her efforts to effect political change, "a process of changing power relationships so that the meaning of power itself is transformed" (Hartsock, "Political Change" 28).

As a mother juggling a family and a career, Schroeder's standpoint allowed her a more accurate knowledge of reality through her first-hand observation of the inequities the social system foisted on working mothers and made her appreciate the daily struggles they had to face. Her male colleagues did not consider the issue of child care important because they never had to find or deal with it. As Schroeder argues, "to such men family issues are too soft and sentimental and don't belong to the no-nonsense world of work" (*Champion* 67). "But," she asserts, "the real point is that children are our most valuable national resource. Taking good care of them is a national responsibility—for parents, for employers, for all of us" (70).

In addition, Schroeder's difficult pregnancies afford her a more accurate view of the health care system. First, she felt bullied by male doctors who didn't really take into account what was happening to her. Moreover, she recognized health care procedures are often based on a male standard. She and her female colleagues had to fight to get women's testing mandated, something her male colleagues didn't consider important. Having seen first-hand the "male-ness" of the health care system, and the political system, Schroeder knows that issues such as women's reproductive health care rights need constant vigilance and advocacy.

Patricia Schroeder broke into the male-dominated power structure of the U.S. government and recognized that it functions to perpetuate itself and to make it difficult for the oppressed to gain entrance, much less power. From her position as an "outsider-within," she realized that, despite their importance, some men, notably the tough officers of the military she dealt with while on the House Armed Services Committee, couldn't bring themselves to even mention family issues when testifying about the needs of their troops because they didn't want to appear "soft." Her male colleagues in Congress generally considered issues like day care to be women's issues. Schroeder's "insider-outsider" placement helped her identify and challenge key gendered political issues.

Once Schroeder moved "inside," she remained baffled by women who didn't support her or her advocacy of important legislation affecting females. Perhaps most disturbing, however, are the women who think that to move from outside to in, they have to attack other women. In an essay she wrote for Robin Morgan's *Sisterhood is Forever*, Schroeder states:

> Some women in politics long to be part of the boys' "gang." When Gerry Ferraro ran for vice president, I saw many a woman attack her, thinking that would be an entry ticket into the gang—but no way. Such a woman accomplishes nothing except selling out another woman. Every time so-called liberal women want something—daycare, pay equity—the gang sends one of "their" women out on attack. On TV it looks as if one woman says it's a great idea, another says it's not, so women haven't made up their minds—therefore, we needn't do anything about it. Unfortunately, Republicans have developed this tactic into an art. On the democratic side, there are women hesitant to push the guys as hard as some of us did, because these men weep all over you, whining, "You don't understand! If I vote pro-choice, ooooh, what will they say!" Then there are the

women who are "trying to move things along." It's not that they lack vision,
but they want to remain players. ("Running" 33)

By virtue of this outsider-within position, Schroeder maintained a "double consciousness" as a congresswoman. She was "at once outside of the dominant
group and intimately within that group in ways that allow[ed] observation and
understanding of that group" (Wood, "Feminist Standpoint Theory" 62).
Schroeder's understanding of her status within the Congress and the larger implications for women's status within the hegemonic U.S. social order guided her
work in the House.

Schroeder achieved her initial understanding of her "location" in society
through the various discriminatory actions she encountered in her educational
and professional endeavors. While she considered herself a wife, mother, and
lawyer, she had never pictured herself in Congress until others prodded her to
run. While campaigning, she learned to ignore the "experts" in Washington,
D.C., and go with the instincts of her friends and family, thus reaching the rank
and file voters in a way that had escaped the incumbent and subsequently led to
his defeat. Her truncated presidential bid exposed her to the pragmatic side of
politics. While she may have had enthusiasm and a desire to improve the country, the bottom line became one of the lack of money, preparation, and a political machine. Rather than run merely a symbolic campaign and become a cau-
tionary tale for future women who seek the highest office, she withdrew from
the race, convinced that some woman would eventually be president, just not her
at that particular time. Thus, her political beliefs and experiences led her to develop an idealistic and pragmatic political consciousness through which she resisted the dominant practice of politics as usual.

Schroeder looked at childcare and family issues from the vantage point of a
working mother, and she discovered and fought the gendered boundaries of law
school and Congress from her position as a working woman determined to make
life better, specifically trying to "create opportunities by correcting inequalities"
(*Champion* 113). Although it can be said that as an attorney, Schroeder was a
member of the privileged class, she embraced and understood the importance of
multiple standpoints, knowing from personal experience, and from listening to
her constituents, that jobs, status, and sometimes even survival require resistance
to dominant ideologies and practices.

Schroeder's two personal narratives present her life through the specific
frame of her political career; she spends precious little time discussing her
childhood or personal life. The latter she meticulously and intentionally links
directly to politics. This places her work squarely in the realm of the political
autobiography, which focuses "overwhelmingly on the political life of the
author with little in the way of personal introspection. . . . [T]he presentation
usually aims to enhance the role of the author in the politics of his or her day"
(Blewett). Gerda Lerner explains the importance of the political autobiography
in an interview with Joan Fischer. Lerner suggests that "thinking, the solving of
problems of mental constructs, can be valid only if validated by experience, by

the application of thought in public life. And that's politics" (Lerner). In other words, the life of a politician and the politics of life are inextricably linked, as "politics determine[s] our lives" (Lerner). Schroeder's experiences as a woman fighting for an education, campaigning for a seat in the male bastion of Congress, and considering a presidential candidacy lend credence to the observations noted above. Politics do not occur in a vacuum. Schroeder entered the political world because of her commitment to improving her community, her state, and her country. She knew from experience that someone needed to work for change. As she worked her way through the intricacies of the House, she gained even more first-hand knowledge that gendered boundaries had to be broken to pave the way for equal opportunity for all.

Since Schroeder left the House, the "face" of Congress has, to some extent, changed. California Congresswoman Nancy Pelosi became the first female Speaker of the House in 2007, and more women now serve in the Senate than during Schroeder's tenure in office. In January 2001, Schroeder attended the Senate ceremony when Hillary Clinton, the newly elected senator from New York, took the oath of office (Lowy 201). She recalls the image vividly: "'It was so funny seeing the president of the United States follow his wife behind like the tail of a kite. . . . It tells you these role models are changing so radically that it makes it a very interesting time to be alive'" (201).

We agree.

Chapter Four

The "Feisty" Feminist from Queens: A Feminist Rhetorical Analysis of the Autobiographies of Geraldine Ferraro

Catherine A. Dobris

Traditionally, autobiography has been the province of rich, white men recanting stories of privilege within the generic constraints of its form in a given time period. Consequently, when women choose to engage in the previously male-dominated genre of autobiographical writing, they may face particular obstacles imposed by the nature of the endeavor. As Jill Ker Conway questions, "how can a woman write an autobiography when to do so requires using a [male privileged] language which denigrates the feminine and using a genre which celebrates the experience of the atomistic Western male hero?" (*When Memory Speaks* 3). In response to this paradoxical challenge, some women autobiographers may struggle to confront the disembodied, reductionistic Westernized male "hero story," by trying to find a woman-centered language which translates "herstory" more effectively. Susan Stanford Friedman observes:

> Individualistic paradigms do not take into account the central role collective consciousness of self plays in the lives of women and minorities. They do not recognize the significance of interpersonal relationships and community in women's self-definition. . . . [T]his autobiographical self often does not oppose herself to all others, . . . does not feel herself to exist outside of others, and still less against others, but very much with others in an interdependent existence that asserts its rhythms everywhere in the community. (79)

Other women authors may mirror the more traditional male narrative approach to story-telling, conforming to mainstream rhetorical standards to guarantee a wider audience for the text resulting from hegemonic unconsciousness that does not afford her insight into the limitations and boundaries of using an inauthentic language. Thus, the study of women's autobiographies, particularly autobiographies of self-proclaimed feminists, presents unique rhetorical challenges that may be explored through a feminist methodology. Specifically, feminist criticism has acted to elevate autobiography to "a privileged site for thinking about issues of writing at the intersection of feminist, postcolonial, and postmodern theories" (Smith and Watson, *Women* 5).

This chapter provides a feminist analysis of Geraldine Ferraro's autobiographical writing to explore how a contemporary public woman integrates traditional female private space, such as family and interpersonal relations, with the public sphere, in this case the presentation of self in the political arena. Contemporary women's autobiographies, such as those written by Ferraro, provide appropriate narratives by which to examine the construction of gender since they offer a gendered worldview of a particular private and public life by a woman who wrestles both with patriarchal constraints as well as her own gender identity.

Ferraro is a significant female voice in the vanguard of 1980s feminism; therefore, feminist critical methods advanced by Foss and Foss are employed in order to understand how her rhetoric both reinforces and challenges the dominant construction of gender in the public sphere. First, a brief historical sketch of Ferraro situates the rhetor as a contextual figure in contemporary culture. Next, the discussion describes Foss and Foss' perspective on feminist analysis. The remainder of this chapter examines Ferraro's major publications for the nature of perceived autobiographical exigencies, the nature of the narratives, including characters, settings, and themes, the nature of the world created through the writings, and the construction of self in relation to feminism and gender.

Geraldine Ferraro: The Rhetor

In *My Name Is Geraldine Ferraro: An Unauthorized Biography*, Lee Michael Katz contends that Geraldine Ferraro was brought up like a "princess" by her Italian American parents, Antonetta and Dominick (23–29). She lived in a beautiful home in Newburgh, New York, in the 1930s and 1940s. Her father's death, when she was only eight, altered her forever, both materially and fatalistically. Her mother found herself with few funds and diminutive means to support her children except through repetitive, low-paying factory work. Education for their children had been a goal of Ferraro's father, and her mother managed to pursue his vision and her own, sending both Ferraro and her brother, Carl, to private Catholic schools where they appear to have obtained high quality educations. Ferraro distinguished herself from grammar school through law school, earning high marks and participating in a wide range of academic and athletic arenas. Ferraro's concomitant goals to obtain a law degree, marry, and raise a family were certainly unusual for white, middle-class women of her 1950s generation who almost universally chose the latter, but if the former then only the former. Less unusual was her choice, after marrying John Zaccaro, to eschew the workplace for more than thirteen years while she assumed the role of a stay-at-home "mom" for the couple's three children. In 1973, initially against her husband's requests that she remain in the home, Ferraro resolved to return to the workplace. Over the next eleven years and allegedly with the full support of her husband and children, Ferraro rose quickly from Assistant District Attorney in Queens, New York, to New York congresswoman. She then became the first female United States vice presidential candidate on a major party ticket, running as a Democrat with Walter Mondale.

Two Autobiographies: The Artifacts

In large part because Ferraro became the first and so far the only woman to run as a vice presidential candidate on a major party ticket in the United States, in 1985 she wrote her autobiography, *Ferraro: My Story*, with the assistance of Linda Bird Francke, covering much of the same ground included in Katz's unauthorized version of her rise to political power. Later, in 1998, she wrote another account of her story, *Framing a Life,* with Catherine Whitney, this time concentrating ostensibly on how the lives of her mother and, to a much lesser extent, her grandmother and daughters, influenced her life story. Finally, in 2004, Ferraro wrote a postscript for a new edition of her initial autobiographical work in order to update current readers on her last twenty years both politically and personally. Ferraro provides no information in either text regarding the background of the ghostwriters or her relationship to them.

While Ferraro's life might have been deemed noteworthy sans her nomination, given her other accomplishments as a pioneering woman in law and politics, both autobiographical works outline her ascendancy to this paramount event. Thus, Ferraro's autobiographies provide essential insights into a woman whose entrance into the political arena placed her on the precipice of the realization of second-wave feminism in her 1980s bid for the second highest office in the United States. While in most ways Ferraro assumed the traditional rhetorical garb of her male counterparts, her very presence in such a visible public contest guaranteed a revisioning of stereotypical female public roles.

Feminist Method

As feminist rhetorical scholar Sonja Foss suggests, even when there is clear evidence that women orators have achieved eloquence equal to or surpassing that of their male peers, their significance is often overlooked (166–67). Ferraro's nomination on the Democratic ticket ensured that her significance would not be disregarded given her incursion into this high-profile public position. A feminist analysis of her autobiographical writing provides insight into her integration of personal and public selves.

In the 1970s and 1980s, feminist scholars in rhetoric and literature began to develop perspectives and methods to study the work of historical and contemporary women from a feminist theoretical model. According to Foss, "feminist criticism is the analysis of rhetoric to discover how the rhetorical construction of gender is used as a means for oppression and how that process can be challenged and resisted" (168). Foss adds that there are three basic principles which frame contemporary American feminism: "women are oppressed by the patriarchy," "women's experiences are different from men's" (166), and "women's perspectives are not now incorporated into our culture" (167). Acknowledging these three observations reveals the potential for feminist rhetoric to be evaluated from a systematic approach that does not impose a hegemonic perspective on the artifact. Geraldine Ferraro's autobiographies are best understood using the theoretical lens of these feminist observations. Specifically, Ferraro explores her conflicts with patriarchal oppression, examines her unique experiences as a woman politician, and documents her career efforts and autobiographical reflections so as to incorporate her experiences as a woman into the dominant culture's historical record.

Foss describes specific procedures for conducting a feminist rhetorical critique (165–74). First, the critic identifies a unit of analysis (169). In this case the two autobiographical texts serve in their totality as the unit of analysis. Second, the scholar poses a gender specific question in order to examine the artifact (169). This chapter evaluates how Ferraro's texts both affirm images of women in public and private life and liberate women from the confines of those stereotypes. Finally, the critic identifies the portrayal of gender in the artifact, thus determining what the artifact suggests about how the patriarchy is maintained, affirmed, challenged, and/or transformed (171). A feminist analysis of Ferraro's autobiographical discourse probes the traditional accounting of "women's communication [as it has been] muted and misinterpreted, producing inaccurate accounts both of women's communication and of women's lives" (Foss and Foss, *Women* 1).

More specifically, the nature of autobiography lends itself well to the rhetorical feminist analysis of "process," because it is a genre that reveals the course of one's life by judiciously presenting the chronological decisions made by the rhetor, starting at birth and continuing either until particular benchmarks are achieved or until she has moved into a new phase of existence. Therefore, an examination of the autobiographies, including Ferraro's most recent postscript, reveals a comprehensive picture of the autobiographer's representation of her public and private gendered identity. The feminist critic restructures the historically male-centered autobiographical form in order to subvert the often linear approach to storytelling. A feminist analysis examines the interconnectedness of knowledge between and among topics that might be less apparent from a more linear patriarchal construction of the text. The principle of "feminist approximation" is achieved, in part, by replacing traditional analysis of autobiographies concerned primarily with judging the veracity of a story, with a feminist perspective that acknowledges the relativity of truth. Finally, the feminist critique acts intersubjectively in cooperatively evaluating the influence the rhetor's story has in constructing and reconstructing images of women in the public sphere. There are three central elements of analysis in studying Ferraro's texts: the nature of the exigence; the nature of the narratives; and the nature of the world created that leads to an assessment of the feminist construction of a public and private self. Her choices within each area reveal reasons, significant ideas, and ultimately, the gendered world Ferraro inhabits.

The Nature of the Autobiographical Exigence

As discussed earlier, autobiographers choose their genre for many reasons. When a controversial political figure becomes the "first" to accomplish a significant socio-political act, unauthorized biographies such as those written about Ferraro by Rosemary Breslin and Joshua Hammer and Katz are inevitable. In the particular case of Ferraro, by her own account she was the target of antagonistic journalists both during and after her bids for public offices. The nature and intensity of these attacks clearly led to Ferraro's major controlling exigence for writing her own autobiography to "set the record straight." Throughout her texts she explicates significant elements of her personal life that were assailed by the press and also defends two particular loved ones, her husband and her deceased father.

In her autobiographical narratives Ferraro takes on key issues of the alleged mob connections and financial misdeeds of her husband, John Zaccaro, to argue emphatically that he, and by implication she, was falsely accused by politicians, the media, and the government. At times she argues that one or the other of them received bad advice from inept or unethical attorneys, and she argues that "any errors . . . were technical matters, not ethical or criminal violations" (*Ferraro* 205).[1] Ferraro admits that following the election, Zaccaro pled guilty to "a single count of a scheme to defraud, a misdemeanor" (278), but she insists that his lawyers would have won had he gone to trial. She contends he pled guilty primarily to avoid further publicity. While her argument may not be particularly convincing—public exoneration would have served as the strongest antidote to the onslaught of negative media exhortation—the autobiographical forum allows Ferraro to have the last word on the topic of her husband's, and by association, her own, purported guilt.

Ferraro also defends her long dead father in response to the explosive editorial published close to the election deadline by journalist Guy Hawtin, who hints at Dominick Ferraro's illegal activities shortly before a purportedly "suspicious" demise (*Framing a Life* 142–44). In the final chapter of *Ferraro* (316–17) and also in *Framing a Life* (160–62), Ferraro recounts how she followed up the journalist's story, disproving his thesis and, in fact, arguing that he lied about his information when he claimed that he was not able to interview the doctor who attended Dominick Ferraro during the time before his death. In both texts she cites her father's undertaker and friend, Mr. Colonie, and an anonymous housekeeper for corroboration. Since the first source is a friend and the second, unnamed, neither makes a strong case to a discerning critic. In *Ferraro* she claims that the investigative reporter admits to an error in the original story and that he did in fact interview Dominick Ferraro's attending doctor. She omits commentary, however, on the possible truth of the significant kernels of the story—that her father's death was suspicious and that he engaged in criminal activity. To the casual reader Ferraro has likely cast enough doubt on the reporter's ethos to refute his accusations, but a close look at her argument reveals that she does not actually challenge the most significant charges leveled at her father. Whether or not he engaged in illegal activities remains a mystery. Instead, she emphasizes that her father's actions some forty years earlier were irrelevant to her bid for the vice presidency, and effectively vilifies the press coverage of this episode.

Whether or not she is ultimately successful in persuading her readership, Ferraro endeavors to exonerate both her husband and father. But what issues does Ferraro attempt to "right" in her own name? In this case, Ferraro focuses on three key points in her campaign: her competence in the political arena, particularly in international affairs, her Italian American heritage, and her pro-choice stance on abortion influenced by her Catholic faith.

International Affairs

By her own account, one of Ferraro's greatest real and perceived weaknesses as a vice presidential candidate was her lack of experience in international politics (*Ferraro* 109, 244). She attempted to compensate for her deficiency by visiting Central America for a ten-day trip designed to increase her actual and perceived foreign policy competence (78). She argues that in reality her competence was no less respectable than her opponents', and posits that it was her gender that provided the grounds for a more rigorous inspection of her international credentials. She quotes a headline during the campaign that questions her credibility in foreign affairs, clearly taking aim at her gender: "Will this Queens Housewife Be the Next Vice President?" (77). Additionally, after the election she writes of giving Ted Koppel his "comeuppance" in a skirmish with Madeleine Albright at Georgetown University. Albright queries, "do you believe that you, as well as other commentators, were harder on Mrs. Ferraro on foreign policy because she was a woman than you might have been on a man?" (qtd. in *Ferraro* 275). Koppel reportedly replies, "Yes, we were" (qtd. in *Ferraro* 275).

While Ferraro makes a compelling case for being a bright woman and a quick study, the retelling of her own candidacy suggests that gender issues not withstanding, foreign policy was ultimately not her political strength. Rather than acknowledge this fully, however, she gives the impression that she held herself to an overly ambitious standard, as did the press, when she says, "I knew as much about foreign policy as most members of Congress, and probably more than some. But I didn't think I knew enough . . . I didn't feel right unless I knew as much as possible about the issues we were voting on in Congress" (*Ferraro* 77). Later she calls foreign policy her "presumed weakness" (109) and finally implies that by doing her homework she became a worthy contender against Bush (244). Whatever her private misgivings, she presents her public self as one who faces up to weaknesses, real or perceived, by conquering them in stereotypical Western male fashion.

Italian American Heritage

Throughout the texts, Ferraro not only tackles gender criticisms but she also addresses and expresses pride in her Italian American immigrant heritage as well as disappointment in the lack of support shown by her ethnic community (*Ferraro* 213, 228–32, 235). For example, she is "very proud of being the first Italian American to run for national office" (5), and she observes that "like countless others from . . . [her] generation . . . [she] reaped the benefits of the sacrifices and hard labor of . . . [her] immigrant legacy" (*Framing a Life* 12). She later explains that, in her view, Italian Americans did not trust the government and therefore did not "vote as a bloc" when it came to her or any other candidate (111). Ferraro acknowledges feeling hurt that she did not receive the unequivocal support of her ethnic group (156–57). She seems taken aback that attacks on her Italian American roots from members of other ethnic groups may have provoked fear of association from her own community, robbing her of further support. Ferraro hoped that Italian Americans would vindicate her when, for example, rumors serviced about possible "mob" connections, but instead felt that they shunned her. She also suggests that her gender was a factor that did not play well in the largely traditional Italian American community where women's participation in public venues might be viewed less favorably. Repeatedly, however, she expresses personal pride at being Italian American. Frequently, she tries to "set the record straight," denying the stereotyping accusations of the media linking her ethnic heritage to possible underworld sources.

Catholicism and Pro-Choice Politics

Ferraro's series of justifications for being both a "good" Catholic and a thoughtful, pro-choice politician serves as a motivating force in her autobiographical writings. Both accounts of her life are heavily inundated with evidence of Ferraro's "good Catholic girl" upbringing, from her education in Catholic schools to her claims that "the furthest I allowed a boy to go was to kiss me . . . As a Catholic-reared-and-educated young woman, I figured that if God didn't get me, my mother surely would" (*Framing* 87). But it appears that one of the most agonizing issues of Ferraro's run for public office was the seeming contradiction between her Catholic beliefs and her support of pro-choice initiatives. As she observes, "my pro-choice stance on abortion had always drawn hecklers, and my standing as a good Catholic had been publicly questioned" (*Ferraro* 33). Her typical defense, repeated throughout the campaign, was to claim, "personally, as a Catholic, I accept my Church's teaching on this issue. I am opposed to abortion as a Catholic. But if I were raped I'm not sure I'd be so self-righteous" (137). In *Ferraro: My Story*, she devotes an entire chapter to "the Conservatives, the Italians, and the Archbishop," illustrating the unfair and sometimes irrational behavior of adversaries she had hoped would be allies. She argues emphatically that "the separation of church and state is one of the founding principles of our Constitution" and that "we are a religious nation because we do not have a state religion, because the government guarantees freedom of religion" (211). She

takes the reader through her own emotional and intellectual journey, affirming
that she took her "faith very seriously" and went to "mass every week" but that
"as an elected official . . . [she] had no right to impose [her faith] on others"
(215). While it is doubtful that her argument would persuade anti-choice readers
to understand her position, the more significant issue seems to be a defense of
Ferraro as a "good Catholic," and on this aim of setting the record straight she
emerges successfully.

The Nature of the Autobiographical Narratives

Ferraro's autobiographies are written with the assistance of professional writers,
yet each seems to capture her forthright oratorical style as "feisty" (*Ferraro* 209,
241), "serious" (241), "honest and direct" (179), and "tough" (43, 51). These
stylistic qualities become apparent in the settings, characters, and themes within
the narratives, which provide a framework for analyzing the interplay of Ferraro's private and public selves in the texts.

Settings

Settings throughout the texts are significant in two senses. Ferraro emphasizes New York City's burroughs and their urban locale as the backdrop for her
family's volatile financial status. Queens in particular provides a robust staging
for her emerging identity as a Catholic, Italian, blue-collar woman from "Archie
Bunker territory" (*Ferraro* 114)—a reference to the 1970s television show
which she uses throughout her narratives to help readers locate her both tempo-
rally and politically. New York City is also the site of her grandmother's immigration, her mother's childhood, and Ferraro's own upbringing. It is the scene
for all of her education and for her eventual upper-middle-class arrival in Forest
Hills, New York. Presumably, the celebrated images of New York City neighborhoods through media references such as *All in the Family* allow the reader an
adequate understanding of the nature of her geographic moves within this small
region; though many of her readers are likely to be lost in the translation of
sights and sounds of a city they have only observed from afar. Moreover, her
public identification as a "New Yorker" serves as an important screen for others
to view her many lifelong rhetorical choices, including "bluntness," "feistiness,"
and her public persona as a "friend of the worker." All of these traits seem to
emerge from the setting of Queens and provide a validation for some of her less
conventional gendered choices. So while a Midwestern woman in her forties
might be judged harshly for being an outspoken politician, it is understandable
that this "New Yorker" might be a feminine female and still possess non-
traditional gendered traits. Moreover, a wealthy upper-class woman may be a
"friend to big business," but a woman from "Archie's neighborhood" will empa-
thize with blue-collar workers.

In contrast, the scene of international travel informs a significant gender issue for Ferraro. In particular, Ferraro describes her travels throughout her presi-

dential campaign and after, both in the United States and internationally, positioning herself as a cosmopolite who vacations in the islands, an Italian American who visits her parents' ancestral Italian homeland, a patriotic American who campaigns from Maryland to Indiana to California, and a knowledgeable politician who explores grave current events by visiting the Middle East. Juxtaposed against her blue-collar upbringing, there emerges an image of a New York aristocrat who remains rooted in her Italian American ethnic heritage. Little description is tendered for any specific voyage because the travel-log backdrop retains importance only as a vehicle to set up Ferraro's public identity. The absence of details constitutes a significant framing device that tells the reader who she is and how, considering where she started, she arrived at her rhetorical public position. Positioning herself as the "first woman," she uses setting to both explain disjuncture in her gender identity, that is "she's not masculine, she's just a New Yorker!" and also to demonstrate her credibility in the public world of men's politics, that is, she's "as good as any man."

Characters

The volume of characters included in *Ferraro: My Story*, a history of Ferraro's life as it led up to her vice presidential campaign, is understandably far greater than the number of characters contained in *Framing a Life*, which focuses more narrowly on the influences of her grandmother and mother. In both books, her mother, her husband, and her children assume significant roles in her chronicles. Specifically, in *Ferraro* groups of characters, including "Italian Americans," "feminists," "the mob," "Republicans," and "Blacks," are presented as they influenced the development of her campaign. Each group fits neatly into a "good guy/bad guy" slot, either detracting from or assisting in her ascendancy to public office. "Italian Americans" fail to support her adequately, in her view, while "feminists" are loyal cohorts. Alleged connections to the "bad guy" mobsters, denied fiercely throughout the text, destroy her bid for office against the "bad guy" Republicans, led by Reagan and Bush. "Blacks" are presented as having questionable allegiances when represented by Jesse Jackson or Shirley Chisholm because they do not seem to fully support her. However, they are ultimately the "good guys" who Ferraro claims to champion as evidenced, she argues, by her appointment of African Americans to key posts when opportunities arise.

Democrats play a less certain role in this drama. Though Ferraro often asserts her party allegiance, apparent Democratic Party leaks that criticize her during the period in which Mondale considers her as his running mate dismay her. She even recounts several run-ins with Mondale himself, but ultimately remains loyal to both the Party and to him.

Ferraro also includes some "celebrity" appearances by well-known public figures like Barbara Bush, George Will, Ted Koppel, Phil Donahue, and Sally Ride, primarily to bolster various arguments concerning how she was attacked by the press and the Republicans, how she was vindicated of all financial wrongdoing, and how she was admired by women everywhere. The First Lady materializes primarily to call Ferraro a name that "rhymes with witch" (*Ferraro* 249) and then to apologize for misspeaking. Koppel and Donahue surface to give credence to her claims that the media, even including these otherwise presumably credible talk show hosts, treated her badly throughout the campaign. Her story about Will involves him apologizing to her for doubting the veracity of her financial disclosures and later sending roses as a request for forgiveness. This act of contrition from a well-known political conservative provides a powerful implicit argument for the truthfulness of Ferraro's claims. Finally, Ride makes a brief entrance in a clandestine lunch because, as Ferraro argues, Ride is a NASA employee and cannot endorse a candidate. Still, support of Ferraro is implied when she tells Ride that in a recent poll they are listed as the top two role models for women in the United States and Ride reportedly replies, "I don't mind being second to you" (293). The "good and bad guys" threaded throughout Ferraro's autobiographies emphasize public and private encounters with public figures, further justifying her choices, her integrity, and her ultimate political worth.

In *Framing a Life*, in addition to the two maternal figures, Maria Giuseppa Caputo and Antonetta Caputo Ferraro, significant characters include her father, Dominick Ferraro, her husband, John Zaccaro, and her three children. Subordinate characters include her brother, Carl, and her cousin, Nick Ferraro, and the Secret Service. Minor characters are mentioned generally to highlight one of Ferraro's accomplishments and serve to provide historical socio-political context rather than acting as fully developed sanctioned characters. Her cousin's references, for example, are included primarily to show how Ferraro became an assistant prosecutor in Queens, New York. We learn very little about Nick Ferraro through her narrative. and once his mention has served its purpose of illuminating her rise to political power, he disappears from the scenario.

Ordinarily, this lack of development of subordinate characters would not be unusual in an autobiography whose purpose is to illuminate the author. It is significant, however, that this particular text alleges to be a "family memoir." Yet, the first part of her title, *Framing a Life*, is by far the controlling metaphor, emphasizing how the existence of other players created the Ferraro story which was illuminated years earlier in her text, *Ferraro: My Story*. What might have been a more subversive feminist account of interpersonal and public success instead relies primarily on a male-centered autobiographical writing style to substantiate her focus on the greatness of her achievements in both contexts, rather than on the relational contributions of the significant figures in her life story.

The major characters emerging from *Framing a Life* include her grandmother, Maria Giuseppa, her mother, her father, and her husband. Ferraro gives a primarily chronological account of how her family arrived from Italy, struggled with poverty, and ultimately made good lives for themselves. She depicts her grandmother as a strong woman who embraces a traditional Italian American role as matriarch of a large, poor family in New York during the early part of the twentieth century. Ferraro does not seem to know a lot about her grandmother's motivations. While she speculates occasionally on her motives, the reader is mostly left with a general sketch of a stereotypical immigrant with excellent survival instincts. Perhaps the most provocative claim in her grandmother's story occurs when Ferraro refers to her grandfather's death as her grandmother's "emancipation" (*Framing* 40). The clear implication is that however much her grandmother capitulated to the patriarchal embodiment of her role in the family and in society, her life improved once she was freed from her captivity as a "wife." This seems to set the stage for Ferraro's mother's more emancipated choices and later for Ferraro's life choices and emancipation from her own duties as housewife. With each subsequent generation, the women in Ferraro's family move further into the public spotlight while continuing their prominent roles in the private sphere.

Ferraro frequently refers to her mother, Antonetta, as a "lonely" woman (*Framing* 56, 76) who suffered from osteoporosis and emphysema, the latter of which eventually killed her. The picture that emerges of Ferraro's mother is far more detailed than is her grandmother's portrayal, though still lacking in dimensionality. She presents Antonetta Ferraro as having no faults. She worked tirelessly to support her daughter, and to a lesser extent, her son, Carl. Ferraro tells her readers that from the beginning she was viewed as "special" because she was a girl (*Framing* 44). By Ferraro's account, her mother seemed devoted to her daughter, providing a stellar education and helping guide her to a solid career and a good marriage. Antonetta Ferraro seemed to want nothing more than to ensure that her daughter was not trapped by the eighth-grade education and early widowhood that had limited her own existence. At no point in Ferraro's story does her mother appear to question Ferraro's leap into public life, despite her traditional upbringing. Ferraro credits her mother with much of her own success, at one point observing, "my mother was forward thinking, an almost unconscious feminist before her time. She provided me with exactly the same opportunities as my brother" (60–61). Ferraro explains that her mother was embarrassed because of her limited education and also that she seemed to balk at the traditional roles assigned to women during her era. Although Ferraro's mother grieved her husband's death, like her own mother, she also seemed freed of some stereotypical gender constraints as she assumed the position of widow and ceased to play the traditional wife role. Ferraro describes her as "strong" and "smart" (15) and emphasizes how hard she worked, how much she loved her daughter, and how her crowning glory was watching her daughter achieve international acclaim. When her mother was chagrined by her lack of formal education Ferraro comforted her saying, "can you name one other person, male or female, who has been to Harvard or Yale or any other university, who can say, 'my daughter was a candidate for vice president of the United States?' Only you" (15). While Ferraro's words of consolation certainly give some credit to her mother for her success, the statement also is oddly egotistical, implying that Ferraro is her ultimate achievement and "never mind" if she did not achieve anything in her own right.

Ferraro's father and husband play "strong, silent" roles in the texts. She portrays her father as a traditional Italian American man who may have traversed an illegal landscape in his business dealings but if so, according to Ferraro, only through his own ignorance of American laws and procedures. She shows him as a strong, proud man who loved his family and died tragically of a heart problem kept secret from his family. She tells her readers that he loved her and she him and that she was his "princess" (*Framing* 44–50). It is his love of her that forms the basis for a healthy, private self-concept, but it is his death when she is young that sets into motion the events that lead her toward a public service career.

Ferraro's husband, John, is presented as a devoted spouse who initially opposes her professional career, advising her that married women, even lawyers, do not work outside the home. He seems to come around without much provocation and, according to Ferraro, becomes her biggest supporter. In her story they do not argue, fight, or disagree. If one cries, the other offers comfort; annoyances, resentments, and antagonisms seem oddly absent from the relationship. Following the election, they renew their marriage vows, affirming their commitment to one another. Ferraro expresses regret at how her husband's life was scrutinized and assailed as a result of her campaign, but in the end asserts that neither of them has regrets about her political choices. His character addresses her shift from private to public identity, and his existence helps construct a gendered public identity for her. In other words, "public women," like their male counterparts, are supposed to have "good men" standing behind them. Her husband's masculine presence also provides presumed evidence of her heterosexuality and femininity, both potential issues for a woman invading the upper echelon of male political power in the 1980s.

The absence or scarcity of male characters in *Framing a Life* also calls attention to Ferraro's theme of female connectedness. The text routinely emphasizes female characters, while male characters are often introduced for the purpose of highlighting the role of women in her life. For example, her father's death is mostly significant as an event that changes her mother's life, and consequently, her own. Her mother was thrust into poverty and, according to Ferraro, made her daughter the focal point of her existence. Her mother worked blue-collar jobs to support her, sent her to well-respected Catholic private schools, and encouraged Ferraro to pursue a career so that she would never experience the financial hardships that widowhood had foisted upon her. Male characters do not shape Ferraro's life to the same degree as do female characters.

Likewise, Ferraro's daughters, Laura and Donna, are emphasized more so than son, John Jr. While we learn that her son was loyal to his parents, Ferraro presents her daughters as the central siblings by emphasizing how they campaigned in subways for her, gave speeches on her behalf, and achieved personal academic success earning advanced degrees from Harvard and the University of Chicago. John Ferraro Jr.'s contributions and career outcomes are more ambiguous. By describing her daughters' accolades, Ferraro further helps her readers appreciate the importance of successful female characters in her life in two major ways. First, though clearly she is a proud mother, the significance of their successes lies more in underscoring how Ferraro is supported by her two strong, smart female progeny. Second, her daughters are to some extent "proof" of Ferraro's effective parenting, much as she is, as she argues in both autobiographies, the "proof" of her mother's extraordinary maternal care.

Throughout this entire "family memoir," Ferraro offers two brief observations about her only surviving brother, Carl, two others having died in infancy before her own birth. He gets scant mention in the books and although she claims to love him, it is never clear if there really is love or any degree of caring between the two. There is a concise depiction of a trip to Italy with her mother in which her brother appears generally uncaring and overly frugal with money. She comments that she "loved . . . [her] . . . brother very much" (*Framing* 96), but it is his aloofness that emerges more starkly in this scene. In a later passage, Ferraro remarks that she is doubtful that her brother had ever recovered from the death of their father, but she does not explore the implications of her statement. Does this imply that Carl Ferraro was always unhappy, felt a void in his life, or did not explore his potential in the public sphere or in human relations? Ferraro does not encourage the reader to ponder these possibilities. Finally, when Ferraro notes that her brother died in his sixties, she comments that "Carl never seemed to find his place in the world" (*Framing* 200). She assumes some responsibility for her seemingly inadequate relationship with him, observing:

> in many ways his whole life had been difficult. . . . I saw that I had been an extremely demanding sister. I wanted Carl to be more considerate of my mother. I wanted him to fulfill his potential. I wanted him to be more successful. I wanted him to be all the things I thought my mother needed to be proud of him. I finally realized that she *was* proud of him. She didn't need him to be different. (*Framing* 199)

Ferraro's statement appears to show a dialectic tension between atonement and judgment. She appears to express repentance and yet, since implied in every sentence is the counter-notion that Carl was not "considerate," did not "fulfill his potential," and was ultimately not "successful," the reader can hardly fault Ferraro for her treatment of her brother. She does not seem to like him particularly well, and she either omits an exploration of their relationship to safeguard the privacy of his children, or she perceives his presence as an insignificant contribution to her life story. She chooses to avoid examining their private relationship publicly, while at least after his death acknowledging her unsettled, unresolved, and unfinished affiliation with her sibling. This is particularly striking against the backdrop of her mother's miscarriages and the deaths of two older brothers in infancy before her birth. It would seem that this surviving brother might have played a significant role in the small Ferraro family history, but the reader is left to her imagination on this point. We cannot be certain what her brother's accomplishments were, in contrast to his highly successful sister—certainly a gender role reversal of particular note in their generation.

Themes and Plotlines

The plotlines in the autobiographical texts are similar and overlapping. *Framing a Life* provides explanation and background for the plot development in *Ferraro: My Story*, but otherwise there is not much difference between the two readings. Subplots in these books stress her mother's orchestration of Ferraro's education, her conflicts with the Catholic Church in her political career, and media allegations regarding her husband's financial and business transactions. In *Framing a Life*, she overtly states that her primary purpose in composing the text is to correct the nation's underrepresentation of immigrant women as major contributors to the creation of the American Dream (16). Again, this seems to be the issue of "setting the record straight," perhaps a cornerstone of many autobiographies. While her attempt to "get things right" adheres to a more traditional genre, her mission to do so for the good of disenfranchised women illustrates a central goal of feminist activism. Whether or not she achieves this goal is questionable. For example, her information on her grandmother is limited. While she does provide a lot of facts and figures about her mother that inevitably lead back to her Italian immigrant roots, the text in its entirety does not add much beyond Ferraro's original assertion that we fail to acknowledge the contributions of immigrant women to our country's development. She might have made the argument that her grandmother and mother represented a significant number of similar women in American history, but other than vague assertions, her focus is primarily on the two women.

As noted earlier, she does credit much of her success to the lives and sacrifices of her foremothers and emphasizes how their forfeitures shaped her destiny as a significant public force, paving the way for millions of American women in public office. Shortly before the election, she gave a final speech at her alma mater, Marymount College, paying tribute to her mother: "Because of her sacrifice, I had the privilege to attend this college. Because of that dedication, I am what I am today. And tonight, I would like to say to her from the bottom of my heart: Thank you for everything" (*Framing* 152).

Ferraro maintains that other purposes for authoring her text are to show how her mother was responsible for her greatness, to explore the confines of women's greatness, and to show how women in the early 1980s, leading up to the 1984 campaign, changed the world for all women (16). These are distinct themes throughout the text, but the major plot of both books is how Ferraro serves as the central and dominant heroine of her own life, which reflects a patriarchal autobiographical authoring style.

Certainly, the campaign for vice president forms the overarching plot throughout her stories, but her emphasis is that she was always a "star," from a much heralded beginning to a glorious older age. Only once does she briefly lose faith in herself, but a tap dancing class with one of her daughters is all it seems to take for the public Ferraro to move back into the political spotlight. Ferraro even reconstructs her private struggle with cancer as an opportunity to shine as she bravely faces her ordeal and becomes a public advocate for healthcare reform. The themes and plotlines that pervade the texts help the audience to conceptualize Ferraro as a heroine, created by women who are also heroines, primarily because of their roles in making her what she is today.

A number of themes permeate Ferraro's autobiographical efforts including: value of education; conflicts between Catholicism and politics; importance and support of family; stereotypes and oppression of women; connectedness among women; and strength and liberation of women challenging stereotypes. From beginning to end, Ferraro emphasizes the value of education in the texts. Both her grandmother and mother suffered financially and relationally as a result of a lack of education. Her mother sacrificed everything so that her children could have good, private Catholic educations. Despite her own poverty, she sent her children to boarding schools so that she could work longer hours at her working-class jobs in order to continue to fund their education. Ferraro speaks with warmth about her educational experiences. She details her academic, athletic, and social triumphs, culminating in a law degree in an era when few women chose such a route. Ferraro also includes characterizations of herself as "pretty," and therefore, capable of "getting a husband" to marry, support her, and with whom to have children. As a successful woman of her generation, she may have felt the need to demonstrate that she was in the public sphere "by choice," rather than because she could not fulfill her traditional role in private life.

The theme of education resounds when she becomes a parent and sends her children to private rather than public schools. When political opponents challenge her selection she does not hesitate to defend her choice. In response to accusations she argues, "are there any parents here who don't want more for their children than they had? I would silence my accusers" (*Ferraro* 32). She connects her own upbringing, which valued education, with her later choices for her family and to her political stance on education, observing:

> It was clear that education was a priority in our lives from the moment we began our schooling. My parents would have it no other way. . . . My father had arrived from Italy with a distinct advantage; his family prized education. . . . My own life had been immeasurably enriched by the education I'd received. . . . I saw to it that each of my children received the very best education. . . . By extension, this became a passion for me in my political life. (212)

She uses the private and public theme of "education" as a bridge between her personal upbringing, her own parental choices, and her political convictions in the public realm.

Ferraro presents her private self as a devout Catholic throughout the books. She speaks positively of her Catholic education, declares her regular Church attendance, and in a few key passages when she is describing highly stressful experiences, makes reference to personal prayer. But her public pro-choice political stance puts her frequently at odds with some of the male clergy while her perceived rejection by the Church causes her intrapersonal strife and also has political consequences. Her stories about the Church are interspersed with conflicting examples in which she is alternately supported, lambasted, praised, and criticized for being a Catholic woman who supports the pro-choice position. She often uses her gender as an explanation for her position, maintaining that if she were raped she was not sure what choice she might make concerning abortion, an argument that is qualitatively different from that of a male colleague who might speculate about a wife or daughter in such a situation.

As suggested earlier, Ferraro expresses disappointment at the lack of un-wavering support from the Catholic Church, the Italian American community, and the Democratic Party. The one group that appears to provide solid support, however, is her family. With the exception of her brother, almost all mention of family members in the narratives is for the public purpose of demonstrating un-qualified support for Ferraro's ambitions. She frequently evokes a "family first" metaphor when writing about whether or not to accept various publicly posed challenges, and many times she claims that she would not undertake a new posi-tion without the support of her family. We learn very little about her husband except that he is a "private man," and little is revealed about her children that is not broadly related to their overarching support of her campaign or more briefly about their own accomplishments.

Absent from the texts are descriptions of contentious family interactions re-garding Ferraro's career choices. She offers a minor exception of a few difficult nights spent comforting her husband concerning the press's unremitting de-mands for him to reveal private business and financial information as well as pressure for him to disclose possible ties to the reported Italian American un-derworld. Even in these instances when Ferraro appears concerned that her hus-band may be depressed or that she has jeopardized her family's security and happiness at their expense, nowhere does any family member seem to take issue with her choices. While this seems improbable, Ferraro is consistent in her pub-lic portrayal of a happy, loving family who "stands behind" all of her decisions with no regrets. Generally, the political families of American male politicians are expected to be devout, loving, supportive "Rockwellesque" groupings, pro-viding unconditional support and "standing behind their man." Female politi-cians may experience this exigence to an even greater degree since they are try-ing to buy public acceptance of their roles in public life. If their families doubt their ability to succeed or question their right to be in the limelight, then how can the rest of the country accept their bids for public office? Thus, her family must appear to support Ferraro unequivocally and in turn, she claims to priori-tize them over her career. For example, when she describes her election triumph to Congress she also writes, "the new title of Congresswoman didn't replace the old title of Mother" (*Framing* 119).

Starting with her grandmother's and mother's stories in *Framing a Life*, Ferraro highlights the victimization, stereotyping, and oppression of women in the United States, noting the hegemonic nature of their situation. While male characters are rarely vilified, female characters are often victimized because of gender and ensnared in personal, economic, and professional traps that may limit their capacities to function at their full potential. This is an interesting rhe-torical balancing act, since women are often portrayed as victims of patriarchy but are rarely the casualties of the actions of particularly identified males. Occa-sionally, she takes aim at sexist comments from members of the Republican Party, or at a former employer, but overall, the patriarchy is an unnamed force.

This strategy allows her to escape the stereotype of a "radical" feminist "male basher."

Throughout her text, she provides examples of how women live within, negotiate, and emerge from male oppression. For example, as noted earlier, the deaths of her grandfather and father seem to provide a kind of liberation for her grandmother and mother. She also describes sexual harassment in an early job, though she does not treat it as a serious threat and instead uses the example to showcase how she skillfully navigated around her boss's threatening overtures. Later, in her successful work as a prosecutor she talks about her expertise in helping young female victims of child abusers with her compassionate female-centered communication approach to a male-dominated legalistic justice system. She mentions getting "indictments" as a measure of her success, yet does not refer to obtaining convictions. This seems an interesting omission if intentional, since she claims to help the young female victims of crime and yet does not explain to what extent this occurs.

Ferraro characterizes both her grandmother and mother as strong women who do not entirely capitulate to the gender stereotypes of their generations. Her grandmother appears to embody the immigrant woman stereotype of "knowing her place," but also is portrayed as a strong woman who protects her large, poverty-stricken family. She also characterizes her mother as a courageous, resolute woman opposing gender stereotypes in key ways. This is illustrated by Antonetta Ferraro's unwavering support of her daughter, who might otherwise have become a high school dropout who married and replicated her mother's life. Her mother's belief that girls should be educated for a career is underscored several times as Ferraro quotes her saying, "it doesn't make any difference whether you're a boy or a girl. You can be whatever you want" (qtd. in *Framing* 60), and "You're right, my Gerry is a beauty. . . . But when you educate a boy, you educate a boy alone. When you educate a girl, you educate a family"(qtd. in *Framing* 72). Still, although Ferraro refers to both maternal figures as strong women, she also notes that her grandmother was "deferential" (83), and while she commends her mother for being dedicated and resilient, she explains that she did not want to follow their stereotypical gender roles (14). Ferraro draws her own strength from both women by emulating their unfaltering determination to protect their families and by challenging herself to go beyond their conventional life choices.

Certainly, Ferraro's primary show of connectedness among women is illustrated by the multigenerational maternal lineage of grandmother, mother, and daughter, only involving male characters as ancillary or supporting characters for the events and achievements of these women actors. Professionally, she also names a small group of five to seven public women called "Team A" whom she credits with being central to her nomination on the Democratic ticket (*Ferraro* 72). These women appear to support her *because* she is a woman. Through the solidarity of their gender, Ferraro believes she can gain visibility and "help all women in politics" (72). She claims improving the political topography for women was a major goal given her "own experiences," in the problematic male-dominated public sphere of politics (72).

Although there are many examples throughout the writings of women coming together for the good of womankind, perhaps the most dramatic occurs when Ferraro speaks at a campaign breakfast and appears to withdraw her support from the Equal Rights Amendment (ERA). She explains:

> I had gone out of my way to prove that the thematic formula of the Platform would not include any specific legislation for any special constituencies, even for women. . . . When asked if "no specific legislation" included the ERA, I said yes. Equal rights for women . . . could be in the platform without using the capital E, the capital R, the capital A. (86–87)

After the breakfast meeting ended, Ferraro realized that she could have supported the ERA as a "constitutional amendment rather than a piece of legislation" (87). But since the "damage was done" (87) she had to think quickly to repair it. She observes:

> As soon as the breakfast ended, I hotfooted it to the nearest phone to call my congressional office. "Call NOW, the NWPC, all the women members of Congress, DNC political director Ann Lewis, and Bella and Steinem," I told them rapidly. "Tell them not to say anything to the press until they talk to me." I could just see the headlines: "Ferraro, First Woman to Head the Platform Committee, Comes Out Against the ERA." . . . We gathered in the Congresswomen's Reading Room in the Capitol at one p.m., where I told them personally about my mistake and what I had done to correct it. And as one, they gave me their support. It was fantastic, really. Any of these high-profile activists could have blasted me in the press. But not one did. The women's support was incredible. (87)

Her extended example defies stereotypes of women as not working cohesively in the public realm and provides an exemplar for women transcending real and perceived social barriers to join together in solidarity.

One of the primary ways that Ferraro challenges stereotypical visions of women in the public sphere is through her frequent referrals to herself as a "first." In many ways, Ferraro is the quintessential 1980s feminist underscored by her insistence that she should be heralded for "having it all." For instance when she wins a seat in Congress she plainly says:

> I was determined to do it all. Be a totally committed congresswoman in Washington and a fully engaged wife and mother in Queens, work for the good of the nation while also caring for the smallest needs of my small district. I promised myself that I could do it, or I wouldn't have taken the job. Others had done it, and so would I. (119)

She does not explain that by "others" she implies "other women," since male politicians rarely provide public justification for their roles as husbands and fathers other than in the most superficial sense. Ferraro bridges the stereotypical role of stay-at-home mom, caring for children and running a household, with the ultimate career woman role who traverses the globe, engages with the most powerful men (and a few women) in the world, and speaks her mind while still maintaining her femininity.

The Nature of the World Created through the Narratives

So what is the world that Ferraro creates through her writing? Almost inevitably, Western autobiography creates an egocentric world in the necessity to place the rhetor at the center of the story by tracing the steps from birth to some culminating event, which in this case is Ferraro's bid for the vice presidency. Certainly, most readers of *Ferraro: My Story* likely expect that Ferraro's account of why and how she became the first woman vice presidential candidate on a major party ticket will follow this rhetorical form. Her egocentric portrayal in this first text, however, is partially reframed by applying Foss and Foss's conception of "wholeness" by having examined her second autobiographical effort in concert with her first. In considering her "family memoir," *Framing a Life,* readers gain greater insight into the private and public worlds Ferraro has created for them. This text presumably explores the worlds of an "Italian American family," as the book jacket proclaims, and yet, it seems primarily to be another exploration of how Ferraro, with the unconditional support of her family, ascended to great heights. The reader discerns that Ferraro knows little about her grandmother and is left to speculate about her grandmother's motives and actions. Ultimately, even her mother's greatest accomplishment, according to Ferraro, is the production of Ferraro herself. She credits her mother for her many personal sacrifices, documented in her books, her stalwart commitment to providing the best education for her daughter *because* and not in spite of Ferraro's gender, and her unwavering support of Ferraro from childhood through middle age. Although there is still a certain degree of ego imbued in making the statement for her mother that she and "no other" is the emblem of her mother's highest worth, would a male autobiographer credit his mother for his success and concomitantly point to himself as proof of her success? If he did so, would the world he created look different than Ferraro's? In Ferraro's world women are strong, powerful people who can do all the things that men can do plus one more—produce children, as her grandmother, her mother, and she herself did. Consequently, they engender strong, powerful individuals who can shape the destinies of millions of citizens.

Does Ferraro provide an alternative vision of a world in which women are equal to men, perhaps even superior to men in their capacity to reproduce and nurture their offspring, or are women in the end reduced to their reproductive functions? She also clearly presents that self-made, determined, hard working women can be authoritative, influential political figures such as herself. This would suggest that women who are traditional wives, do household chores, raise children, and take care of their mothers, grandmothers, and families, can succeed in their professional careers as long as they can balance all of their traditional female roles and adapt to the juxtaposition of male-centric professional roles.

A key to understanding Ferraro's perspective may lie in what she does not say in her narratives. While clearly a proud and devoted mother, Ferraro does *not* say that *her* greatest accomplishment is her children, however superbly they have emerged from her devoted care. Her greatest accomplishment in these public texts, from her view, seems unequivocally her history-making, though unsuccessful, bid for the vice presidency. To that extent, Ferraro shows that she has been victorious in the traditional private realm consigned to women, while simultaneously succeeding in the male-centered public sphere. If the latter is deemed to be more worthy, is it because she values the public over the private, or because, as she notes frequently, she is the "first" to achieve success in this venue, therefore paving the way for others to come after her?

Perhaps the answer to this question lies somewhere between the two poles of possibility. Ultimately, however, despite Ferraro's protestations that "family comes first," certainly a view that few male politicians would choose to emphasize unless pressed, the success she seems to value is the observable, calculable public success of her political exploits. Consequently, by what standards, if any, is the world Ferraro creates a feminist one? And to the extent that it is indeed feminist, whose feminism is it?

Construction of a Gendered Feminist Self

Ferraro is really her own heroine in the stories of her life and, in a sense, that, in and of itself, may qualify her as a feminist, even as she tells her life in a traditional, patriarchal fashion. She refutes stereotypes of women, challenges oppression, and eventually adopts a feminist persona. She supports the pro-choice standpoint and the Equal Rights Amendment for women, touts the solidarity of her feminist colleagues, and lives her life exactly as she chooses. And she does all this despite a social script that probably would have otherwise consigned her to a traditional existence as a Forest Hills matron in an upper-middle-class suburb of New York.

Of course, Ferraro narrates her feminist story in a traditional chronological style and champions a "fair haired" heroine who leads a charmed life, encounters resistance, meets with failure, and in the euphemistic tradition of Rocky Balboa—"lives to fight another day." But while *Ferraro: My Story* could in part be read as emblematic of her 1980s bid for office thus justifying her focus on self, *Framing a Life* might have developed differently because of its presumed function as a "family memoir." Because of the time lapse between her bid for office and when she wrote the later chronicle, she might have reflected on her life through utilizing contemporary redefinitions of feminism as a movement for equal opportunity rather than repeating the outmoded and unattainable ideal of "having," and therefore doing, "it all." But this does not occur.

Against this backdrop of tradition and challenges to convention, we also read a story of "Gerry the star," who seems to do everything right and always for the right reasons. She only notes a few mistakes such as calling herself the "presidential candidate" instead of "vice presidential" candidate at the Democratic National Convention, and in making a potentially racist joke about Italian American men at a press conference, when her finances and alleged mob connections were being investigated by journalists. These infrequent foibles serve primarily to humanize an otherwise apparently "perfect" woman who achieved success in every arena, despite failing in her bid for the vice presidency. Her earlier references to herself as "not a feminist" even allow the more traditional women of her generation to identify with and possibly share Ferraro's feminist evolution. Early in her accounts of her public life she notes that she was not a "total" feminist (*Framing* 98), but one wonders what her definition of feminism is when she also writes that as a child, "I knew I could do whatever I wanted to do. I lived in a world without limits" (14). Certainly, most women of her generation saw their lives as much more circumscribed. Her narratives both affirm images of 1980s women in public and private life and simultaneously liberate women from the confines of those stereotypes. This illuminates a phase in the development of second-wave feminism. Her feminism advocates maintaining traditional female values of "home and hearth," and it details her invasion of one of the more sacred male bastions of public life, the political arena. She challenges some of the most sacrosanct principles of mainstream male culture, pushing the boundaries of women's existence, particularly the limitations on Italian American women's lives, by becoming "the first woman" of her or any other generation to rise to one of the highest of political aspirations. As Ferraro herself observes in the Postscript to the New Edition of *Ferraro: My Story*:

> So here I am in 2004, twenty years after that historic run. I'm the executive vice president and head of the public affairs division of the Global Consulting Group, an investor relations communications firm. . . . I continue to do television, now as a Fox political analyst, and I have become an advocate for cancer research. I am frequently asked if I had it to do all over again, would I? The answer is the same as it was on election day in 1984. Yes. (337)

Ferraro challenges the stereotypes of women in the public realm, including taken-for-granted assumptions that women could not successfully combine private lives with rigorous public life. She lost the election, but she appears to have won the rhetorical campaign to liberate women from various oppressive stereotypes. In the early twenty-first century we still question when there will be a female president. Ferraro's candidacy broke significant barriers for all women, and her autobiographies give us insight into the creation of a 1980s feminist. Ferraro writes that shortly after her nomination for vice president, feminist activist Gloria Steinem encountered a black male jogger who yelled, "'Isn't it great? Now *you* can be president.'" And she yelled back, 'No, *you* can be president.' The black man grinned and said, 'Now *any of us* can be president'" (qtd. in *Framing* 123). Thanks to pioneers like Ferraro, now perhaps anyone *can* be president. And perhaps, the current generation will improve upon the blueprints she leaves behind, but with an appropriate nod of gratitude to this remarkable and noteworthy "first."

Notes

The author offers special thanks to her number one student, Martha A. Meeker, M.A., for her work in gathering and annotating sources for this chapter.

1. References to the book, *Ferraro: My Story*, are to the 2004 edition.

Chapter Five

Just Like "Azaleas in the Spring": Elizabeth Dole as a Daughter of the South

Nichola D. Gutgold

North Carolina's state motto, "To be rather than to seem," sums up the goal-oriented nature of one of the state's most productive natives, Elizabeth Dole. To guide her career path and decisions, she continues to draw from the experiences of her youth in genteel Salisbury, North Carolina, even though she has lived most of her life in Washington, D.C. She also speaks and writes about the influence of her Southern upbringing, retains her caramel North Carolina drawl, and capitalizes on her Southern roots to boost her husband's and her own political goals. Elizabeth Dole's use of narratives describing her experiences in her home state of North Carolina have shaped her definition of herself, helped her to identify with her audiences, and facilitated her rise to prominence as a Republican who became Secretary of Transportation, Secretary of Labor, and President of the American Red Cross. As the spouse of former presidential candidate Bob Dole, she campaigned vigorously for her husband, becoming as well known as he. In 1999, Elizabeth Dole made an exploratory bid for the presidency and currently serves as a Republican senator from North Carolina.

The American South has long enjoyed a romantic place in literature and popular culture. It has had a dramatic impact on American history through colonization, slavery, Reconstruction, the forced relocation of Native Americans, the Civil War, and the Civil Rights Movement. Cultural aspects of the South also are well known and documented. We often hear of Southern hospitality and chivalry, agrarianism, and evangelical Christianity as having originated in the South, commonly called the "Bible Belt." Authors such as Edgar Allan Poe and Mark Twain recount characteristics of the region of the South in their writing. The book and movie *Gone with the Wind* portray the South and its people in a way that remains indelibly marked in the minds of readers and moviegoers worldwide. Even the home décor industry boasts

"Southern style" goods to make homes that are located anywhere in the country reminiscent of the charm and lure of the South.

Although Elizabeth Hanford Dole has been away from her home state for most of her career, her Southern heritage remains a focus of her speeches and autobiography.[1] She has clung to her Southern roots, thus gaining political advantage from her distinct Southern persona. This chapter illustrates how Elizabeth Dole projects a Southern communication style that fosters political relationships through its inherently warm, inclusive, and engaging methods. Her speeches, replete with autobiographical narratives, detail her Southern upbringing and define her ideology. As the wife of a prominent Washington, D.C., politician, Elizabeth Dole easily could have let go of her Southern heritage and fashioned herself as a Washington politico. By fostering her Southern feminine image, Elizabeth Dole makes herself a more interesting and novel figure. She hasn't faded into the background by adopting the acceptable navy and black dress favored in Washington, D.C. Instead, she dresses resplendently, attired in bright colors and feminine styles.

Historically, Southern women who spoke in public were nothing less than "shocking" (Shelby 223). For Dole to speak eloquently and intelligently in public attracts attention and helps to broaden the accepted sphere of influence for women. She continues to trumpet her Southern heritage, and through her optimistic words and purpose-driven deeds she encourages others to follow in her footsteps in a career in public service and leadership. Although Dole began her Washington career as a Democrat, she is one of the most well-known Republicans in the country. She has championed conservative causes for her husband, many Republican candidates, and herself.

Biographical Overview

Mary Elizabeth Alexander Hanford was born on July 29, 1936, the only daughter of John and Mary Hanford. A precocious child, she nicknamed herself "Liddy" when she was no more than two years old; the name stuck throughout her childhood and even throughout her early Washington career ("Dole" 146). She led a comfortable life, and her parents indulged her with lessons in areas that interested her, such as dancing and horseback riding. Her real strengths, however, were her academic interests; she showed tremendous intellectual promise very early in life. "I learned a strong work ethic on South Fulton Street. Self-improvement was a measure of personal growth. It was also a way to satisfy my goal-oriented parents" (Dole and Dole, *Unlimited* 51). She lived up to that promise through high school, where she actively participated in student government and even ran for president of the senior class. Comparing Hanford to Elizabeth II, "Britain's newly crowned monarch," her campaign manager stated, "more and more . . . the modern world is giving women a big part to play. Boyden [High School] must keep pace in this world" (52). Although she lost her bid for office, her classmates observed qualities in Hanford that prompted them to vote her "most likely to succeed" ("Dole" 146), and Hanford writes that from this experience she took away important lessons about being prepared.

After high school, Hanford followed in her brother's footsteps and attended Duke University. She studied government and was one of a select few women who enrolled in political science courses in order to fulfill the requirements of her degree program. Her choice of political science as a major sent a "ripple of concern" (Dole and Dole, *Unlimited* 54) back home, since her mother had wished that she would major in home economics and take a more traditional route that would conclude with marriage, children, and home-making (54). As a freshman at Duke, she ran unsuccessfully for class representative. However, her classmates later elected her president of the women's student government association (Pope). She came out as a debutante in Raleigh (Dole and Dole, *Unlimited* 78) and became a member of the "White Duchy," which served as a "primitive sort of old girls' network" (79). In her senior year at Duke in 1958, the student body elected Elizabeth Hanford "Leader of the Year" (Pope) and May Queen (Dole and Dole, *Unlimited* 80). She graduated Phi Beta Kappa from Duke ("Dole" 146), and although many of her female classmates pursued careers as wives and mothers, Hanford remained unsure of her future goals. She next finished a Master's degree in education and government at Harvard (146), completed student teaching, and then realized that she didn't want a career as a teacher (Dole and Dole, *Unlimited* 85).

Drawn to Washington, D.C., "like a magnet" (Leishman 131) according to her mother, in the summer of 1960, Elizabeth Hanford worked in Washington, D.C., as a secretary for North Carolina Democratic Senator B. Everett Jordon (Dole and Dole, *Unlimited* 85). While in Washington, D.C., she sought the advice of several high-powered women to learn their opinions about what career path she should pursue (86). In 1962, Elizabeth Hanford entered Harvard Law School. While one of only twenty-four women in a class of 550 ("Dole" 146; Dole and Dole, *Unlimited* 90), there were rules at Harvard Law that prevented women from participating fully in student life. For example, women could not eat at the Lincoln Dining Hall and a sexist professor had "Ladies Day" in class, where women students would be grilled with difficult questions that were not asked of their male counterparts (Dole and Dole, *Unlimited* 90). She recalls a male classmate asking her, in a tone of indignation, "Elizabeth, what are you doing here? . . . Don't you realize that there are *men* who would give their right arm to be in this law school, men who would *use* their legal education?" (90). She missed the warm atmosphere she found at Duke University, but she didn't let the chilly climate derail her education. She earned her law degree and moved to Washington, D.C., when she was twenty-nine years old. Her first job was a temporary position with Health, Education, and Welfare (HEW), where she organized a conference on deaf education, "the first of its kind held under government auspices" (135). She also passed the Washington, D.C., bar exam and tried her hand as public defender in night court (136). Her next position was with the Johnson Administration in the Office of Consumer Affairs, where her boss, Betty Furness, saw her exceptional talent and rewarded her by giving her increased opportunities to make speeches and to learn everything about consumer protection (139–40). After Lyndon Johnson declined to run for re-election, Richard Nixon won the presidency, and Elizabeth Hanford was able to keep her position, although she had a new boss, Virginia Knauer. Like Furness, Knauer recognized Hanford's ability and promoted her to deputy in the office, which was renamed the President's Committee on Consumer Interests (141). In 1973, after much lobbying, she won a position on the Federal Trade Commission (FTC) (147–48).

In 1972, Virginia Knauer introduced Elizabeth Hanford to Kansas Senator Robert Dole, who was serving as the national chairman of the Republican Party (148). Although they didn't start dating until several months after they met, Elizabeth Hanford became Mrs. Robert Dole on December 6, 1975, when Bob Dole was fifty-two and Hanford was thirty-nine ("Dole" 146).

In August 1976, Gerald Ford, who had become president in 1974 when President Richard Nixon resigned, invited Bob Dole to serve as his vice presidential running mate. When Dole accepted, Elizabeth Dole's life changed dramatically, for she entered the often-whirlwind world of a campaigning spouse. The Ford-Dole ticket lost to the Democratic ticket of Jimmy Carter and Walter Mondale, but Elizabeth Dole got a taste of political campaigning, and she found it exhilarating. She recounts a campaign moment in Florida:

> A woman took my hand and asked me where in the world I get the energy to do what I was doing.
> "I get it from you," I told her.
> It was true. Something about a campaign sweeps you up on an emotional current and hurtles you from one situation to the next. That something is the high-voltage support that charges a live audience and inspires a candidate. (Dole and Dole, *Unlimited* 173)

In 1979, Bob Dole announced his candidacy for the 1980 presidential election. Elizabeth Dole resigned from the FTC to campaign for her husband. When Ronald Reagan won the presidency in 1980, he appointed Elizabeth Dole as the head of the Office of Public Liaison (196). In 1983, he invited her to serve as Secretary of Transportation ("Dole" 147). She served for five years until she resigned in 1988 to help her husband make another bid for the presidency. George Bush won the 1988 presidential race and tapped Elizabeth Dole to serve as the Secretary of Labor (147). She served in that position until she stepped down in 1991 to become President of the American Red Cross. In 1996, Bob Dole won the Republican nomination for President of the United States, and Elizabeth Dole took a one-year leave from the Red Cross to help him campaign. Her campaign skills won rave reviews from the press and the public. When Bob Dole lost the election to Bill Clinton, Elizabeth Dole returned to the Red Cross where she worked until she resigned in 1999. That year she made a nine-month exploratory bid for the Presidency of the United States. Then, in 2002, she won the first Senate seat ever held by a woman from her home state of North Carolina.

Elizabeth and Robert Dole penned their combined autobiographies, *The Doles: Unlimited Partners*, in 1988, at the height of the presidential campaign and a revised version, *Unlimited Partners: Our American Story*, during the 1996 presidential contest. Although the Doles share the book, they present their narratives individually. For example, the book begins with chapter one, "The Doles of Russell," followed by chapter two, "The Hanfords of Salisbury." Each subsequent chapter highlights their individual stories until their lives begin to intertwine through marriage and political campaigning. The presentation of their lives in one volume is significant for two reasons. As Kerry Tymchuk, the Doles' speechwriter and collaborator on the second edition, notes, including Elizabeth's story added to the persuasive power of the political autobiography. "She was out on the campaign trail as much as he was—sometimes more, and she was extremely popular" (Tymchuk). In addition, this unique literary convention underscores Elizabeth Dole's role as a political spouse. In her writing, she constitutes "a new female subject" (Watson, *Lives* 2), recognizing her dual status as a candidate's spouse and an independent, political self.

Elizabeth Hanford's Early Southern Upbringing

Elizabeth Dole fosters and maintains political relationships by using a variety of communication strategies that she learned as a young daughter of the South. She begins her autobiography by sharing details about her life as a young girl in North Carolina. She says, "while I was growing up, the [Charlotte] *Observer* had been a morning ritual in the Hanford household, like breakfast ham and grits."(Dole and Dole, *Unlimited* 40). She also describes her prize, a silver loving cup, in an essay-writing contest sponsored by the "United Daughters of the Confederacy" (40). Of her birthplace and the town where she still keeps her childhood home, Elizabeth Dole notes:

> Local residents nurtured a distinctive southern ambience. The pace of life was a little slower here, the greeting extended to a stranger a little warmer, than in Northern cities. Salisbury is still the kind of place where people on the street tip their hat in welcome, and where conversations start with a friendly "Hey." (42–43)

She argues that the communication style of the South is warmer and friendlier than communication in the North. This stylistic difference appears noteworthy in Elizabeth Dole's speeches. For example, walking around audiences, which has become a trademark of Elizabeth Dole's communication strategy, can be seen as an extension of the warm style of communication. She describes the rationale behind her decision to move around the audience when she speaks:

Another principle I have kept in mind is the importance of speaking from the heart. As president of the American Red Cross, I barnstormed the country, asking Americans for three important personal resources: their time, their money, and yes, their blood, for the Red Cross provides almost half of America's blood supply. In order for individuals to donate these resources, a personal connection had to be made—and I quickly came to see a podium as a barrier to making that connection. (E. Dole, *Hearts* 4)

A fundamental teaching that Elizabeth Dole's early life offered came from a deeply rooted religious faith. She recounts her personal experiences, particularly those with her grandmother, that express the Christian ideology for which Dole is known. Her maternal grandparents, Mom and Pop Cathey, lived just two doors down from her, and young Elizabeth spent many days at Mom Cathey's home, where children munched on cookies, drank lemonade, and happily listened to Bible stories (E. Dole, "National Prayer" 134). Dole recalls her grandmother's faith and strong religious convictions. Mom Cathey, who faithfully read the Bible, also kept a radio next to her bed that was tuned to a religious station. Elizabeth Dole notes that "through her I was encouraged to have a vital, living faith," and to understand that "we were each pilgrims on the road to grace" (Dole and Dole, *Unlimited* 49). She makes it clear that she learned "a strong work ethic on South Fulton Street," where "self-improvement was a measure of personal growth" (51). To this day, Elizabeth Dole notes in her autobiography, one of her most cherished possessions is her Mom Cathey's Bible. She also recounts how she renewed her strong Methodist upbringing in the early 1980s through "spiritual growth" meetings (Stengel 30). Elizabeth Dole intertwines her definition of home with the religious beliefs that were a central part of her girlhood. She even makes the distinction that while "Washington is full of excitement and professional challenges. . . . Salisbury is home" (Dole and Dole, *Unlimited* 43). As a youngster, her work to collect stamps, tinfoil, and wastepaper during World War II illustrates an early commitment to humanitarian work that still characterizes her life. She writes: "However ignorant I was of the war's larger implications, I found it a continuing lesson in sensitivity to the feelings of others" (51). These two functions of ideology, faith in God and a commitment to humanitarian causes, were taught and modeled to her when she was a young girl and have become instrumental to her in her life's work. She credits her grandmother for teaching her the most important lesson about faith: "What we do on our own matters little—what counts is what God chooses to do through us" (215). Elizabeth Dole's work for humanitarian causes, as president of the American Red Cross and as a United States senator, demonstrates her practical application of her faith. This commitment resembles that of the Southern ladies whose "advocacy of benevolent causes . . . helped to counter theological predispositions and traditional notions about woman's place" (Shelby 220).

Elizabeth Dole's Southern Style Meets D.C.

Just as a traveler to a new region can feel surprised and disoriented by the different environment found in a new land, meeting someone who characterizes the essence of a different region can be jarring. Some of the press that Elizabeth Dole has received suggests that her effusive Southern style does not appeal to them or, even worse, represents a false performance on the part of Dole. For example:

> Carl Anthony, an expert on first ladies, said that Dole's "Southerness" [*sic*] helps to define her as a public figure. And, further, that she uses that quality to protect her from rude attacks, much as did Lady Bird Johnson, who traveled through the South campaigning for her husband's pro-Civil Rights position. Dole "wears" her Southerness, [*sic*] according to Anthony, "like a suit of armor." For her, everything is wonderful, and she is happy to see every person. But this seems to be her way of steeling herself against anyone who wants to probe beneath the surface. (Wertheimer and Gutgold 14)

Another article describes her presentation style as "Southern fried Kabuki: every line, every smile, every knowing aside, every haa-haa-haa has been tested and practiced until the timing is just so" (Stengel 33).

Yet, for all the detractors, one aspect of Elizabeth Dole's style is undeniably true: she evokes her Southern heritage and pays tribute to good lessons learned from her youth in North Carolina. Perhaps even more impressively, she successfully ran for a senate seat from her home state of North Carolina after having worked in Washington, D.C., for more than a quarter of a century. Her ability to "go home again" after residing in the capitol for so long indicates that citizens of her home state still view her as one of their own. Her speeches, often autobiographical, recount significant periods of her life. In one of her earliest speeches that gained national attention, the National Prayer Breakfast Speech given in Washington, D.C., in 1987, Elizabeth Dole tells the stories of her religious upbringing in North Carolina and her spiritual journey. She shares how her grandmother "practiced what she preached, and lived her life for others" (134). Dole also recounts how she moved away from the church and how she learned to get back to the faith that was the center of her life as a child:

> From an early age, I had an active church life. But as we move along, how often in our busy lives something becomes a barrier to total commitment of one's life to the lord! In some cases, it may be money, power or prestige.
> In my case, my career became of paramount importance. I worked very hard, to excel, to achieve. My goal was to do my best, which was all fine and well. But I'm inclined to be a perfectionist. And it's very hard, you know, to try to control everything, surmount every difficulty, foresee every problem, realize every opportunity. That can be pretty tough on your family, your friends, your fellow workers and on yourself. In my case, it began crowding out what Mom Cathey had taught me were life's most important priorities.

I was blessed with a beautiful marriage, a challenging career . . . and yet
. . . only gradually, over many years, did I realize what I was missing. My life
was threatened by spiritual starvation. (E. Dole, "National Prayer" 134–35)[2]

In her autobiography, she explains the story of the spiritual starvation she
described in her "National Prayer Breakfast Speech." "Growing up in Salisbury,
I had cherished the ties that bind a permanent congregation. It was a feeling I
missed in the non-denominational atmosphere at Duke and Harvard" (Dole and
Dole, *Unlimited* 214). She describes how her high-powered Washington, D.C.,
career and perfectionist tendencies pulled her away from the church and her
strong commitment to faith that she learned early in her life. "Ironically, this
form of perfectionism, so different from my grandmother's selfless spirituality,
began crowding out what Mom Cathey had taught me were life's most important
objectives" (214). Elizabeth Dole also acknowledges her continuing struggle
with religious fulfillment: "I'm a long way from where I want to be. At times I
have even wondered whether I am trying to tackle spiritual growth with that
same perfectionist zeal that prompts a man to pray: 'Please Lord, give me
patience—and I need it right now!'" (215)

Elizabeth Dole's ideology has been deeply ingrained in her life's work.
Whether it was her first significant job in Washington, D.C., on the President's
Committee of Consumer Interests or the position she holds today as Senator, she
has integrated what she learned early on into her work. "What began as just a
job soon turned into something of a personal crusade," she writes about her
work on consumer affairs (143). Her American Red Cross presidency allowed
her to make her job a "mission" where she could "help those in need on a full-
time basis" (283). As a North Carolina senator, Elizabeth Dole has championed
the cause of hunger prevention, once again making her work in Washington a
humanitarian effort.

The Republican National Committee selected Elizabeth Dole to serve as the
temporary chair and opening night speaker at the 1988 national convention.
Theresa Esposito, then a state representative from Dole's home state of North
Carolina, introduced her, reminding the audience of her impressive resume and
Southern background:

The jobs she took on at [the Department of] Transportation were awesomely
demanding. This Phi Beta Kappa from Duke University, this Harvard Law
School educated daughter of the South did not duck the issues, making safety at
Transportation her highest priority. . . . Though a frequent speaker at political,
business and charity events, she cherishes most last year's keynote speech at
the president's prayer breakfast. It is a great privilege to introduce fellow North
Carolinian, the temporary chair of our convention, the honorable Elizabeth
Dole. (qtd. in Gutgold, "Rhetoric" Appendix B 11)[3]

In the speech, Elizabeth Dole appeals to the women of America to "have an
open mind" about George Bush. She tries to appeal to both traditionalists and

feminists when she describes the setbacks that could face American women if liberals are elected. She states, "if we let the liberals in we lose all that progress, your progress. We women would be especially vulnerable. We're always vulnerable when jobs are cut back and the economy stagnates" (E. Dole, "Republican, 1988" 149). This speech is important in Dole's career because it shows her identification with her audience. In *Lives of Their Own*, Martha Watson reminds us that the Burkean notion of identification is at work in many autobiographies. In the 1988 speech, Elizabeth Dole persuades others by establishing common ground. In this case, the shared experience of being a woman becomes the "basis for cooperation" (Watson 11).

Throughout her autobiography, Elizabeth Dole calls attention to many of the situations she faced in her various government positions. She also recounts many of the stories in her speeches. Her personal life intersects with her political career as illustrated in her example of a controversial multibillion-dollar arms deal with Saudi Arabia. She took on the job of persuading her husband, who was one of the undecided lawmakers on the issue. She recounts this humorous story in both her autobiography and her speech, "An America We Can Be":

> The session came to an abrupt end when I said I was going home to cook a candlelight dinner. "That's great, Elizabeth," said my deputy. "But it's only 6:00 p.m.! Isn't it a bit early for you to be going home? Don't you want to finish targeting those undecided Senators?"
>
> "You don't understand," I said. "Tonight, I'm targeting Bob Dole." And for those of you wondering, I did get Bob's vote. And even though the candlelight dinner was successful, I never tried it out on any other Senator! (E. Dole, "An America" 199–200)

Dole's penchant for storytelling permeates her autobiography. She fills each chapter with charmingly told events in her personal and political life. The political and personal intertwine. For example, when faced with career decisions, Elizabeth Dole describes how being at home in Salisbury helped her think objectively about her future. In 1988, after she had stepped down from her position as Secretary of Transportation, she describes her thinking about what she would do next:

> Christmas 1988 found me where I always spend part of the holidays—with my mother in Salisbury. In between shopping for gifts, and visiting family and friends, I was also thinking about my future. I had devoted twenty-three years of my life to government service. Perhaps now was the time, I thought, to try and make a difference somewhere else. (Dole and Dole, *Unlimited* 272)

Dole describes how her decision to become Red Cross president was affirmed by her mother's experience with volunteer work for the American Red Cross. She explains:

> Shortly after accepting the presidency of the Red Cross, I was reminded by my mother of her own service as a Red Cross volunteer during World War II.

"Elizabeth," she said, "Nothing I ever did made me feel so important." Flying home from Kuwait, only one month into my job, I knew that Mother was right. I had found a job that filled me with a sense of mission like I had never known. (290)

Becoming a Powerhouse Campaigner

In 1976, Elizabeth Dole entered the world of political campaigning when her husband became the vice presidential candidate on the Republican ticket with Gerald Ford. In the beginning, the Ford campaign wasn't sure what role Elizabeth Dole would play in the campaign, since traditionally, spouses would look lovely and smile adoringly at their spouse-candidate, and not much else. But, Elizabeth Dole proved unlike most wives, because even though she didn't think that voters were electing her, "as an independent career woman, and an FTC commissioner with ten years of government experience," she wanted to be able to express herself on the campaign trail (Dole and Dole, *Unlimited* 171). She comments: "I wasn't going to spend the whole campaign answering reporters' questions with a demure 'I don't do issues.' *I did do issues*. Six days a week. The genie couldn't be put back into the bottle" (171). Bob Dole wanted his wife to campaign with him, but women at the Republican National Committee argued that Elizabeth Dole should use her considerable persuasive talents by covering as much ground as possible on her own. At first, the Doles struck a compromise: they went to the same cities and then split up with separate agendas and met up together in the evening. After a few days, Elizabeth Dole decided to strike out on her own, and she often received more favorable and plentiful media coverage than her husband. During 1980, Dole campaigned ardently for the Reagan/Bush ticket. In 1984, she served an important role as a speaker at the Republican National Convention, providing a woman's voice to counter Democrat Geraldine Ferraro's candidacy.

As the years went by, Elizabeth Dole became an enthusiastic voice for the Republican Party, promoting her husband's efforts to become president in 1996. Her campaigning and blockbuster speech at the 1996 Republican National Convention drew rave reviews. She strolled the convention hall and warmly mingled with supporters as she spoke. The speech, a narrative that described her husband's life, received extensive press coverage. Even former president Bill Clinton, in his memoir *My Life*, notes the excellence of Elizabeth Dole's oratory: "Elizabeth Dole gave an impressive and effective nominating speech for her husband, leaving the podium to speak in a conversational way as she walked among the delegates" (721). Reflecting on some of the thinking and planning that went into the speech, Dole writes: "As the Republican National Convention in San Diego approached, I told the campaign staff and convention planners that it would be much more comfortable for me to deliver my speech from the floor of the convention, rather than from the rostrum. My idea was met with a great deal of opposition from well-meaning individuals" (E. Dole, *Hearts* 5). She explains how the risk she took in making the speech paid off: "I concluded that giving the best speech I could for Bob was worth the risk" (6). She observes that successful speeches require "making an emotional connection with the audience" (7).

Partly because of the attention she received as a campaigner for her husband and at the urging of many supporters, some of whom created a "Draft Elizabeth for President" Web site, Elizabeth Dole launched an exploratory bid for the presidency from March through October 1999, campaigning vigorously. Ralph Reed, the former Christian Coalition leader, said that she "could be a 'very formidable' candidate if she emphasizes her North Carolina Bible-belt roots" (qtd. in "2000" 4). She dropped out of the race when her fundraising efforts could not match that of front-runner George W. Bush. When she stepped down from the race she said optimistically: "To my friends, I say, take heart. We will meet again and often—in the unending struggle to realize America's promise as a land whose greatness lies, not in the power of her government, but in the freedom of her people" (E. Dole, "Presidential" 225). Elizabeth Dole entered the public stage again when she ran for the U.S. Senate from her home state of North Carolina. When she "went home again" to campaign, she noted the difference a Southern audience makes when it comes to appreciating her spirituality:

> I attempted to bring in something because I am a person of faith, and I would see heads nodding. And at the end of my campaign, I made the comment that North Carolina is the buckle of the Bible Belt and it really is true. A lot of your humanitarian yearnings flow from that and some people might think, "oh, you should never say a word about faith." Maybe in the South, and especially North Carolina, that isn't hard to do, because your audience is agreeing with you. (E. Dole, Interview)

Elizabeth Dole's Narratives

Throughout her life-story, Elizabeth Dole encourages others to follow in her footsteps in a career in public service and leadership. She describes herself:

> My husband once described himself as "the most optimistic man in America." Well, I consider myself to be the most optimistic woman in America. I believe in our country. I believe in the innate goodness of the American people. I believe in the values that made this country what it is: courage, perseverance, generosity, faith, and a commitment to service. (E. Dole, *Hearts* 9)

At more than seventy years old, she has retained exuberance for her work as a public servant and through her speeches and her autobiography encourages others to serve. Her optimistic discourse serves to instruct and empower future women leaders because she points out that during her long career she has experienced and witnessed significant progress for women in politics despite the challenges that still remain. As she does on many occasions, she again recalls her first day at Harvard:

> Of all the changes I have witnessed during my nearly four decades in public service, the change in opportunities available to women and minorities is probably the greatest. I will never forget my first day at Harvard Law School. There were 550 members of the class of 1965—only two dozen of them women. A male student approached me and asked, "Elizabeth, what are you doing here? Don't you realize that there are men who would give their right arm to be in law school, men who would use their legal education?" I guarantee you that question is not asked of the women who now comprise roughly 50 percent of each Harvard Law School class! (161)

Elizabeth Dole also makes a point to tell readers that as a young woman she enjoyed the support of women mentors. Shortly after she graduated from Duke University, she called upon Maine Senator Margaret Chase Smith, who advised her to obtain a law degree. Senator Dole says that her "way of repaying a debt to the lady from Skowhegan" (Dole and Dole, *Unlimited* 86) is to make time to meet with young women who ask to speak with her about public service careers.

Conclusion

Elizabeth Dole likely will write another autobiography before she exits public life, since none of her writings chronicle her most recent political contribution as a United States senator. Her story is one of longevity; she constantly seeks a new way to challenge herself, make a contribution, and stay active—much like she was taught as a young girl growing up in Salisbury, North Carolina. Elizabeth Dole's values and beliefs permeate both the public and private spheres. Her work as a public servant embodies the belief system with which she was raised. It is likely that her next autobiography will include her characteristic storytelling, rich with many examples from her North Carolina roots. These tales will describe, undoubtedly, a Southern belle who grew into an educated and worldly woman, eventually returning to her home state to continue to make a difference by living the principles and strong work ethic ingrained in her from birth.

Notes

1. For example, Elizabeth Dole used the phrase, "Azaleas in the spring," in a speech at the National Prayer Breakfast meeting in 1987 to describe how important the gospel was in her life growing up in Salisbury, North Carolina. The speech transcript is reprinted in Wertheimer and Gutgold's *Elizabeth Hanford Dole, Speaking from the Heart*, 134.

2. The ellipses are included in the original transcript of the speech.

3. For use in her dissertation, Gutgold transcribed the text of Theresa Esposito's introduction from a personal videotape of Elizabeth's Dole's speech.

Chapter Six

All Our Relations: Wilma Mankiller's Rhetoric of Feminist Ecology and Indian Sovereignty

Emily Plec

Women can help turn the world right side up. We bring a more collaborative approach to government. And if we do not participate, then decisions will be made without us.

—Wilma Mankiller (Mankiller and Wallis 242)

Wilma Mankiller, the former Principal Chief of the Cherokee Nation, opens each chapter of her autobiography, *Mankiller: A Chief and Her People*, with a story, quotation, or glimpse into Cherokee tradition. Sometimes historical, sometimes mythical, always personal, these excerpts frame the chronological chapters of her life. The epigraph above, originally delivered by Mankiller in September of 1984, offers a useful framework for consideration of her work as a political leader as well as the larger issues addressed in this volume. A prominent public figure and frequent lecturer, Wilma Mankiller has addressed diverse groups, sharing her Cherokee perspective on policy, governance, economics, spirituality, feminism, and community. Her discourse frequently emphasizes the role of women in the maintenance of family, community, and, by extension, nation. Wilma Mankiller herself embodies the greatest fulfillment of these obligations and responsibilities in terms of her devotion as a parent and partner, public servant, and political leader. No matter the specific subject matter, Wilma Mankiller's public discourse, which includes numerous speeches, lectures, essays, articles, and two important books, is ultimately about community and sovereignty, finding balance, coming to be of good mind, and seeing the connections among all our relations.

As illustrated throughout this volume, autobiographies do much more than tell us about the life history of an individual. They communicate ideologies, they help us to identify and understand other communities, and they have the potential to shape the way we perceive and relate to others. Wilma Mankiller's autobiography achieves all three of these rhetorical feats and does so in a way that has the potential to transform the realities and lifeworlds of people from many cultures. As Richard Dyer points out in his review of the book, "the best thing about Wilma Mankiller, and her book, is that she isn't a parable; instead she's a person" (47).

Moreover, as Sarah Turner contends, "the autobiographical project of Native Americans is unique in the sense that it is a reaction against a politically sanctioned attempt at extermination and a denial of culture, language, and beliefs" (109). Mankiller herself laments that "the voices of our grandmothers are silenced by most of the written history of our people. How I long to hear their voices!" (Mankiller and Wallis 20). Or, as Inés Hernández-Ávila writes, "through language, Native people, Native women, have been disgraced and violated in our own home(land) and robbed of our sovereignty. In our own home(land), we recover our grace and our sovereignty through language and through struggle, even if that language is the enemy's made ours" (502). Mankiller writes against the erasure of Cherokee histories and the silence surrounding Native women's lives. She writes within a long tradition of autobiographical work by Indian women. She also writes within particular colonial frameworks in ways that problematize interpretation of the text(s).[1] This chapter contributes to the rapidly growing body of scholarly literature on Indian women's autobiography by focusing on significant aspects of Mankiller's discourse.[2]

Mankiller's autobiography, as well as her edited volume, *every day is a good day*, makes important contributions to Native American nonfiction. In these books, Mankiller communicates an indigenous ecofeminist consciousness that is informed by a political history of genocide, broken treaties, relocation, and termination. She also articulates a vision of Indian sovereignty grounded in an ecological model of social and environmental justice that highlights balance and interconnection. Mankiller's ecofeminism and theory of sovereignty have tremendous significance for non-indigenous peoples whose failures to achieve balance and recognize interconnection enable and exacerbate many of our social and planetary crises. In particular, Mankiller's understanding and elaboration of the meaning of sovereignty challenges the dominant U.S. American government's tendency to assert and rely upon false dichotomies, oversimplification, and circular definitions. Her discourse also opens constructive possibilities for rethinking and rearticulating the relationships all people have with each other and with the earth.

Following a biographical section that highlights the trials and triumphs of Mankiller's personal and political career, this chapter examines her autobiography and edited volume as significant instances of Native American and ecofeminist rhetoric. Mankiller's parallel presentation of personal events and Cherokee history in her autobiography provides the foundation for her broader message of interconnection and balance. Through these themes, she articulates her perspectives on feminism, nature, and the role of history and non-Indian allies in Indian struggles for social justice. Finally, Mankiller's edited collection of indigenous women's wisdom, when interpreted in conjunction with her autobiography, presents a polyvocal perspective on sovereignty that makes important contributions to (inter)national and (inter)tribal dialogues. By speaking with other indigenous women leaders in *everyday is a good day*, she builds upon considerable ethos developed both in her memoir and through her work as Principal Chief of the Cherokee Nation. In fact, from a Cherokee perspective, *every day is a good day* may be understood as an extension of the autobiographical project.[3] This collection of *Reflections by Contemporary Indigenous Women* stands as a multivoiced echo of Mankiller's own spirit of inspiration—drawn from land, community, ceremony, and family.

The Strength of Suffering

We are survivors of a battle to gain control of our own lives and create our own paths instead of following someone else's.

(Mankiller and Wallis 212)

Wilma Pearl Mankiller's childhood began on November 18, 1945, in Tahlequah, the capital of the Cherokee Nation in Oklahoma. She was the sixth child of her Dutch-Irish mother, Irene, and Cherokee father, Charley Mankiller. With eleven children in all, and poverty rampant across the nation, the Mankillers struggled financially. Their third daughter recalls, "we were not well off, at least when it came to money. Like many of the people in Adair County, we were really poor—'dirt poor' is how they say it in Oklahoma. I suppose there are degrees of poverty just as there are degrees of wealth. If so, we were on the bottom rung of the poverty ladder" (Mankiller and Wallis 33).

The Mankillers made a living by growing fruits and vegetables, cutting timber and harvesting crops seasonally, and supplementing their garden with wild game (Mankiller and Wallis 35; Reaves 181). As Brad Agnew states in his examination of Wilma Mankiller's leadership of the Cherokee Nation, "the family barely eked out an existence on the flinty foothills of the Ozarks where Mankiller's early years were spent in a four-room, tin-roofed house built of rough lumber with no electricity or running water" (211). Like many children born to poverty but surrounded by a loving family and rich, bountiful natural world, Wilma Mankiller was initially oblivious to her family's poverty until a schoolmate teased her about her flour-sack underwear. Her world, at that time, was filled with the creative games of children and the colorful stories of elders. Nonetheless, the difficulties they faced and their hopes for a better life for their children would eventually force the family to leave Mankiller Flats in Adair County for a Bureau of Indian Affairs (BIA) relocation program in San Francisco. Mankiller calls the experience her own "little Trail of Tears," a microcosm of the Cherokee experience of removal. She recalls, "I wept tears that came from deep within the Cherokee part of me. They were tears from my history, from my tribe's past. They were Cherokee tears" (qtd. in D. Wilson 257).

In her autobiography, she describes the culture shock she and her family encountered upon their arrival in San Francisco:

> The noises of the city, especially at night, were bewildering. We had left behind the sounds of roosters, dogs, coyotes, bobcats, owls, crickets, and other animals moving through the woods. We knew the sounds of nature. Now we heard traffic and other noises that were foreign. The police and ambulance sirens were the worst. That very first night in the big city we were all huddled under the covers, and we heard sirens outside in the street. We had never heard sirens before. I thought it was some sort of wild creature screaming. The sirens reminded me of wolves. . . . Everything was new to us. For instance, we had never seen neon lights before. No one had bothered to even try to prepare us for city living. (Mankiller and Wallis 71, 72)

The abrupt and uneven transition to city life combined to make the Mankillers' acculturation more difficult than their departure. Wilma Mankiller attended the fifth through seventh grades in Daly City. Then, after living on her grandmother's farm in Riverside for a year, she returned to the Bay Area to find her parents had been forced to relocate again; this time to Hunter's Point, a low-income housing project. According to Mankiller, "living there was really like one long, hot, boring, lazy afternoon—nothing to do, no place to go, and no promise of anything better in the future" (109). She recalls a community where ambulances refused to go and where the police were "the enemy" (109).

Mankiller weaves numerous quotations into her autobiographical recollections. One of these, from Michael Harrington's *The Culture of Poverty*, suggests the impact of her experience living at Hunter's Point: "there are tens of millions of Americans who are beyond the welfare state. Taken as a whole there is a culture of poverty . . . bad health, poor housing, low levels of aspiration and high levels of mental distress" (qtd. in Mankiller and Wallis 110). It was during her adolescent years in the Bay Area that Mankiller's involvement with the San Francisco Indian Center began to develop into a political and explicitly cultural consciousness (111, 112).

After graduating from high school, Mankiller moved in with her sister, Frances, and took a clerical job with a finance company. Her sense of personal freedom and independence was soon curtailed, however. A few days before her eighteenth birthday, Wilma Mankiller married Hector Hugo Olaya de Bardi, or Hugo Olaya. Her Ecuadorian suitor was four years older and "dashing and different and good-looking" (146). He also was rather traditional in his expectations of his wife. Soon after the birth of her first daughter, who was conceived during their honeymoon, Mankiller grew discontented with her domestic life. She recalls:

> Hugo kept up his schedule of going to school by day and working for the airline every night. I stayed home with my baby daughter. I kept house, shopped, cooked, and cleaned. I evolved into my role of young wife and mother. I felt there was some order, perhaps some of that old Cherokee balance, in my life, but I was not completely sure I was comfortable with my situation. That feeling would nag at me for a long time (150)

Mankiller's passive description of her daily routines are drab in comparison to her vivid accounts of visits to Alcatraz Island during the occupation of the late 1960s and early 1970s and her disappointingly brief descriptions of her work with the Pit River Tribe in Northern California. In 1974, shortly before the Cherokees were granted self-determination by the U.S. government, Mankiller left Olaya. She describes the dissolution of her marriage alongside a "rebellion" which involved the purchase of a "little red Mazda" (202). In some ways, Mankiller's "rebellion" can better be understood as a microcosmic example of the exercising of sovereignty and feminist self-determination since the purchase of the car enabled her to continue her work with Indian communities. A few years later, she moved with her daughters, Gina and Felicia, back to Oklahoma (D. Wilson 257; Lisa 161). Her experience advocating with the Pit River people led her to seek employment with the Cherokee Nation in 1977 as an "economic stimulus coordinator," earning $11,000 a year (Reaves 183). Mankiller also completed her bachelor's degree in 1979 and began to pursue a graduate degree at the University of Arkansas at Fayetteville.

In November of 1979, she was seriously injured in a head-on automobile collision and was forced to undergo several painful surgeries. The other driver, who Mankiller later learned had been her close friend Sherrye Morris, was killed in the accident. Several pages of her autobiography are devoted to the tragedy, and her near-death experience clearly affected Mankiller's outlook on life. In *every day is a good day* she says, "after that, I no longer feared death, and I no longer feared life" (149). Less than a year after the accident, Mankiller was diagnosed with myasthenia gravis, which had caused her to experience severe muscle weakness. After yet another surgery, Mankiller returned to the Cherokee Nation and accepted a position as Community Development Director. In this capacity, she initiated volunteer programs and grant applications to support efforts such as the revitalization of the small town of Bell, Oklahoma. Mankiller recalls:

> We established a partnership between the Cherokee people living at Bell and the Cherokee Nation. Our goal was to bring members of the community together so they could solve their common problems. From the beginning, the Bell residents realized they were responsible for the success or failure of the project. . . . It turned into a massive community-renewal effort using local labor and talent and about a million dollars in hard costs, funded by grants. (Mankiller and Wallis 234)

Unlike many development officers, Wilma Mankiller preferred to let the Cherokee people decide what needed to be done in their communities, then encourage their active participation in the work to accomplish their goals. She writes:

> For me, the Bell project also validated a lot of the things that I believed about our people. I have always known that Cherokee people—particularly those in more traditional communities—have retained a great sense of interdependence, and a willingness to pitch in and help one another. I also knew that we had the

capacity to solve our own problems, given the right set of circumstances and resources. The Bell project affirmed those beliefs. (235)

In his biography of Mankiller, Michael Crawford Reaves succinctly summarizes the "two pivotal occurrences" that evolved from Mankiller's work with the Nation:

> First, she met a Cherokee named Charlie Soap on the Bell community project. After finding that they worked well together, the relationship grew, and they married in October 1986. The second important change also involved the work Mankiller contributed to the Bell project. She attracted the attention of Chief Ross Swimmer, who asked her to run as his deputy chief in 1983. (Reaves 184, 185)

In her autobiography, Mankiller devotes considerable attention to the difficulties she faced in the election, many due to gender discrimination. She recalls people saying that "having a female run our tribe would make the Cherokees the laughingstock of the tribal world" (Mankiller and Wallis 241). Still today, Mankiller makes a point of educating audiences about the long tradition of female leadership in Cherokee history. She recounts the tradition of female warriors and advisors known as "War Women," "Pretty Women," and "Most Honored" or "Beloved Woman" (207). As Theda Perdue notes, "the reemergence of Cherokee women onto a public stage at the end of the twentieth century is testimony to the endurance of that culture. Service to community rather than individual achievement still distinguishes Cherokee women and brings them acclaim" (195).

Political opponents and many community members opposed Swimmer's selection of Mankiller as his preferred candidate for Deputy Chief, forcing a runoff election for the position (Mankiller and Wallis 242). Mankiller's political opponents were even more distressed when, midway through their term in office, Swimmer accepted a position with the BIA, thus promoting Mankiller to Principal Chief for the remaining two years of the term (243). In 1987, she chose to formally run for the office of Principal Chief and was victorious, following a tense runoff election with a former deputy chief and political rival, Perry Wheeler (248). The election was significant for many reasons, including its novelty. "Finally," Mankiller recalls, "I felt the question of gender had been put to rest" (249). She also notes the importance of "returning the balance to the role of women in our tribe . . . young Cherokee girls never thought they might be able to grow up and become Chief themselves" (246).

Additionally, Janis King, in her examination of Wilma Mankiller's "justificatory rhetoric," argues, "Ms. Mankiller's election and terms of office are important for American women because her communicative style helped her to overcome conflict and verbal assaults upon her character and to win the election" (21). One of the primary attacks against Mankiller, aside from those on her gender, was the accusation by her opponent Perry Wheeler that she lied to the public about her health when she was hospitalized for a kidney infection during the campaign. After several unsuccessful attempts to quell discussion of her health, Mankiller effectively countered the attack by turning Wheeler's self-identification as a traditional Cherokee against him. She argued that it was a breach of Cherokee tradition to think ill of another and to wage a negative campaign against an opponent. Instead, the Cherokee tradition required that a person hold "a good mind toward all people" (J. King 33). As a result of this rhetorical strategy, Wheeler may have been perceived as less traditional, and therefore less qualified to represent the Cherokee people. Mankiller's rhetoric of transcendence both educated her audience and diverted their attention from the criticisms of her leadership. King summarizes Mankiller's approach during the election:

> She enlightened her rhetorical audience about their tradition in history, culture, and values as the way to rebuild her credibility after her character has been called into question. She informed her audience that women in Cherokee history were the planners and decision-makers. She reminded her audience that the tribe had been progressive in the past when their ancestors were self-reliant and self-sufficient, and these characteristics were what her progressive leadership ideas of today were designed to achieve. Lastly, she educated her audience about the relationship between illnesses and the tribe's tests of leadership/manhood concerned with perseverance and tolerance and also with the tradition of having a good mind toward all people. (J. King 35)

During her first full term as Principal Chief, Mankiller revised tax laws affecting businesses operating on Cherokee land, expanded health services, and signed an historic agreement with the BIA to "allow the Cherokee Nation to participate in a self-governance demonstration project" (Agnew 224). Three years after her victory in the runoff election, Mankiller was hospitalized with kidney failure. Her older brother Don volunteered to be a donor and, following her recovery and return to office, Mankiller chose to run for a second full term. This time she was reelected with almost 83 percent of the vote. In April of 1994, Mankiller was invited to moderate a presidential summit that included 322 tribal leaders from all 545 federally recognized tribes. After the summit, President Clinton promised to "fulfill trust obligations the government had made, respect tribal sovereignty, and protect the religious freedom of Native Americans" (227). The meeting was followed by a "listening conference" in Albuquerque, New Mexico, which led to the creation of the U.S. Justice Department's Office of Indian Justice (227).

After ten years as Principal Chief of the Cherokee Nation, Mankiller decided "it was time to move on" ("Guest Essay" 5). She recites some of the achievements of her administration, including "exponential growth in virtually every area of the Cherokee Nation" (5). She counts increases in membership, expanded tribal services (including health care), Cherokee language and literacy projects, and the doubling of both direct employment and the tribal budget among the most important areas of growth (5). She also describes difficulties with particular economic projects, such as the Cherokee Nation Industries, and Housing Authority proposals to the Department of Housing and Urban Development. At the conclusion of her final term in office, Mankiller was plagued by accusations that she misappropriated funds to authorize severance pay for eleven executives (Mankiller, *every day* 153). Mankiller and her employees defended the practice as customary; they believed the incoming chief, Joe Byrd, would fire them (Mankiller and Wallis 265). Incidentally, Byrd had run uncontested in the runoff election with the Chief's endorsed candidate and the leader in the June election, George Bearpaw, after Bearpaw was disqualified for pleading guilty to a twenty-year-old felony (263). Byrd assumed office and promptly cleaned house, firing numerous long-time Nation employees. Eventually, federal investigation into charges of misappropriations and the conviction of Byrd's campaign manager on 22 felony counts led to widespread calls for Byrd's resignation (268).

Meanwhile, Mankiller had moved to Hanover, New Hampshire, to assume the Montgomery Fellowship at Dartmouth College. While there, she contracted pneumonia and was soon diagnosed with second-stage large-cell lymphoma (269–71). She underwent chemotherapy, which was abruptly stopped when her oncologist discovered a severe lung infection due to her lowered immune system. In January of 1998, in the midst of her treatment, President Clinton awarded Mankiller the Presidential Medal of Freedom, which she accepted "on behalf of all Native American people" (274). Unfortunately, soon after she resumed chemotherapy, her transplanted kidney failed. Mankiller's niece, Virlee Williamson, stepped forward to donate one of her kidneys because "it seemed like the right thing to do" (qtd. in Mankiller and Wallis 273). Through all these trials and tributes, Mankiller remained active in social and political life. Among other projects, she co-edited *The Reader's Companion to the History of American Women* with Gwendolyn Mink, Marysa Navarro, Barbara Smith, and Gloria Steinem.

In the summer of 1999, Chad Smith defeated Joe Byrd and became Principal Chief, a victory that Mankiller views as a step toward the restoration of "financial and political stability" for the Cherokee Nation. In two passages from his first Inaugural Address, Chief Smith alludes to Mankiller's life and legacy: "along this journey, we must pray not for an easier path or a lighter load. Instead, we must ask for strength to face challenges, wisdom to make the right decisions, and perseverance to never give up." (qtd. in Mankiller and Wallis 260). He continues, "let us, armed with our indomitable Cherokee spirit and ancestral pride, proceed on our journey, relying on the strength and wisdom of our Cherokee women and guided by our Creator" (qtd. in Mankiller and Wallis 274).

Native American Rhetoric: Interconnection and Implication

The discourse of Native Americans has long attracted the attention of rhetorical critics and theorists. As early as 1953, A. M. Drummond and Richard Moody argue in their essay, "Indian Treaties: The First American Dramas," that "metaphorical expression" and "poetic invention" marked the "red man's rhetoric" (16). Two decades later, Ruth Arrington suggests that speech scholars examine "worthwhile materials written by the American Indian [which] are available in newspapers, journals and diaries, and magazines" (191). Arrington reinforces her argument by briefly surveying a variety of publications produced by Cherokees in Oklahoma. Several other examinations of "Indian Rhetoric" were undertaken in the 1970s. In 1973, for example, the Speech Communication Association hosted a "Dimension Series Program" at their New York convention. The program, titled "Rhetoric of Discontent: The American Indian," featured Dr. Barnard Old Coyote, then-President of the American Indian National Bank, and Earl Old Person, the former head of the Blackfeet Tribal Council (Blanche 86). Also appearing in the 1970s, the essays of Marjorie Murphy demonstrate a common interest in identifying key characteristics of Indian rhetoric. As Murphy notes, "Indian rhetoric is rooted in the tradition of eloquence being essential to tribal government where the power of public opinion takes the place of coercion" (358). She also mentions "a natural reticence to too much talk" (359) as an attribute that impacts Indian rhetoric.

Similarly, but with closer attention to culture and context, Gerry Phillipsen examines features of Navajo rhetoric in terms of the larger Navajo cultural system. In "Navajo World View and Culture Patterns of Speech," Philipsen argues that "rhetoric, for the Navajo, is functional as a means to restore and maintain order, balance, and harmony. . . . Harmony can thus be seen as the dominating function of effective expression and the dominating motive of rhetorical appeal" (139). Notably, the concept of harmony, in the form of balance and "being of good mind," also is featured prominently in Wilma Mankiller's rhetoric and in the discourse of the indigenous women interviewed for *every day is a good day*. The Cherokee approach to life requires one to endeavor to maintain a constructive attitude. The search for balance and the maintenance of harmony become remarkable feats when set against experiences of genocide, removal, and assimilation. Later scholars examine the ways in which Cherokee speakers used the power of language to resist the decimation of their culture, land, and people.

Writing about the cultural context of nineteenth-century Cherokee removal known as the "Trail of Tears," William Strickland examines the rhetorical response to the Indian removal policies of President Andrew Jackson. The power of the spoken word, in addition to efforts to maintain tribal unity, guided Cherokee arguments for resistance to the removal campaign. Strickland illustrates how Cherokee rhetors such as Major Ridge and John Ross aimed to convince Cherokees to remain unified against removal, which would force them to leave their ancestral lands and ultimately lead to further relocations ("Rhetoric" 294–300). The first part of the argument was based on fact; Jackson's policy would move the Cherokee people from their homes in Georgia to the territory now known as Oklahoma. The latter part of the argument (about further relocations), a potential slippery slope, would prove prophetic for many Cherokees, such as Wilma Mankiller and her family, who experienced the ongoing trauma of relocation and removal.[4] Strickland points out the fact that Ridge's and Ross' appeals to Cherokee unity were generally successful. He states, "Harmony was basic to the Cherokee character, and rhetorical appeals were based upon this shared tribal value" (299). In many ways, the larger rhetorical, social, and spiritual value of harmony accounts for particular characteristics of Indian discourse, such as the eloquence and use of silence (listening) identified by Drummond, Moody, Murphy, Philipsen, Strickland, and others.

More recent work in the communication field by scholars such as Randall Lake, Richard Morris, and Philip Wander continue this project of defining contemporary Native American rhetoric. Their essays also point to the significance of indigenous discourse for reconsidering the uses of rhetoric. Philipsen's discussion of "ritual speech," for example, is implicitly taken up by Lake in his discussion of naming and ritual activity within the naturalist framework, in which "symbol and thing are naturally and empirically related" ("Rhetor" 203). Morris and Wander remind us that, within the context of Native American rhetoric, "the spoken word possesses the power of community" (186), thus reinforcing the potency of Cherokee oral (and literary) traditions. Kathleen German links indigenous rhetorical practices to the natural environment. She suggests that "figurative expression drawn from the natural world assumed that human life was part of the cycle of natural events, blending past and future with present time" (34). Moreover, "For most Native Americans, harmony and balance in nature were highly prized and subject to intervention through ritualized human utterances" (34).

Many of the features of Native American rhetoric identified by communication scholars are present within Mankiller's autobiography and edited volume. More importantly, Mankiller's discourse highlights the theme of balance and harmony in nature from a feminist standpoint. She proffers a rhetoric of feminist ecology that unites the past and present, the individual and community, humor[5] and gravity, women and men, nature and technology, and Indians and non-Indians. In short, hers is a rhetoric of interconnection.

In the early sections of her autobiography, Wilma Mankiller introduces herself and her people to the reader. She begins in the first chapter by explaining the origin of her surname and her pride in her family's cultural legacy. One literal Cherokee version of the name Mankiller is *Asgaya-dihi*; another is an honorary title, *Outacity*, conferred upon a person with exceptional skill in warfare. Mankiller, in the Cherokee tradition, was used not only to label people who excel militarily; the title also sometimes refers to persons who could change minds and affect bodies in order to avenge wrongs committed against themselves or others (Mankiller and Wallis 12). Wilma Mankiller describes the teasing she received (and still occasionally receives) because the English interpretation of the word conjures a backlash to American feminism.[6] She describes her eventual acceptance, then pride, in her family's name and history then abruptly states, "But I have started my story far too early. Especially in the context of a tribal people, no individual's life stands apart and alone from the rest. My own story has meaning only as long as it is a part of the overall story of my people. For above all else, I am a Cherokee woman" (14). In an examination of what he terms "rhetorical sovereignty," Scott Richard Lyons explains:

> A people is a group of human beings united together by history, language, culture, or some combination therein—a community joined in unison for a common purpose: the survival and flourishing of the people itself. It has always

been from an understanding of themselves as a people that Indian groups have constructed themselves as a nation. (454)

Mankiller draws upon the history of her people, in alternating chapters, to show the connection between her life and the past and present of the Cherokee people. She educates her reader about issues ranging from invasion and conquest to broken treaties and Indian activism. She notes, for example, the fact that at the time of the Spanish conquest, "there were *more than seventy-five million native people* in the Western Hemisphere, with six million of those residing in the United States" (italics original, Mankiller and Wallis 21). Mankiller also describes how conditions among the Cherokee worsened in the eighteenth century, as Cherokees adopted the practice of slavery, fell victim to massive smallpox epidemics, and succumbed to the introduction of alcohol. Her discussion suggests that these were all significant signs of a people's life falling out of balance, out of harmony. She indicates:

> Continual warfare with other tribes and with whites took an intolerable toll, and so did infectious diseases and alcoholism. Cherokees and other native people no longer thought of themselves as partners in any sort of compatible liaison with the world around them. . . . It seemed as if the spiritual and social tapestry they had created for centuries was unraveling. Everything lost that sacred balance. . . . There is an old Cherokee prophecy which instructs us that as long as the Cherokees continue traditional dances, the world will remain as it is, but when the dances stop, the world will come to an end. Everyone should hope that the Cherokees continue to dance. (28–29)

A series of U.S. political maneuvers in the late nineteenth century further compromised harmony and balance in Cherokee communities. These tactics, engineered by bureaucrats such as retired Senator Henry Dawes and conservative Congressman Charles Curtis, amounted to little more than theft and imperialist expansion. The Dawes Commission sought to terminate tribal governments, negotiate allotments and land sales with a National Council, and acculturate the Indian to the lifeways of rural White America. The Allotment Act, passed in 1887 and amended several times in the subsequent decades, resulted in an agreement under which all enrolled members of the Cherokee Nation were to receive 110 acres each of average land from tribal domain (the remainder, presumably, would be made available to White settlement). In *Custer Died for Your Sins*, Vine Deloria Jr. remarks, "if, it was thought, the Indian had his [sic] own piece of land, he would forsake his tribal ways and become just like the white homesteaders who were then flooding the unsettled areas of the western United States. . . . By 1934 Indians had lost nearly 90 million acres through land sales, many of them fraudulent" (52–53).

Most Cherokees opposed the Allotment Act, holding instead the position that lands held in common by the Nation were the strongest guarantee of equality and balance. In her autobiography, Wilma Mankiller recounts a passage from a letter published by W. A. Duncan in the October 5, 1892, *Cherokee Advocate*, highlighting the inequality that results from the individual allotment of lands.

If the system of owning land in severalty has the effect to exclude so many people among the whites from the enjoyment of a home, it seems to me that the same system among the Cherokees would soon have the effect to render many of them homeless. Business knows no pity, and cares for justice only when justice is seen to be better policy. If it had power to control the elements, it would grasp in its iron clutches the waters, sunshine and air and resell them by measure, and at exorbitant prices to the millions of famished men, women and children. (qtd. in Mankiller and Wallis 167)

For Cherokees, the "final blow" to national sovereignty came in 1898 with the passage of the Curtis Act, which "effectively ended tribal rule" (137). As Mankiller notes:

The Curtis Act not only abolished tribal laws and courts, but made native people subject to federal courts. It also provided for the survey of townsites; the extension of voting rights to hundreds of thousands of nonnative people, although denying native people the right to vote; and the establishment of free public schools for the white children in Indian Territory. (137)

In November of 1907, when President Theodore Roosevelt declared Oklahoma a state, it was "a sad day for the Cherokee Nation" and "a very dark page, not only in Cherokee history but in the history of the United States" (139, 166–67).

By tracing Cherokees survival and resistance to U.S. imperialism, Mankiller illustrates the ongoing tensions between the needs of Indian communities and the impositions of federal institutions. Turning to her own recent past, Mankiller examines the inconsistencies among policies affecting Indians and tribes in the mid-twentieth century. For example, "the Economic Opportunity Act of 1965 allowed Native American organizations and tribes to bypass the BIA while they planned, developed, and implemented their own social, educational, and economic initiatives" (188). A few years later, Congress passed an Indian Civil Rights Act that ironically "brought further federal intervention into tribal governments and courts" (189). Mankiller summarizes the situation as the source of Native American activism: "Before any balance or harmony could be achieved, the archaic federal system that dominated our lives had to fully rehabilitated. That reform needed to come from within" (189).

Indian activism, particularly the occupation of Alcatraz Island, plays a prominent role in Mankiller's autobiography. She recalls:

The Alcatraz experience nurtured a sense among us that anything was possible—even, perhaps, justice for native people. . . . I, too, would become totally engulfed by the Native American movement, largely because of the impact that the Alcatraz occupation made on me. . . . As a result, I consciously took a path I still find myself on today as I continue to work for the revitalization of tribal communities. (192)

Mankiller also mentions the influence of the movement in *every day is a good day*: "the morning I made the short journey to Alcatraz, my heart and mind made a quantum leap forward" (80). She describes her visits to the island, and her interactions with the indigenous activists who occupied it, as "a watershed" which inspired her involvement with the Pit River Tribe's fight to regain land near Mount Shasta. "At Pit River," Mankiller recalls in *every day*, "I learned that sovereignty was more than a legal concept. It represents the ability of the People to articulate their own vision of the future, control their destiny, and watch over their lands. It means freedom and responsibility" (82).

In her autobiography, Mankiller weaves the personal and political together by alternating, in successive chapters, her story with the story of her people. Therefore, she illustrates the interconnection between her life and the life of her people and thus, exposes readers to significant events and important facets of the Cherokee experience and helps them see the ways in which their lives are tied to such histories. In her edited volume, *every day is a good day,* Mankiller extends her examination of interconnections to consideration of the natural world.

Toward a Feminist Ecology

For the Cherokee, like many indigenous peoples, the connections between humans and nature continued to flourish despite genocide, colonialism, relocation, and efforts at assimilation into White society. As Perdue suggests:

> Many Cherokee women as well as men continued to adhere to a traditional belief system that linked the spiritual and physical worlds into a coherent balanced whole, emphasized the importance of community and harmony, and sanctioned the autonomy, complementarity, prestige, and even power of women. . . . Because the activities of women have not usually constituted what we think of as "history," the women themselves have slipped from view. . . . Their association with the land and their opposition to selling it strengthened the Cherokee concept of and commitment to common landholding as well as the Nation's refusal to negotiate removal. (185–86)

Cherokee women traditionally held land and controlled the produce that came from the working of it. Yet, balance and complementarity characterized Cherokee gender relations more than hierarchy and contest (Sattler 223).

Mankiller states that "women even occasionally accompanied men to the battle field as warriors. We were also profoundly religious, believing that the world existed in a precarious balance and that only right or correct actions kept it from tumbling. Wrong actions could disturb the balance" (Mankiller and Wallis 20). Moreover, it was "the new values Europeans brought to the Cherokees" that led to the decline of the role of women in Cherokee society (20). The "lack of balance and harmony between men and women," she asserts, is "what we today call sexism. This was not a Cherokee concept. Sexism was borrowed from Europeans" (20). In *every day is a good day*, Oneida artist and activist Joanne Shenandoah explains the prominent role women play in Oneida politics and social life:

> Early in life I learned that women are in charge, that they make the final deci-
> sions about everything. I thought it was that way for everyone. When I went
> into the corporate world, it was a rude awakening to discover that women are
> not respected or listened to. Until that time, I didn't realize the difficulty most
> women have in the world. (qtd. in Mankiller, *every day* 111)

Mankiller's own feminist consciousness, fostered by the American feminist movement of the 1960s and 1970s and deeply linked to the matriarchal structure of her Cherokee heritage, illustrates the convergence among many feminisms. For example, her close friendship with Gloria Steinem and her advocacy for women's groups and organizations have positioned her within the mainstream feminist movement. At the same time, Mankiller's feminism is uniquely Indian and Cherokee. In her essay "Native American Women," Rayna Green calls attention to the collectivistic quality of Indian feminism: "for Indian feminists, every women's issue is framed in the larger context of Native American people" (264). This characterization of Indian feminism is consistent with Mankiller's focus upon the history, activism, and ethnic renewal of Native people. She also emphasizes the importance of "having a good mind" (Mankiller and Wallis 196) or "being of good mind," which is "what our elders call 'a Cherokee approach' to life" (226). Mankiller states that she "found the way to be of good mind" by facing adversity and turning it into "a positive experience—a better path" (229). After many tragedies and challenges, Mankiller concludes, "I don't spend a lot of time dwelling on the negative. I believe that having a good, peaceful mind is the basic premise for a good life" (Mankiller 148). Joy Harjo comments upon the practice required by this path: "being a good human being is an art" (qtd. in Mankiller 158).

Indian feminism and the "Cherokee approach to life" share several features in common. In addition to an eschewal of negativity, egocentrism, and imbalance, a deep reverence for the land and all its inhabitants characterizes this perspective. Mankiller quotes Jenny Leading Cloud, a White River Sioux, in her autobiography: "we Indians think of the earth and the whole universe as a never-ending circle, and in this circle man is just another animal. The buffalo and the coyote are our brothers, the birds, our cousins. From the tiniest ant, even a louse, even the smallest flower you can find—they are all relatives" (qtd. in Mankiller and Wallis 42–43). David Rich Lewis surveys some of the most pressing environmental issues facing indigenous people within the United States. He acknowledges the ways in which Native American cultural attitudes toward nature inspired early environmentalists but also calls attention to the stereotypical use of Indians as token environmental symbols. More importantly, he suggests that indigenous lifeways have much to contribute to non-Indians' understanding of ecological balance and sustainability, stating that:

> Indians were never properly "ecologists." . . . They were, however, careful stu-
> dents of their functional environments. . . . They developed an elaborate land
> ethic based on long-term experience, tied to a cosmological view of the world
> with all its animate and inanimate, natural and supernatural inhabitants as an in-

terrelated whole. They recognized that they were part of creation and acted accordingly. (Lewis 439)

Late-twentieth-century ecofeminists such as Greta Gaard, Val Plumwood, Karen Warren, Carolyn Merchant, Starhawk, Charlene Spretnak, and Ynestra King argue that Western patriarchy produces dualisms and dichotomies that undermine the ecological connections among all entities. Some of these theorists also elaborate a unique relationship that women have with nature, due in part to their dual oppression under patriarchy. Sisters Mary and Carrie Dann explain this idea in the chapter of *every day is a good day* titled "Womanhood":

> *Western Shoshone women are taught that a woman is like the Earth: she gives and nurtures life. The Earth and women have the same properties. The Earth provides for us, just as we provide for our children. . . . Most people in power are men. They are irresponsible. When they rape the Earth, they are raping us as well. Physical rape comes to women because men have no respect for the female spirit. Before the coming of white people, one didn't hear about men violating women. . . . Things are way off balance.* (italics original, qtd. in Mankiller, *every day* 103)

Ecofeminism embraces community, wholeness, and interconnection as alternatives to what Plumwood calls the "master model" (23, 28) of identity posited by Western philosophy. In *every day is a good day*, Rosalie Little Thunder, who has dedicated herself to the survival of buffalo and bison, articulates an ecofeminist understanding of interconnection: "*and so, all things, all beings are interrelated, not only among human beings. For indigenous peoples, that sense of responsibility is for our relatives, the keystone species that shape and guide our lives. We heed the lessons of the ants and the trees and the wind and the Moon*" (italics original, qtd. in Mankiller, *every day* 166). Jaune Quick-to-See Smith, a Flathead Salish artist, explains that "our families and our tribes are ecosystems—a community together, functioning as a unit" (qtd. in Mankiller, *every day* 136). Likewise, LaDonna Harris says, "We even think about animals, the Earth, the Sun, in relational terms, in kinship terms. And when one thinks of others in kinship terms, one has a responsibility for them" (qtd. in Mankiller, *every day* 68). Echoing the concern expressed by the Dann sisters, Audrey Shenandoah cautions, "Man thinks he is superior and dominant over everything, even moving the Earth or trees at his discretion, and that everything else in Creation is a commodity that he can use of make money on. And that is why the world is out of balance" (qtd. in Mankiller, *every day* 53, 200).

Sarah James, a leading advocate for animal habitat in the Arctic National Wildlife Refuge, states:

> We must all work together in balance with each other. We must educate all people about respect for who we are and respect for our Earth. We must work hard to know our non-Native friends. It is so important to find the common ground of all people. . . . We drink the same water, breathe the same air, and want to eat healthy food. We all have children, and we want them to survive in a healthy and just world. (qtd. in Mankiller, *every day* 71)

James' call for partnerships and Native/non-Native alliances supports Mankiller's efforts to acknowledge White people who "made attempts to help Native Americans" (Mankiller and Wallis 100). In *every day is a good day*, Mankiller notes that there are "many examples of outstanding white partners and supporters such as historian Angie Debo, who made a profound positive difference in the lives of Native people" (46).

Mankiller mentions "noteworthy political leaders of conscience such as Henry Clay and Daniel Webster," who opposed Andrew Jackson's Indian Removal Act (87), early twentieth century champion of Seqouyah linguistics Charles Lummis and author Helen Hunt Jackson (100), as well as activists such as Kate Barnard, who spoke out against the abuse of Native Americans. Following a similar line of reasoning, Rayna Green calls for non-Native scholars "to listen and hear instead of talking. . . . It is now time for feminist scholars to ask Native American women—indeed all groups of women they study—what their agendas are and how feminist scholars might lend themselves to the task" (267). Indian sovereignty remains an important part of Mankiller's ecofeminist agenda, and the priority of the indigenous women represented in *every day is a good day*. For, as David Richard Lewis reminds us in his study of Native Americans and environmental issues, "land—*place*—remains the essence of Native identity and sovereignty" (440). Gail Small echoes this idea, noting that "our land is what we coalesce around. . . . I have a hard time envisioning a living culture without a land base, without our ancestors' land" (qtd. in Mankiller 56). Joanne Shenandoah summarizes, *"the indigenous interpretation is neither fixed nor absolute, but a free-flowing concept that involves many elements, the most important of which is our responsibility to act as custodians of the natural world in trust for other species and those yet unborn"* (italics original, qtd. in Mankiller 86).

Act Like You're Sovereign: Articulating Indian Sovereignty

Arguably, the most contested and critical term in contemporary Native American Studies is *sovereignty*[7] (Lyons 450, 451). In his speech delivered at the 1973 Speech Communication Association Convention in New York, Dr. Barney Old Coyote states that "beginning with the Continental Congress and until the present date, there is one thing, a very nebulous thing, that has made the American Indian minority different than any other minority. It's something that's called tribal sovereignty" (Old Coyote 89). Wilma Mankiller, in a speech delivered in 1989, recalls testifying before a Senate Subcommittee that was examining Indian Affairs. After giving her testimony, she was asked by Hawaii Senator Daniel Inouye to "define Tribal Sovereignty" ("Tribal Sovereignty" 1). She recounts, "I told him, 'honestly,' which is honestly the way I feel, that . . . asking someone like me to define Sovereignty is sort of like asking someone to define the meaning of life" (1). Deloria expresses his concern about the positioning of "intellectual sovereignty and individual self-determination as broad avenues by which the whole issue of being Indian is being subverted" ("Intellectual" 30). He claims that the concept of sovereignty, "having lost its political moorings," is now "adrift on the currents of individual fancy" (27). Certainly, U.S. national political discourse seems to confirm this perception.

In an August 6, 2004, appearance before the Unity Journalists of Color Convention, President George W. Bush commented on tribal sovereignty in response to a question posed by journalist Mark Trahant. Trahant asked, "what do you think tribal sovereignty means in the twenty-first century, and how do we resolve conflicts between tribes and the federal and the state governments?" (Bush). Bush replied, haltingly, "tribal sovereignty means that; it's sovereign. I mean, you're a—you've been given sovereignty, and you're viewed as a sovereign entity. And therefore the relationship between the federal government and tribes is one between sovereign entities" (Bush). Bush then proceeds to briefly mention several forms of federal intervention in tribal life, including federally administered small business loans, education programs, and health care. The circularity, redundancy, and ambiguity of Bush's discourse on sovereignty illustrate a serious lack of understanding of key tribal issues at the highest levels of U.S. government.

In contrast to Deloria's concerns about the indeterminate quality of the term sovereignty, and in response to President Bush's apparent lack of familiarity with the term's usage within Native communities, Mankiller provides a multiple, polyvocal perspective on sovereignty which offers a productive and politically savvy rhetorical strategy for Indian rhetors. Mankiller's edited volume *every day is a good day*, in conjunction with her autobiography, presents a perspective on sovereignty that is rooted in indigenous understandings of the meaning of life. The autobiography serves as a microcosmic study of self-determination. Mankiller's indigenous ecofeminist perspective situates the Cherokee Nation, and Indian communities in general, as responsive to and inseparable from the natural world. Thus, sovereignty is ultimately about communities finding harmony and balance in their relations with one another. In order to achieve such balance, however, a wide variety of perspectives on sovereignty must be considered. Mankiller's *every day is a good day* offers a collage of indigenous women's definitions of sovereignty, which work together to create a complex unity of articulations of the Indian experience of self and Other. For instance, Audrey Shenandoah defines sovereignty and, in so doing, addresses one of the difficulties of dialogues about sovereignty:

> *Many people don't understand the word sovereignty. Sovereignty is the ability to carry out your own direction. If you think sovereign, you can be sovereign. People use the word all the time, but I don't think they know what it means to act sovereign. Part of sovereignty is being able to see the things you know are right and fight for them.* (italics original, qtd. in Mankiller, *every day* 93)

Writer and poet Harjo elaborates, "*sovereignty is a state of mind, or I should say, a state of heart. It has more to do with how we conduct daily mundane actions than the heroic acts of war*" (italics original, qtd. in Mankiller, *every day* 89). Based upon this definition, Mankiller's contributions and legacy as organizer, then Deputy Chief, and finally Principal Chief of the Cherokee Nation (for successive elected terms) stand as an emblem of sovereign governance. Likewise, her emphasis upon the community-based economic and cultural growth of the Cherokee Nation suggests, as Lurline Wailana McGregor puts it, *"The stronger we become in our culture, the healthier we will become as a people and the more sovereign we can become in our thinking"* (italics original, qtd. in Mankiller, *every day* 163).

Lyons admits that sovereignty has "long been a contested term in Native discourse, and its shifting meanings over time attest to an ongoing struggle between Americans and the hundreds of Indian nations that occupy this land" (449). In fact, he argues, "For indigenous people everywhere, sovereignty is an ideal principle, the beacon by which we seek the paths to agency and power and community renewal. . . . the pursuit of sovereignty is an attempt to revive not our past, but our possibilities" (449). He elaborates:

> Sovereignty . . . denotes the right of a people to conduct its own affairs, in its own place, in its own way. . . . While the meanings of sovereignty have shifted and continue to shift over time, the concept has nonetheless carried with it a sense of locatable and recognizable power. In fact, the location of power has depended upon the crucial act of recognition—and vice versa. (450)

The United Nations General Assembly Resolution 1514 states, "all peoples have the right to self-determination. By virtue of that right they freely determine their political status and freely pursue their economic social and cultural developments" (qtd. in Mankiller, *every day* 83). Early legal decisions against the Cherokee such as *Cherokee Nation v. Georgia* and *Worcester v. Georgia* indicated profound inconsistencies in the government's understanding of sovereignty. Chief Justice John Marshall claimed that the Cherokees constituted a "distinct political society, separated by others, capable of managing its own affairs and governing itself" (qtd. in Lyons 451). At the same time, he characterized the Cherokees as a "domestic dependent nation" (qtd. in Lyons 451) considered to be "distinct, independent political communities, retaining their original natural rights, as the undisputed possessors of the soil, from time immemorial, with the single exception imposed by irresistible power" (qtd. in Lyons 452). Nonetheless, as Lyons points out, "Indian nations still possess, and are still recognized to possess, varying and constantly shifting degrees of sovereignty" (453).

The multidimensional discourse on sovereignty offered by Mankiller both complicates and enhances understanding of the issues that most immediately affect the lives of Native Americans in the United States. Rather than being a simple assertion of an assumed relationship between federal and tribal "sovereign entities," Mankiller's discourse provides readers with a way of linking Native American sovereignty with feminism and ecological sustainability, through the principles of harmony, balance, empowerment, and being of good mind.

Conclusion

In *American Epic: The Story of the American Indian*, Alice Marriott and Carol Rachlin state, "It is in their oratory and their oral literature that the Indians have left their lasting monument, and it shall endure" (228). Marriott and Rachlin are correct in identifying Indian rhetoric as a "lasting monument" but too hastily limit the influence of such discourse and its impact upon the United States as well as other nations. Wilma Mankiller continues a long tradition of Native American eloquence by sharing the story of her life as it intertwines with the life of the Cherokee people and by articulating her vision of feminist ecology and Indian sovereignty. She stands as the first of many indigenous women who will lead the contemporary Cherokee Nation and transform ideas about nature and power.

Mankiller's rhetoric also forces readers to question dominant readings of Indian history as she points out the "woeful absence of accurate information about tribal people, either historical or contemporary" (Mankiller and Wallis 22). She notes:

> Remembering those Cherokees and others who were forced to move to Indian Territory and how they persisted brings me at least some relief whenever I feel distressed or afraid. Through the years, I have learned to use my memory and the historical memory of my people to help me endure the most difficult and trying periods of my life. (77)

Few, if any, scholars of rhetoric, political science, or women's history would dispute the importance of studying Wilma Mankiller's rhetorical legacy. Green highlights the fact that "the study of Native American women is flowering" (248) but expresses concern that they "have been studied to death or distraction" (249). In her review of studies of Native American women's lives, Green commends a number of works "for their portrayal of tribal leaders, women who used their power to become agents of change for their communities" (259). Clearly, Wilma Mankiller may be counted among such luminaries, yet, with the exception of Janis King's analysis of her campaign for the 1987 election, Mankiller's discourse has gone largely unexamined. As Green notes, however, "the real flowering of work on Indian women is represented in . . . modern autobiography, and by Native American women leaders and writers talking about their own lives" (262).

In her autobiography as well as her edited volume, which is arguably an (auto)biographical text, Mankiller represents the Cherokee approach to life as a methodology for enacting her theories of feminist ecology and Indian sovereignty. She uses her personal experiences and her identity as a Cherokee woman to forge a political agenda that has significant implications for the ways in which humanity responds to the natural world. Her personal challenges and triumphs, alongside the wisdom of her contemporaries, encourage readers to consider constructive possibilities for renewing, rethinking, and rearticulating the relationships all people have with each other, with our cohabitants, and with the earth.

Notes

1. Among the few criticisms of Mankiller's autobiography, Richard Dyer claims that the narrative, at times, appears "glib and ghostwriterly" (47). Indeed, the dynamics of Mankiller and Wallis' co-authorship is ill defined and unclear. The role of the publisher is increasingly important in examining the process through which the personal is made public (and hence political). Publishing houses can serve as sites of intellectual colonialism when commodifying and reproducing Native stories and indigenous wisdom for profit. Moreover, Gloria Steinem, the poster feminist for the second wave of White feminism, penned the introduction to *every day is a good day*. Despite these potential concerns, Wilma Mankiller's discourse articulates a Cherokee perspective that is simultaneously traditional and progressive. In doing so, she makes a space for the articulation of indigenous values to nonnative social and cultural ideals.

2. Among the recent scholarly examinations of Native American autobiographical writings are Sarah Turner's and Kathleen Mullen Sands' articles in a special issue on ethnic autobiography in the journal *Melus*, Hertha Dawn Wong's *Sending My Heart Back Across the Years: Tradition and Innovation in Native American Autobiography*, David Brumble's *American Indian Autobiography*, Arnold Krupat's *For Those Who Come After: A Study of American Indian Autobiography*, and Gretchen Bataille and Kathleen Sands' *American Indian Women: Telling Their Lives*.

3. An illustration of the collapse of individual/collective boundaries in some Cherokee discourse is provided in Rennard and William Strickland's "Beyond the Trail of Tears: One Hundred Fifty Years of Cherokee Survival" in William Anderson's *Cherokee Removal: Before and After*. A Cherokee farmer speaking against the Dawes Commission allotments entreated, "Senators: You will not forget that when I use the word 'I' I mean the whole Cherokee people. I am in that fix. What am I to do?" (D. W. C. Duncan, qtd. in Strickland and Strickland 126).

4. Like many other Indians relocated from reservations to urban areas, Mankiller eventually returned to her family's home in Adair County, Oklahoma. A popular joke about relocation describes the pervasiveness of the failure of relocation programs: "When the space program began, there was a great deal of talk about sending men to the moon. Discussion often centered about the difficulty of returning the men from the moon to the earth, as re-entry procedures were considered to be very tricky. One Indian suggested that they send an Indian to the moon on relocation. 'He'll figure out some way to get back'" (Deloria, *Custer* 159).

5. Humor is a prominent aspect of much Native American rhetoric. As Vine Deloria Jr. illustrates in *Custer Died for Your Sins*, "in humor, life is redefined and accepted" (148). In conjunction with the spirit of harmony, he points out, "teasing was a method of control of social situations by Indian people" (149). It was also a rhetorical strategy: "Gradually people learned to anticipate teasing and began to tease themselves as a means of showing humility and at the same time advocating a course of action they deeply believed in" (149).

6. Commenting on her 1992 invitation by President-elect Clinton to an economic summit meeting in Little Rock, Arkansas, *The Wall Street Journal* editorialized: "Our favorite name on the list . . . is Chief Wilma Mankiller . . . we hope not a feminist economic priority" (Mankiller and Wallis 13). Mankiller invokes several humorous quips as responses to such slights, many of which serve as subtle reminders of the functions of humor described above.

7. Vine Deloria Jr. explains his association of the term "sovereignty" with the Native American fish-ins of the 1960s and 1970s. "Their slogan was 'if you act like you're a sovereign, eventually you will be treated as one.' *U.S. v. Washington* proved they were

right. The issue simply boils down to making another political entity respect your rights deriving from a contractual arrangement you have made with them" ("Intellectual" 26).

Chapter Seven

The Personal Is Political: Negotiating Publicity and Privacy in Hillary Rodham Clinton's *Living History*

Karrin Vasby Anderson

When *Living History*, Hillary Rodham Clinton's memoir of her tenure as U.S. first lady, was published in June of 2003, it came on the heels of what *USA Today* labeled "a risky $8 million advance" (Minzesheimer 10D). With an amount seldom equaled in the realm of nonfiction publishing (at least, until her husband's reported $10 million advance from Random House for his autobiography, *My Life*), Simon & Schuster signaled its belief that this history-making first lady turned U.S. Senator would make history again in the world of publishing. And she did. By December 2003, the book sold 1.4 million of its 1.6 million first-run copies and became the best-selling nonfiction book of the year (10D). Some critics speculated that healthy initial sales could be attributed to the prospect that Rodham Clinton[1] would provide the reader with the inside scoop on the personal and political scandals that plagued the Clinton presidency. Prior to the book's release, an unnamed source "close to the former First Lady" told the New York *Daily News* that "it's going to be more candid than people think. . . . She's going to lay out more of her feelings on certain [embarrassing] things than her critics expect, and she does not shy away from Monica Lewinsky" (Colford and DeFrank 3).

When the volume appeared, however, reviews were predictably mixed. Mary Leonard of the *Boston Globe* charges that "time after disappointing time . . . Hillary Rodham Clinton heeds that cautious inner voice . . . and ducks the yawning questions or dismisses the controversies that made her the most enigmatic character in an eight-year American political drama and the most polarizing first lady since Eleanor Roosevelt" (H8). Conversely, Lynn Bronikowski of the Denver *Rocky Mountain News* claims that the book is "Hillary Rodham

Clinton's frank, vividly-written portrait of the Clintons' controversial White House years—addressing far more than her husband's infidelities and the deep anger and hurt that followed" (9D).

Although the book reviews, themselves, reinforce Betty Friedan's claim that media coverage of Rodham Clinton functions as a "massive Rorschach test of the evolution of women in our society" (qtd. in Jamieson 22), what they omit is a thorough understanding of how Rodham Clinton uses the autobiographical genre to negotiate complex issues of publicity and privacy that can be especially problematic for women politicians. This chapter argues that in her autobiography, *Living History*, Hillary Rodham Clinton employs personal narrative as a rhetorical strategy to outline her political ideology. Further, the discussion contends that the autobiography suggests the ways in which Rodham Clinton's political ideology, shaped both by liberal feminism and by Methodism, focuses on human welfare, broadly, and the well-being of women and children more specifically. As a study in women's political agency, *Living History* valorizes women's public political power, as well as the symbolic power accorded to figures such as the United States first lady.

Autobiography: The Political as Necessarily Personal

Generically, the autobiographical form emphasizes personal narrative as authentic and authoritative. Martha Watson explains, "the author's voice carries unusual weight in an autobiography. Simply put, the author tells her side of the story. Certainly, the reader can and will . . . test some of the details against her or his own experience. But the author is free and, indeed, is fully expected to explain her perceptions and her interpretations of events" (11). Rodham Clinton acknowledges the advantages and limitations of this unique perspective in the preface to *Living History*, stating:

> This book is the story of how I experienced those eight years as First Lady and as the wife of the President. Some may ask how I could write an accurate account of events, people and places that are so recent and of which I am still a part. I have done my best to convey my observations, thoughts, and feelings as I experienced them. This is not meant to be a comprehensive history, but a personal memoir that offers an inside look at an extraordinary time in my life and in the life of America. (xi)

Watson explores the paradox inherent in every autobiography between authenticity and mythology. On one hand, autobiography is "an at least partially fictionalized account of a life because looking back in retrospect the author imposes a meaning and coherence on events she did not possess at the moment they occurred. Thus, writing an autobiography entails the creation of a personal mythology" (4). Conversely, however, this "personal mythology" also can function as "public moral argument." Watson continues that the "generic features of autobiographies—their chronological structure with a basis in real events and the status of the narrator as the central character—give them distinctive strengths and potentials as public moral argument" (9).

When a woman politician authors an autobiographical text, she is uniquely positioned to narrate public, political events through this personal lens. This invokes the tension that historically has existed for women between publicity and privacy, with women who have chosen to act in the public sphere being labeled as inappropriate, transgressive, and/or unwomanly (Jamieson; Zaeske). This was particularly problematic for female leaders of social movements writing in the nineteenth century, as Watson's study aptly illustrates. Watson refers to the analysis of Patricia Meyer Spacks, who "argues that the language, the tone, and the details of [narratives in women's autobiographies] as well as their form reflect a tension between their public and private roles not found in the works of men" (20). One might conclude that the political gains made by women in the twentieth century would have mitigated this tension. However, the *New York Times* editorial review of Rodham Clinton's memoir suggests the ways in which the tension persists:

> Every autobiographical writer struggles with the question of how to create a portrait of the self. But for Senator Clinton, the portrait she is trying to create is both personal and political. Too personal, and the political self is compromised. Too political, and she risks sounding like a campaign poster. How she balances those two Hillarys creates the real tension in her book. ("Reading Senator Clinton" 30)

Complicating this tension is the fact that *Living History* is not a "memoir," per se, but instead combines the characteristics of autobiography with the demands of a campaign history. Rodham Clinton wrote her book as a newly elected U.S. Senator rather than as a first lady exiting public life. Leonard observes that "like *Faith of My Fathers*, Senator John McCain's 1999 autobiography, the self-serving *Living History* is a required prop if or when Clinton, now the junior senator from New York, launches her own presidential campaign" (H8). *Denver Post* books editor Tom Walker notes that "Clinton spends a lot of time in the book talking about trips abroad during her tenure as first lady, often in official capacity. Presidential candidates often take well-publicized grand tours of the world in advance of their campaigns to at least appear statesman-like" (F1). Elizabeth Auster of the Cleveland *Plain Dealer* concurs, contending that "[few people] after all, expect[ed] Clinton to step down after one term in the Senate. Few expect[ed] her to bypass a run for the presidency. . . . And few who have watched her careful attempt to walk a somewhat centrist line in the Senate . . . can dismiss her chances of winning out of hand" (G3). Michiko Kakutani of the *New York Times* states it most succinctly, calling the book the "carefully rehearsed and elided statements of a professional pol intent on turning a book tour into the first leg of another campaign" ("Books" E1).

In this respect, *Living History* exhibits rhetorical fidelity with what John M. Murphy has described as the "campaign history," a genre of writing that exemplifies the "intersection of literary form (the need to craft a marketable 'novel'), rhetorical style (the need to make the story persuasive), and historical realism (the need to account for indisputable facts)" (24). Rodham Clinton seems to have crafted her "memoir . . . about the eight years [she] spent in the White House living history with Bill Clinton" (ix) with two sets of exigencies in mind: the formal expectations of the autobiographical and campaign history genres and the political exigencies created by the need to contextualize the Clinton scandals, establish an independent political persona, and position herself for continued public, political leadership, either in the U.S. Senate or as a presidential candidate. The result is an autobiography that articulates a political ideology focused on human welfare, shaped both by liberal feminism and by Methodism. Additionally, Rodham Clinton examines women's political agency, valorizing women's public political power, as well as the symbolic power accorded to figures such as the first lady of the United States.

Living History: A Public Private Life

The exigencies that called forth Hillary Rodham Clinton's autobiography provided her with the opportunity to articulate her political ideology through personal narration. Although the book focuses on the Clintons' White House years, Rodham Clinton acknowledges that she could not do that without "going back to the beginning—how I became the woman I was that first day I walked into the White House on January 20, 1993" (ix). Thus, the narrative begins with Rodham Clinton's childhood. Personal anecdotes address a variety of public policy issues and underscore the common theme uniting Rodham Clinton's political ideology: human welfare, with emphasis on the well-being of women and children. Rodham Clinton attributes her political values, first, to her mother with descriptions like the following: "My mother was offended by the mistreatment of any human being, especially children. She understood from personal experience that many children—through no fault of their own—were disadvantaged and discriminated against from birth" (11). Dorothy Howell Rodham's influence stood in marked contrast to the values of father Hugh. Rodham Clinton contends that the "gender gap started in families like mine. My mother was basically a Democrat, although she kept it quiet in Republican Park Ridge. My dad was a rock-ribbed, up-by-your-bootstraps, conservative Republican and proud of it" (11). Perhaps it was this politically oppositional household that prompted Rodham Clinton to view herself as a political moderate. She explains that during the civil unrest of 1969–1970, while she was a student at Yale Law School, she resisted the impulse to engage in radical protest. Rather, "true to my upbringing, I advocated engagement, not disruption or 'revolution'" (46).

As Rodham Clinton grew into adulthood, her broadening realm of personal experience honed her perspectives on policy. Shortly after college, Rodham Clinton traveled to Alaska where she took a job "sliming fish in Valdez in a temporary salmon factory on a pier." She recounts the experience:

> My job required me to wear knee-high boots and stand in bloody water while removing guts from the salmon with a spoon. When I didn't slime fast enough,

the supervisors yelled at me to speed up. Then I was moved to the assembly packing line, where I helped pack the salmon in boxes for shipping to the large floating processing plant offshore. I noticed that some of the fish looked bad. When I told the manager, he fired me and told me to come back the next afternoon to pick up my last check. When I showed up, the entire operation was gone. (42–43)

The anecdote functions strategically to position Rodham Clinton as an opponent of corporate corruption, a useful persona in the wake of Enron and other corporate scandals of the early twenty-first century.

Early in the book's narration, Rodham Clinton connects her personal experiences with specific policy initiatives. For example, her description of her own pregnancy is used to commend the Family and Medical Leave Act. Rodham Clinton states:

I was able to take four months off from full-time work to stay home with our new daughter, though with less income. . . . I never forgot how much more fortunate I was than many women to be given this time with my child. Bill and I both recognized the need for parental leave, preferably paid. We emerged from our experience committed to ensuring that all parents have the option to stay home with their newborn children and to have reliable child care when they return to work. That's why I was so thrilled when the first bill he signed as President was the Family and Medical Leave Act. (85)

Repeatedly, throughout the book, Rodham Clinton suggests that her views on public policy have been shaped by personal interactions. For example, before a speech for the Rajiv Ghandi Foundation, First Lady Hillary Rodham Clinton was searching for a theme. She recounts an anecdote of a secondary school principal handing her a poem penned by student Anasuya Sengupta. The poem was called "Silence," and it began:

> *Too many women*
> *In too many countries*
> *Speak the same language.*
> *Of silence . . .* (277)

Rodham Clinton continues:

I couldn't get the poem out of my head. As I worked on my speech late into the night, I realized that I could use the poem to convey my belief that issues affecting women and girls should not be dismissed as "soft" or marginal but should be integrated fully into domestic and foreign policy decisions. Denying or curtailing education and basic health care for women is a human rights issue. Restricting women's economic, political and social participation is a human rights issue. (277)

Similarly, Rodham Clinton endorsed the policy of microcredit lending by describing her personal interaction with a pioneer of the program and with villagers who benefited from it. She states:

I had first learned about the Grameen Bank more than a decade earlier, when Bill and I invited the bank's founder, Dr. Muhammad Yunus, to Little Rock to discuss how microcredit lending programs might help some of the poorest rural communities in Arkansas. . . . I helped set up a development bank and micro-lending groups in Arkansas, and I wanted to promote micro-lending throughout the United States, modeled on the success of Yunus and the Grameen Bank. (284)

Later, referring to her interaction with women and girls in the rural village of Mashinhata, Rodham Clinton recounts, "I was struck by the positive spirit of the people I met in this poor, isolated village who lived without electricity or running water, but with hope, thanks, in part, to the work of the Grameen Bank" (286). The autobiographical narrative echoes this endorsement of microcredit lending when Rodham Clinton describes her interaction with women and children in Nicaragua, as follows:

In one of Managua's poorest barrios, I visited women who had formed a micro-credit borrowing group called "Mothers United." Supported by USAID and run by the Foundation for International Community Assistance (FINCA), these women were an excellent example of successful American foreign aid at work. They showed me the products they made or purchased to re-sell—mosquito netting, baked goods, automobile parts. One of the women surprised me when she said she had seen me on television, visiting the site of the SEWA project in Ahmadabad, India. "Are Indian women like us?" she asked. I told her that the Indian women I met also wanted to improve their lives by earning money that would enable them to send their children to school, fix up their homes and re-invest profits in their businesses. The encounter made me more determined in my efforts to increase the amount of money our government invested in micro-credit projects in our country. (312–13)

Microcredit and family leave are just two of the many specific policy initiatives that Rodham Clinton endorses as part of a larger articulation of a human rights political ideology. The chapter entitled "Second Term" presents a laundry list of policy initiatives, including enhancing after school care programs, curbing media violence, preserving child support obligations, and responding to the global crisis of child prostitution. Rodham Clinton balances personal narration with economic analysis in excerpts like the following from a trip to Thailand:

I met one girl at the [New Life Center in Chiang Mai] who had been sold by her opium-addicted father when she was eight years old. After a few years, she escaped and returned home—only to be sold again to a whorehouse. Now only twelve, she was dying of AIDS at the Center. Her skin hung off her bones, and I watched helplessly as she summoned all her strength to draw her tiny hands together in the traditional Thai greeting when I approached her. I knelt next to her chair and tried to speak to her through a translator. She did not have the strength to talk. All I could do was hold her hand. She died shortly after my visit.

On a tour of a local village, I witnessed disturbing evidence of local supply-and-demand economics that brought this girl to her death. (389)

Some critics and reviewers of *Living History* characterized pejoratively Rodham Clinton's choice to articulate her human rights ideology, which foregrounded the needs of women and children, through detailed descriptions of her interpersonal interactions at home and abroad. The *Boston Globe*'s Leonard states:

> The details political junkies crave about the former first lady's role in firing the White House travel office staff, the discovery of her missing and subpoenaed Rose law firm billing records, or the suicide of Vince Foster, Clinton's old friend and White House counsel, are few. Yet she devotes many pages to total recalls of visits to remote villages in India, tete-a-tetes with world leaders, policy speeches, and the curse of many bad-hair days. (H8)

In a review for the *New York Times*, Kakutani complains that Rodham Clinton "expend[s] a startling amount of space on her trips abroad" ("Books" E1), and the *Ottawa Citizen*'s Andrew Cohen refers to her discussions of her international women's rights rhetoric dismissively as a "travelogue" (C5).

At least one reviewer reflected upon the media's own trivialization of Rodham Clinton's political ideology. Ruth Rosen, writing in the *San Francisco Chronicle*, observes:

> For the most part, the American media ignored or trivialized what [Rodham Clinton] did and said in these distant countries. We saw photographs of her and Chelsea riding atop an elephant, but we didn't read that she had denounced crimes against half of humanity. We saw pictures of her in elegant Indian saris and colorful African robes, but we didn't know that she had advocated microloans to advance women's economic independence. (A21)

Both initial media coverage of Rodham Clinton's first ladyship and subsequent critical response to her autobiography reveal a resistance to the feminist politics and Methodist values that shape Rodham Clinton's political ideology. The following discussion outlines how these two ideological influences emerge as themes in *Living History*.

As she tells it, Rodham Clinton was a budding feminist at the age of four, when she was bullied by a neighborhood girl, Suzy O'Callaghan. After standing up to Suzy at her parents' direction, Rodham Clinton explained that she "returned a few minutes later, glowing with victory. 'I can play with the boys now,' [she] said, 'and Suzy will be my friend!' She was and she still is" (12). That seemingly inconsequential anecdote resonates with liberal feminist philosophy insofar as it presents the ideal world as one where women and men coexist equally, and where women have agency if they choose to exercise it.[2]

The impulse to "play with the boys" followed Rodham Clinton to Arkansas, where she became the first woman associate at the prestigious Rose Law Firm. She claims, "not all the Rose Firm lawyers were as enthusiastic as Vince [Foster] and Herb [Rule III] about having a woman join them. . . . When the partners voted to hire me, Vince and Herb gave me a copy of *Hard Times* by Charles Dickens. But who could have known what an appropriate gift that would be?"

(79). During her early years in Arkansas, when Bill Clinton was in his first term as Arkansas governor, Rodham Clinton articulates a liberal feminist philosophy as justification for keeping her maiden name. She states:

> Because I knew I had my own professional interests and did not want to create any confusion or conflict of interest with my husband's public career, it made perfect sense to me to continue using my own name. . . . Brides who kept their maiden names were becoming more common in some places in the mid-1970s, but they were still rare in most of the country. And that included Arkansas. It was a personal decision, a small (I thought) gesture to acknowledge that while I was committed to our union, I was still me. (92)

Although Bill Clinton's first gubernatorial defeat prompted her to begin using the married name "Clinton" after her given name "Hillary Rodham," the issue of naming continued to be troublesome through the 1992 presidential campaign. Rodham Clinton explains that:

> I had ordered new stationery to answer all the campaign mail I was receiving. I had chosen cream paper with my name, *Hillary Rodham Clinton*, printed neatly across the top in navy blue. When I opened the box I saw that the order had been changed so that the name on it was *Hillary Clinton*. Evidently someone on Bill's staff decided that it was more politically expedient to drop "Rodham" as if it were no longer part of my identity. I returned the stationery and ordered another batch. (111–12)

Another tenant of liberal feminism posits the notion that women and men are equally capable of succeeding in all professions and contexts, provided institutional barriers to women's advancement are removed. Throughout the book, Rodham Clinton recounts times during which she was viewed as an "exceptional" woman whenever her talents met or exceeded the expectations of male colleagues. In the following example, which is representative of similar anecdotes throughout the book, Rodham Clinton defines what she has dubbed the "Talking Dog Syndrome":

> I stepped before a joint session of the Arkansas legislature's House and Senate to plead our case for improving all schools, big and small. For whatever reason—probably a combination of skill and lots of practice—public speaking has always been one of my strong suits. I laughed when Representative Lloyd George, a legislator from rural Yell County, later announced to the assembly: "Well, fellas, it looks like we might have elected the wrong Clinton!" It was another example of a phenomenon I call "the talking dog syndrome." Some people are still amazed that any woman (this includes Governors' wives, corporate CEOs, sports stars and rock singers) can hold her own under pressure and be articulate and knowledgeable. The dog can talk! (94–95)

One rhetorical task Rodham Clinton assumes as the author of this particular autobiography is to challenge the "Talking Dog Syndrome," not only by disproving it in her own life, but also by valorizing the contributions of other women, some with recognizable names and many without.

As Rodham Clinton's personal narrative moves from description of her policymaking roles in Arkansas (with education reform) and as U.S. first lady (with health-care reform), her liberal feminist perspective prompts her to discuss problems of world poverty, hunger, AIDS, and other crises in terms of how women are implicated specifically. She shares a Chinese saying that "women hold up half the sky, but in most of the world, it's really more than half. Women handle a large share of the responsibility for the welfare of their families. Yet their work often goes unrecognized and unrewarded inside the family or by the formal economy" (269). Similarly, in a section that explains her support for the U.S. Agency for International Development, Rodham Clinton asserts, "when women suffer, their children suffer and their economies stagnate, ultimately weakening potential markets for U.S. products. And when women are victimized, the stability of families, communities and nations is eroded, jeopardizing the prospects for democracy and prosperity globally" (269–70).

Few readers would be surprised that liberal feminism emerges as an influence on Rodham Clinton's political ideology. What is less expected is the way in which her Methodist faith comfortably complements her feminist politics. Rodham Clinton is up front about the pervasiveness of faith in her life during times of success and times of trial. In the same way that athletes and entertainers credit "God" during moments of achievement, there is a cultural expectation that America's national leaders exhibit a religious consciousness. Rodham Clinton does not challenge that norm, noting that shortly after George Bush conceded the 1992 election, "Bill and I went into our bedroom, closed the door and prayed together for God's help as he took on this awesome honor and responsibility" (117). Similarly, she states that at the inauguration, "Chelsea and I reverently held the Bible as Bill took the oath of office" (114).

Beyond the expected acknowledgment of "God" in the abstract, however, Rodham Clinton emphasizes the ways in which her faith informed and shaped her political ideology. On one occasion, when visiting with British Prime Minister Tony Blair and his wife Cherie, Rodham Clinton states that the group "discussed . . . the connection between our religious faith and public service." She continues:

> Both of us rooted our political beliefs in our faith, which molded our commitment to social action. I talked about John Wesley's invocation, which I had taken to heart when I was confirmed in the Methodist faith—Live every day doing as much good as you can, in every way that you can—and about what theologians have described as "the push of duty and the pull of grace." (428)

The preceding anecdote is the second example in the book where Wesley's invocation was quoted in full. It first appeared much earlier in the book, when Rodham Clinton described her introduction to Methodism. She states:

> My active involvement in the First United Methodist Church of Park Ridge opened my eyes and heart to the needs of others and helped instill a sense of social responsibility rooted in my faith. My father's parents claimed they became Methodists because their great-grandparents were converted in the small

coal-mining villages around Newcastle in the north of England and in South Wales by John Wesley, who founded the Methodist Church in the eighteenth century. Wesley taught that God's love is expressed through good works, which he explained with a simple rule: "Do all the good you can, by all the means you can, in all the ways you can, in all the places you can, at all the times you can, to all the people you can, as long as ever you can." (21–22)

Tacitly acknowledging the contradictions that sometimes arise between religious faith and political stances, Rodham Clinton continues: "there will always be worthy debates about whose definition of 'good' one follows, but as a young girl, I took Wesley's admonition to heart. My father prayed by his bed every night, and prayer became a source of solace and guidance for me even as a child" (22).

In addition to Methodism providing a religious foundation for Rodham Clinton's political ideology promoting human welfare, her faith served as justification for her response to the Lewinsky scandal—the portion of the book that got the most attention from reporters and reviewers when it was first released. Rodham Clinton briefly describes her reaction to her husband's confession that he did violate his marriage vows. The passage, oft quoted by critics in reviews of the book, read, "I could hardly breathe. Gulping for air, I started crying and yelling at him, 'What do you mean? What are you saying? Why did you lie to me?'" (466). The part of the controversy that Rodham Clinton spends more time addressing, however, is the rationale for her staying with, and ultimately forgiving, Bill Clinton. For that, she turned to her faith:

> I was thankful for the support and counsel I received during this time, particularly from Don Jones, my youth minister, who had become a lifelong friend. Don reminded me of a classic sermon by the theologian Paul Tillich, "You are Accepted," which Don had once read to our youth group in Park Ridge. Its premise is how sin and grace exist through life in constant interplay; neither is possible without the other. The mystery of grace is that you cannot look for it. "Grace strikes us when we are in great pain and restlessness," Tillich wrote. "It happens; or it does not happen." Grace happens. Until it did, my main job was to put one foot in front of the other and get through another day. (470)

A political challenge dogging Rodham Clinton during her own campaigns for public office is the critique leveled by some feminists that she should not have stayed with a philandering husband. Worse yet, her loyalty has been interpreted by some as a sign of an "understanding" between the two Clintons. Karen Sandstrom writes, "Hillary wants us to believe she did not view Lewinsky as simply one especially obnoxious episode in the life of a career philanderer. Accurate or not, though, there is an assumption that don't-ask-don't-tell was policy in the Clintons' bedroom long before it hit the military" (J13). The rhetorical advantage provided by Rodham Clinton's emphasis on her faith is that it provides a rationale for reconciliation—one that complements, rather than challenges, her agency as a woman. She ends the chapter entitled "Waiting for Grace"—the chapter that addresses the Clinton impeachment and transitions to Rodham Clinton's run for the U.S. Senate—with the following statement: "I was relying more on my faith every day. It reminded me of an old saying from Sunday school: Faith is like stepping off a cliff and expecting one of two outcomes—you will either land on solid ground or you will be taught to fly" (494). For Rodham Clinton, "grace" is synonymous with forgiveness, reconciliation, and ultimately the agency to choose a life both with her husband and in pursuit of her own political ambitions. Her faith provides her with the rationale and the courage to continue down the path of political achievement. To that extent, faith and feminism coalesce—not as competing discourses in Rodham Clinton's narrative, but as the twin pillars of her political ideology.

Rodham Clinton makes clear, then, that both feminism and Methodism inform her political ideology, despite the notion that those represent competing, rather than complementary, worldviews. The final theme Rodham Clinton articulates in *Living History* is her gradual acknowledgment that women's political power is paradoxical, comprised of many features that some might consider oppositional. In fact, Rodham Clinton's autobiography articulates a vision of women's political agency that resists the public/private sphere distinction, valorizing both public political power and the "symbolic influence" that traditionally has constituted the power of the feminized role of U.S. first lady.

Rodham Clinton's discussion of her political agency as action in the public policy sphere is illustrated first by the tone of the chapter entitled "Health Care." The chapter on health-care reform focuses on the history of previous presidential health-care reform efforts and the political challenge posed by the Clinton administration's efforts. Rodham Clinton takes time to explain the Clinton proposal for "managed composition," contrasting it with a completely federally funded "single-payer" system. It has a more policy-oriented tone than other chapters, which often opt to provide a behind-the-scenes glimpse at more personal aspects of famous moments or official activities. Later, during her discussion of the 1994 midterm election, Rodham Clinton returns to public policy discussion, this time stressing smaller, more incremental gains made as a result of her public policy efforts. She states:

> I worked behind the scenes with Senator Kennedy to help create the Children's Health Insurance Program (CHIP), which by 2003 provided coverage to more than 5 million children of working parents too well off for Medicaid but unable to afford private insurance. CHIP represented the largest expansion of public health insurance coverage since the passage of Medicaid in 1965, and it helped reduce the number of Americans without health insurance for the first time in twelve years. Bill signed a series of bills that I had worked for, including laws ensuring that women be allowed to stay in the hospital for more than twenty-four hours after childbirth, promoting mammography and prostate screening, increasing research into diabetes and improving childhood vaccination rates so that 90 percent of all two-year-olds were immunized against the most serious childhood illnesses for the first time ever. (248)

Similarly, the "Second Term" chapter is a laundry list of policy measures championed by the First Lady, with emphasis on Rodham Clinton's prioritization of children and families. Rodham Clinton acknowledges the less publicized nature of her activities after the 1994 election, but emphasizes her role as squarely centered within the realm of public policy. She states:

> I had moved from a highly visible role as Bill's chief health care adviser, testifying before Congress, delivering speeches, traveling around the country and meeting with congressional leaders, to a more private—but equally active—role during the two years following the mid-term elections in 1994.
>
> I had begun working inside the White House and with other Administration officials to save vital services and programs targeted by Gingrich and the Republicans. I also spent two years helping the President's top advisers refine welfare reform and stave off cuts in legal services, arts, education, Medicare, and Medicaid. As part of our continuing effort on health care reform, I lobbied Democrats and Republicans on Capitol Hill to initiate a comprehensive program to make vaccines available at low or no cost for children. (380)

Passages like the preceding one sound like the words of a prospective presidential candidate discussing her qualifications for public service rather than like the typical former first lady narrating her "sphere of influence" on the president.

Despite Rodham Clinton's emphasis on her public policy agenda as the President's wife, she also discussed explicitly the advantage of the "symbolic" power accorded the U.S. first lady. Recounting the early ambivalence she felt about utilizing the symbolic power of the first ladyship, Rodham Clinton stated, "I had resisted the idea of exploiting the First Lady title, preferring to concentrate on specific policies and actions" (264). The source of her ambivalence appeared to come not only from an uneasiness about the role of first lady, itself, but also from Rodham Clinton's personal identity, as she had worked to define it since childhood. Rodham Clinton explains that a "First Lady occupies a vicarious position: her power is derivative, not independent, of the President's. This partly explained my sometimes awkward fit in the role of First Lady. Ever since I was a little girl, I had worked to be my own person and maintain my independence" (265). Nevertheless, after some prodding by friends and confidants, Rodham Clinton began to explore the ways in which "symbolic" power could further policy goals. She states:

> [Scholar and author Mary Catherine Bateson] argued that symbolic actions were legitimate and that "symbolism can be efficacious." She believed, for example, that merely by traveling to South Asia as First Lady with Chelsea would send a message about the importance of daughters. Visiting poor rural women would underscore their significance. I understood her point, and I soon became a convert to the view that I could advance the Clinton agenda through symbolic action. (265)

She articulates the same rationale to justify taking Chelsea along with her on a trip to Africa, where, in a rare break from convention, the press was allowed to photograph and interview the first daughter. Rodham Clinton states:

> I had agreed to write the [*Vogue*] article that would accompany the [Annie] Leibovitz photographs, and I wanted to shine a spotlight on self-help efforts

supported by American foreign assistance and private charities, speak out about women's rights, support democracy and encourage Americans to learn more about Africa. . . . Bringing Chelsea along was, as always, a special treat for me, and her presence sent a message in places where the needs and abilities of young girls were too often overlooked: The President of the United States has a daughter whom he considers valuable and worthy of the education and health care she needs to help her fulfill her own God-given potential. (400)

Rodham Clinton details a number of trips abroad with her daughter, occasions that allowed her both to spend time with her teenaged daughter before she headed off to college and enabled her to showcase the importance of women and girls. According to Rodham Clinton's narrative, before long, the State Department was on board with this policy-oriented application of the "symbolic" role of the first lady. She explained that her 1995 trip to South Asia included a stop in Pakistan because the "State Department has asked me to visit the subcontinent to highlight the administration's commitment to the region, because neither the President nor the Vice President could make the trip soon. . . . My physical presence in the region was considered a sign of concern and commitment" (268). This rationale emerges again in reference to a 1996 trip to Bosnia, prompting the first lady's staff to reflect humorously on her utility to the administration. Rodham Clinton states:

The administration wanted to send a strong signal that the peace accords [between Serbs, Croats, and Muslims] were to be honored and would be enforced. My staff used to tease me, suggesting that the State Department had a directive: If the place was too small, too dangerous or too poor—send Hillary. That was fine with me, because the out-of-the-way and dicey venues were often the most compelling. I was honored to go to Bosnia. (341–42)

Rodham Clinton is not, however, unreflective about the irony that she garnered favorable publicity for the administration when she was acting as a more traditional first lady. She describes one encounter with Clinton adviser James Carville that occurred shortly after a trip to Nepal where she and Chelsea were photographed atop an elephant. She explains, "when we got back to Washington, James Carville remarked: 'Don't you just love it? You spent two years trying to get people better health care and they tried to kill you. You and Chelsea rode an elephant, and they loved you!'" (qtd. in H. R. Clinton 283).

During this phase, when Rodham Clinton relied on a more symbolic enactment of power, she began to explore policy issues framed in characteristically "feminine" terms. For example, she recounts a lengthy example taken from a 1995 visit to war-torn Ireland, where a teapot came to stand for the women's peace movement:

While Bill met with the various factions, I split off to meet with women leaders of the peace movement. Because they were willing to work across the religious divide, they had found common ground. At the Lamplighter Traditional Fish and Chips restaurant, I met sixty-five-year-old Joyce McCartan, a remarkable woman who had founded the Women's Information Drop-in Center in 1987 af-

ter her seventeen-year-old son was shot dead by Protestant gunmen. She had
lost more than a dozen family members to violence. Joyce and other women
had set up the center as a safe house. . . . "It takes women to bring men to their
senses," Joyce said.

These women hoped that the cease-fire would continue and that the violence would end once and for all. They poured tea from ordinary stainless steel
teapots, and when I remarked how well they kept the tea warm, Joyce insisted I
take a pot to remember them by. I used that dented teapot every day in our
small family kitchen at the White House. When Joyce died shortly after our
visit, I was honored to be asked to return to Belfast in 1997 to deliver the first
Joyce McCartan Memorial Lecture at the University of Ulster. I brought the
teapot with me and put it on the podium as I spoke of the courage of Irish
women like Joyce who, at kitchen tables and over pots of tea, had helped chart
a path to peace. (321–22)

During the 1996 presidential campaign, Rodham Clinton coined the phrase
"kitchen table issues," a term that fuses public and private realms with a metaphor that is, at first glance, symbolic of women's experiences. Rodham Clinton
made clear, however, that she used the term to encompass the family realm, a
sphere of experience to which all humans belong. She states:

I began describing Democratic Party issues as "kitchen table issues," which became a catchphrase in the [1996 presidential] campaign. The discussion of
kitchen table issues led some Washington pundits to talk derisively about "the
feminization of politics," an attempt to marginalize, even trivialize, policies
such as family leave or extended mammogram coverage for older women or
adequate hospital stays for mothers after delivering their babies. With that in
mind, I coined my own term—"the humanization of politics"—to publicly advance the idea that kitchen table issues mattered to everybody, not just to
women. (364)

The political ideology Rodham Clinton articulates in *Living History* is perhaps
best encompassed by the powerful refrain which echoes throughout her much-
publicized address to the United Nations Fourth World Conference on Women,
in Beijing, China, where she reminds her domestic and international audiences
that "human rights are women's rights . . . and women's rights are human rights,
once and for all" (305).

The Paradox of Women's Political Voice

As a book, *Living History* has been a publishing sensation in part because reviews before and after the book's release have emphasized the more sensational
aspects of the narrative: Rodham Clinton's personal angst after her husband's
Lewinsky confession; her first-hand evaluation of historical figures and events;
her history-making bid for the U.S. Senate. What is perhaps more "sensational"
about this autobiography, however, are the ways in which it interrogates the
paradox of women's political voice. Though positioned as a feminist, Rodham

Clinton's political identity can be more accurately defined as articulating *human* welfare, and she was derided by feminists for making a choice in her marriage that she explains and defends as profoundly spiritual. Similarly, during a phase in her first ladyship where she purported to exert power through primarily "symbolic" means, she re-defined public policy to illustrate how limiting and oversimplified are models of human agency that divide human activity into either "public" or "private" realms. Karlyn Kohrs Campbell argues that women's political voice has always been fundamentally oxymoronic, and Hillary Rodham Clinton's *Living History* both enacts and examines the paradox of women's political power. Molly A. Mayhead and Brenda DeVore Marshall theorize the "in-between space" occupied by women in politics, explaining that "many women, while understanding and experiencing the binary impulse [of public vs. private spheres], also appreciate a more synergistic comprehension of the world in which existence can be seen as a 'both/and' phenomenon" (13). They continue, contending:

> since their earliest involvement in politics women not only have negotiated these binary boundaries, they have attempted to create a new site in which the personal and public spheres, specifically in the political arena, transmute into an increasingly androgynous in-between space—informed by a synergistic understanding of the inability to segregate these dimensions of human existence. (13)

Perpetually contradictory, *Living History*, like its author, exemplifies the "both/and" that makes women's political leadership so productive (Anderson and Sheeler). Unlike with many autobiographies, however, the past, in Rodham Clinton's case, is just the beginning. As the Cleveland *Plain Dealer*'s Elizabeth Auster muses, "that, in the end, is the simple secret to her book's success—that it may be prologue to a bigger, more historic story yet to be written" (G3).

Notes

1. The issue of naming is a complex one, especially when referencing this particular subject. The first-name only reference is considered, correctly, to be diminutive. Using the subject's marital title, "Mrs.," identifies her in relationship to her spouse and marital circumstance. As her autobiography acknowledges, she has preferred various last-name configurations during different points in her lifetime: "Rodham," "Rodham Clinton," and "Clinton." Because "Rodham Clinton" is the name she uses as author of this autobiography, its use has the advantage of clearly distinguishing the subject from President Bill Clinton, and it adheres to the standard of gender parity, that is the reference used in this chapter.

2. Scholars recognize many different types of "feminism(s)," acknowledging that the goals and methods of some forms of feminism may be oppositional, even antithetical, to others. Julia Wood explains that liberal feminism hails from the "liberal ideology that women and men are alike in important respects and, therefore, entitled to equal rights and opportunities" (*Gendered* 72). Liberal feminism can be distinguished, for example, from structural feminism, which assumes that "women are different from men" and that

"women's traditional position in the domestic sphere of life has led them to develop more nurturing, supportive, cooperative, and live-giving values than those men learn through participation in the public sphere" (76).

Chapter Eight

Madeleine Albright and the Rhetoric of *Madame Secretary*

C. Brant Short

The writing of political autobiography in the United States has increased significantly in recent decades, prompted by Harry Truman's decision to write his memoirs to finance his retirement, given the lack of a federal pension when he left office. This practice has become commonplace as many American political leaders, including most U.S. presidents, have published their autobiographies. In post World War II America, many Secretaries of State also have written autobiographies, in part to shape their legacy as well as to offer their own vision for American foreign policy. Henry Kissinger has been the most prolific former secretary, writing multiple volumes about his time in office as well as other books on foreign affairs. In contrast, most secretaries, including Dean Acheson, Cyrus Vance, George Schulz, and Warren Christopher, have written a single volume with their service in the State Department serving as the dominant feature of their narrative. Colin Powell published his autobiography prior to his selection as Secretary of State for George W. Bush.

In 2003, Madeleine Albright published her autobiography. Entitled *Madame Secretary*, Albright's memoir details her life story with a concentration upon her life in government, first as an advisor to various Democratic candidates and then her work in the Carter and Clinton administrations. She served the Clinton administration for eight years, first as Ambassador to the United Nations and later as Secretary of State, a position that made her the most powerful female in the history of the U.S. government. As one of the most influential women in the world from 1993 to 2001, Albright's life story demands scholarly inquiry. At the most fundamental level, her autobiography provides a historical treatise that will be used to assess the Clinton administration and world affairs in the last decade of the twentieth century. The fact that she was a part of nearly every major global policy decision in the 1990s is a political rarity; her eight years as the nation's highest official at the United Nations and later at the State Department qualify her as one of the longest serving diplomatic leaders in American history. Moreover, Albright's life story personifies the American dream: the immigrant forced from her homeland who not only succeeds in the United States, but becomes one of its greatest citizens. Finally, Albright's rise to power cannot be separated from gender; she is willing to allow the personal and public spheres of her life as a daughter, wife, mother, student, professor, advisor, and diplomat to be read as a complete text.

This chapter examines Albright's book and discusses the rhetorical implications of political autobiography. Initially, the text includes a review of two theories relevant to analyzing *Madame Secretary* as a form of rhetoric. Next, the chapter describes key elements guiding Albright's autobiography and analyzes its rhetorical dimensions in the context of gender, power, and legacy. After reviewing the book, the investigation examines critical reaction to *Madame Secretary* by identifying themes that emerge from reviews in scholarly and public forums. Finally, the discussion offers conclusions about the rhetorical aspects of *Madame Secretary* as well as women's autobiography in general.

A rhetorical analysis of *Madame Secretary* can be justified in three areas. First, it offers insight into the rhetorical dimensions of gender and politics and the challenges faced by women who seek positions of power. Second, such a study furthers work on the rhetoric of collective memory and, in this case, the persuasive dimensions of political autobiography as a rhetorical genre. Third, this investigation explores the manner in which men and women in public life communicate and interrogates how they construct their political life through public and private narratives.

Autobiography, Standpoint Theory, and the Narrative Paradigm

Thomas Benson concludes that certain conventions guide the construction of an autobiography and that such texts differ from literature and history. The conventions of the autobiography are "constantly working to focus the reader's attention upon an individual who is created in the work" (Benson, "Rhetoric" 8) and not upon what others would define as "real life." The "external world" of the autobiography can only be understood as a "part of the author's experience, rather than as a real place shared with the reader" (8). As a result of such conventions, the critic is less interested in assessing the apparent truth or accuracy of an autobiography, but instead focuses on analyzing the life writing as a narrative intended to shape the worldview of its readers. Since autobiographies are written texts that detail selected events of a single life story, classical notions of rhetoric offer limited utility in the analysis of such texts. In contrast, two recent scholarly perspectives offer useful alternatives to capture the rhetorical meanings of autobiography: standpoint theory and the narrative paradigm.

Scholars in varied disciplines have turned to standpoint theory to illuminate the dynamic connections between discourse and identity. It appears that such an approach would work well in discussions of autobiography as well, as an individual both reviews and explains his or her life in a chronological narrative. "Standpoint theorists posit a reciprocal relationship between communication and standpoints," observes Julia Wood (*Communication* 217). Communication is central to creating one's identity as "we learn the values, meanings, and ways of interpreting the world that are common to our groups" (217). Because one's social location is a "primary influence on the experiences, opportunities, and understanding of group members" (217), an individual's autobiography will reveal his or her standpoints through the process of explaining a life story. Significantly, a core belief of standpoint theory is that "members of subordinate groups are more complete and thus better than those of privileged groups in a society" (217). In regard to which groups might be considered subordinate, gender remains one of the central markers of being marginalized. Wood observes that a central tenet of feminist standpoint theory contends that "women's lives are systematically and structurally different from men's lives and, that these differences produce different (and differently) complete knowledges" ("Feminist Standpoint Theory" 61).

Susan Hekman critiques the evolution of standpoint theory and suggests it is more than a feminist theory. She notes that from its beginnings in the 1970s, many feminists have embraced standpoint because it replaces masculine falsity with an "alternative vision of truth and, with it, hope for a less repressive society" (356). Instead of providing a vehicle for finding truth, claims Hekman, standpoint theory offers rich insights for scholars studying discourse and culture. She concludes that feminist standpoint theory "defines knowledge as particular rather than universal" and "subjects as constructed by relational forces rather than as transcendent" (356). As a result, standpoint theory's "original tension between social construction and universal truth has dissolved" (356). From a political orientation, standpoint theory provides a new vantage. For the traditionalist in political discourse, "politics must be grounded in absolute, universal principles and enacted by political agents defined as universal subjects" (357). In contrast, standpoint theory views politics as a "local and situated activity undertaken by discursively constituted subjects" (357). As a result, it offers a useful way to conceptualize rhetoric and power, two themes central to any political autobiography.

Applying standpoint theory to the analysis of literature and rhetoric, Glen McClish and Jacqueline Bacon conclude that standpoint theory must "attend to the social and historical components of texts. Context is particularly important to rhetoricians, who since the ancient Greeks have emphasized the situatedness of argument and its special relationship with audience. We should not overlook cultural assumptions about race, class, gender, language, epistemology, and worldview that influence any rhetor" (32). As a result, standpoint theory gains strength when scholars are sensitive to the multiple influences that shape a given narrative, especially an individual's life story.

Standpoint theory appears grounded in the social constructionist perspective many communication theorists embrace. As such, standpoint theory emphasizes the pragmatic functions of discourse, which, in turn, explains how individuals from marginalized groups communicate their views of reality. A related theory, the narrative paradigm, helps critics explore the rhetorical dimensions of autobiography. Identified by Walter Fisher in a series of works in the 1980s, this paradigm has presented a layered method to understand the rhetorical dynamics of many different kinds of texts, including speeches, advertisements, songs, and films. At its core, the narrative paradigm assumes that humans are storytelling creatures and that our willingness to embrace narrative is a striking alternative to classical rhetorical methods of persuasion.

Fisher notes that a narrative achieves rhetorical meaning by fulfilling two functions: narrative fidelity and narrative probability. Although each overlaps to a degree, the two functions merge to turn a narrative into a powerful statement of how an audience ought to view the world and even change behaviors. Fisher claims people determine rationality by ascertaining *"narrative probability . . .* [that is] what constitutes a coherent story" (8). In addition, they test *narrative fidelity . . .* [to decide] whether the stories they experience ring true with the stories they know to be true in their [own] lives" (8). In this manner, the narrative paradigm offers a means of "resolving the dualisms of modern life: fact-value, intellect-imagination, reason-emotion, and so on" (10). In the case of autobiography, the dualism governing any life story is the tension between public and private spheres. This tension plays out in setting boundaries of a narrative. In other words, the rhetor crafting a text must consider when one's private life should be revealed in order to explain the public sphere and when one's private life should remain untold in a narrative. At one time an individual had clear rules to govern what topics might be appropriate and inappropriate in an autobiography, but as postmodernism redefines how we create collective memory, such rules fade away. The narrative paradigm provides a rich method to identify and analyze the tensions that guide the construction of autobiography, especially a text that explains the life of any person moving from marginalized status to legitimate power in society.

This chapter combines standpoint theory and the narrative paradigm into a critical lens to evaluate Albright's autobiography and her quest to explain her life story in the context of gender and social status. As a woman at the highest echelons of foreign affairs, she saw the world differently than men of similar rank; as an immigrant and social outsider she had the added burden of challenging social hierarchies related to class, religion, and societal status.

Narrative Themes in *Madame Secretary*

Like others who have held the title of Secretary of State, Madeleine Albright has a clearly defined view of world affairs as well as an ability to guide American foreign policy. Moreover, Albright shares another characteristic of many former

Secretaries: no electoral experience in local, state, or national politics. Albright's experiences as a scholar and political advisor propelled her to national levels of attention, although her personal life also explains the legitimacy she held as a diplomat. Born in Prague on May 15, 1937, and named Marie Anna Korbel, she was nicknamed Madla after a character in a popular show and was called "Madlenka" by her mother. She writes, "it took me years to figure out what my actual name was. Not until I was ten, and learning French, did I find the version that pleased me: Madeleine" (Albright 4). But she also explains that she never altered her "original name, and [her] naturalization certificate and marriage license both read 'Marie Jana Korbel'" (4).

For Albright, her life story must be viewed in the context of her family and birthplace. She observes: "To understand me, you must understand my father. To understand him, you must understand that my parents grew up in what they thought was a golden place" (5). Czechoslovakia, the only functioning democracy in Europe between world wars, had a "wise leader, peacefully competing political parties, and a sound economy" (5). Albright's birthplace became a defining part of her life, even though she spent much of her youth in other locations, such as London during World War II. After the war her father was assigned to the embassy in Yugoslavia. At ten years of age, her parents sent her to a boarding school in Switzerland in order to learn French. As communism took over central Europe, Albright's father worked to secure a United Nations appointment and in 1948 he was able to move the family to the United States. Albright writes, "I am still described as a 'refugee,' which is accurate, but in contrast to many who came to America before and after us, my family wasn't a hardship case" (19). Her personal struggle to fit in was revealing to eleven-year-old Madeleine: "I first became aware of a dilemma I would face throughout my life: given my personal experiences and drive to do well, how could I overcome my inherent seriousness and fit in?" (18). Time and again Albright highlights her early life in Europe and her father's work as a diplomat and later university professor of international politics as central to her life in politics, especially her career as a diplomat.

Albright found her life as a teenager challenging. On the one hand she "increasingly" saw herself as an "average American girl," but she never could remove her connection to Europe in terms of her parents' behavior, her family traditions, and even her appearance. Given the fact that she "was more apple-cheeked and round than tall and blond [she] couldn't compete with the more sophisticated, all-American-type girls. [She] clearly was not Denver Country Club material" (24). Her father set strict requirements on her dating based, in her eyes, upon old world standards. "My social life was further curtailed by my parents' insistence on staging family outings every Sunday," she recalls. "We drove into the mountains and picnicked" with her father fishing in a suit and tie and her mother picking mushrooms. The family had to have "what my father called 'family solidarity,' because we had come to America with most of our family left behind" (25). As a result, the family had remained isolated at times and outsiders were sometimes feared. Albright remembers that her father was "eager" to write and talk about his life as a refugee from communism. He helped shape his daughter's views of the world: "My father talked to me about history and foreign policy whenever he got the chance and his convictions became mine" (26). Her father also told her a lot about the Holocaust. Although it was a topic not discussed much in the 1950s, Albright remembers her father discussing it in detail and telling her that "anti-Semitism was unacceptable and tolerance essential" (27).

Albright applied to many colleges and received admission and scholarships to her first choice, Wellesley, which she entered in 1955. She observes that her class appeared to represent two groups, the "dutiful daughters" of the upper-class who were prepared to become the "dutiful wives" of America's leading men, or who were the "independent individuals" looking for success, not husbands (31). In reality, Albright was a member of both groups, "preparing for a career in journalism or diplomacy," at the same time she "wanted to get married as soon as possible to the perfect partner" (31). From the vantage of her current place in life, she notes that the "notion that there might be a contradiction between these two aspirations didn't occur to [her]" (31).

Gender, class, and politics shaped Albright's college experiences in significant ways. She believes that attending a women's college made a great difference for her because women held all the leadership positions on campus. "We were the student council presidents, newspaper editors, athletic team captains, and valedictorians. No one had to pretend to be dumb in class in order not to show up the boys" (34). Although she sought success in high school, Albright also did not want to draw attention to herself. But at Wellesley, she "was surrounded by girls who had been first in their high schools, many of whom matched [her] seriousness" (34). Moreover, Albright notes in hindsight that women professors held special status, and although she did not see them as "role models" at the time, she recalls four outstanding women mentors who had a profound effect on her education and future. Despite her ability to fit in as just one of many intelligent and ambitious women, Albright "was still part of one minority" (34). While most Wellesley students were Republicans, she and a small group were public in supporting the Democratic Party. We "thought we were brave and outspoken," she remembers (34).

Although Albright continued to assimilate into American culture as a typical 1950s college student, she found that her cultural heritage never left her. She wrote her senior thesis on her birthplace: "Although I had become an American, I couldn't separate myself from the struggles in Europe" (43). Her memories of the war and her family's displacement from Europe "made [her] a strong person with strong opinions," who had been "born with a tendency to express them" (43). As such, her autobiography was a place for her to recount the dualism of being an insider and outsider at the same time, although she may not have realized this status.

Albright's marriage forced her to consider her identity in the context of social status, religion, and gender roles. She fell in love with Joseph Albright, a member of an upper-class and powerful American family that held similar status to the Kennedy or Bush families. She recalls an extremely embarrassing situation in which she was taken to lunch with Joe's aunt before their marriage. Aunt Gaga asked her what she would like to do in Chicago, and Albright mentioned that she would like to buy a new hat for Easter. Aunt Gaga agreed and took Albright to an upscale milliner shop where hats were over $200 each, an amount of money she did not have. The hat was ordered, and Albright was unsure if this was to be a gift or if she was expected to pay. She planned to use her wedding savings to avoid revealing her lack of money, but she "was saved" when Aunt Gaga told her later it was a "little Easter present" (46).

As her wedding approached, "Joe broached a sensitive subject—would I mind becoming an Episcopalian?" (46). Her family told her it was her decision. What concerned her father "more than conversion was the fact that everyone in her fiancé's family seemed to have been divorced at least once" (46). Her father had a blunt talk with his future son-in-law who told Albright's father that "he didn't believe in divorce" (46), a claim of great irony given the couple's future together. Albright writes that conversion was not difficult except for her abiding belief that the Virgin Mary "could carry one's prayer to God. I said the rosary and every year celebrated my name day, which as Marie Jana was on August 15, Feast of Assumption of the Blessed Virgin" (46). Although she converted to please her husband's family, she writes, "I did not think I could give Mary up, and I never have" (46).

Because of her conversion, Albright's wedding could not take place at her Catholic Church in Denver; instead, the couple selected the Episcopal chapel at Wellesley. Her marriage seemed to fulfill her transition from European refugee to an all-American woman. She notes:

> I had graduated with honors from a top-notch college that specialized in equipping women with leadership skills. I had married an American prince whom I adored and who loved me. I had tried the glass slipper, and it fit. In the fairy tale that is where the story ends. In life it's merely the beginning of a new chapter. (47)

Joe Albright's family owned several major newspapers and after a stint in the Army and work at the Chicago *Sun-Times*, he was offered a position at Long Island's *Newsday*, a successful newspaper owned by his Aunt Alicia Guggenheim and her husband, Harry. As their three children arrived, Albright became restless. She took an intensive course in Russian at Hofstra University to keep her mind evolving. When Aunt Alicia told Albright of a session at Radcliffe College to discuss issues relevant to young women in the early 1960s, Albright wrote an essay that she reported was "factual and depressing" (53). In preparing the essay, she confronted the "classic women's dilemma: juggling marriage, motherhood, and profession" (53). The essay reflected the challenges many women faced in the 1960s, and by reprinting a large verbatim section of the essay in *Madame Secretary* Albright highlights a growing discomfort in her own life. In the essay, the young mother, with a college education and a clear sense of ambition who married an "American prince" concludes:

Twice in two years, I have had to leave good jobs with good futures to follow my husband's path. And that was even before I had children. Now, even to get a job, I would have to find and hire a dependable nurse and pay her perhaps more than I could make myself. Perhaps I am being overly pessimistic. Perhaps I could go out tomorrow and get a job as a typist. The next question is, why bother? Do I want a job merely to have a job, or do I want to work in order to be doing something worthwhile? (53)

The family spent a year in Washington, D.C., and then in 1963, Joe Albright returned to *Newsday*'s Long Island office to become assistant editor. This move was fortuitous for Albright, who was able to pursue a Ph.D. at Columbia University. She added courses in Russian and decided to write a master's thesis, although this was not a requirement in her doctoral program. She concludes that writing a thesis with a heavy course load "was an academic challenge that carried over to my personal life" (60). She wanted good grades and to be a good wife at the same time. No matter what she was doing, she "thought [she] should be doing something else. Along with other women, [she] had a common middle name: guilt" (60).

In 1968 after the newspaper hired a new editor, Joe Albright took over the bureau in Washington, D.C., so once again the Albright family was on the move. As her husband continued to grow professionally as a journalist, Albright found herself raising her children, volunteering in the community, and pursuing graduate degrees. Her life was happy; a portrait of the Albright family in the 1970s "would have shown a happily married couple with three smart and beautiful daughters" (75). The family vacationed in Georgia and Colorado, had a farmhouse in Virginia, went to parties, and enjoyed life. Albright notes, "we had a pleasant and varied group of friends, but our best times were when we were together. Joe and I were not only husband and wife but also best friends" (76).

The 1970s also were important because with a doctorate in hand, Albright had the credentials to work in foreign affairs in Washington, D.C. She joined the office of Senator Edmund Muskie as a volunteer and later as a legislative aide. In 1976, her connections paid off again when her former professor, Zbigniew Brzezinski, asked her to join him at the Carter White House. Working long hours in the White House, Albright depended on her husband to keep the family routine. "Joe was great," she writes. "He took over homework supervision and eating meals with the kids prepared by our parade of housekeepers. I tried to get home by dinner every night but didn't always succeed" (90). Although filled with guilt about her lack of time with the family, she states, "as far as I could tell no one was suffering" (90).

Albright's life was fundamentally changed on January 13, 1982, when her husband asked for a divorce. She recalls that Washington was in a blizzard and an Air Florida flight crashed into the Potomac River, injuring twenty-five passengers and killing three. As they watched the news, Joe Albright announced, "this marriage is dead and I am in love with someone else" (94). He told her that he was moving out and headed for Atlanta to be with the woman he loved. "Beyond saying that she was considerably younger, and beautiful, Joe didn't volunteer more information" (95). Albright was stunned by his decision. It was a "thunderbolt" to her; she had no clue the marriage was in trouble. She was angry because he refused to talk about how they could stay together, he called her old-looking, and he did not understand why she was upset. After being in Atlanta with his new love, Joe Albright had second thoughts, calling Albright daily to say he loved her or he did not love her. "He actually described his feelings in percentages. 'I love you sixty percent and her forty percent,' or the next, 'I love her seventy percent and you thirty percent'" (95). As the year wore on, he received a nomination for a Pulitzer Prize and became "fixated with winning" (96). Moreover, "he came up with a startling proposition: If he got the Pulitzer, he would stay with me. If not, he would leave and we would get a divorce" (96). Although she reports she did not understand her husband and his lack of stability, she seemed to go along with his plan. When he learned he had lost, Joe called and declared the divorce needed to go through (97).

Like many other women in her generation, the divorce overwhelmed Albright's sense of identity. She was forty-five years old and had spent half her life with Joe. "I had never lived by myself," she notes, "even the three days between graduation from Wellesley and marriage I had spent with Mary Jane in the dormitory" (98). As a single mother, she found it hard to think in terms of "I" instead of "we." Her ability to make decisions was shattered, albeit temporarily. "I could not make up my mind about what groceries to buy," she observes. "Joe's tastes had become mine. I stood in the cereal aisle, struggling to choose between Cheerios and Shredded Wheat. I rediscovered I really didn't like beef, even though for years that is what we had eaten nearly every night" (99). Realizing that she was in fact "indecisive" and "vulnerable" in many ways, Albright concludes, "I didn't want to become the person I thought I might have to be in order to survive. I did not want to become cynical or stoical or hard-bitten, or to stop wondering whether what I was doing would please somebody else" (99). As her divorce became final and she started to rebuild her life, Albright "found refuge in two places, one as a professor, and one as a participant in politics" (99). As she contemplated divorce, she was offered a job in the presidential campaign of Walter Mondale as well as a teaching position at Georgetown University. She realized she did not have to choose between teaching and politics and for the next decade combined them, finding they complemented her strengths. Albright found teaching was more challenging and more fulfilling than she had thought it would be, and she gained greater respect for her father's life as a university professor. She also became an advisor to vice presidential candidate Geraldine Ferraro in 1984 and developed a close friendship that came back to help her in 1996 when Albright asked Ferraro to assist in promoting her candidacy for Secretary of State.

Albright rarely found her status as a female detrimental in her official role as ambassador and secretary. On occasion, however, others raised issues that she had to manage to maintain her position. In February 1996, Cuban jets shot down two small American planes used by an anti-Castro group. The Cuban pilots knew they were going to fire upon an unarmed plane and one pilot reported back to Havana: "First launch. We hit him! Cojones! We hit him. Cojones! We busted his cojones!" (202). At the United Nations, Albright, angered by the death of three Americans and one legal resident, debated with the Cuban representative. After outlining the events, she told the United Nations, "I was struck by the joy of these pilots in committing cold-murder. Frankly, this is not *cojones*. This is cowardice" (205). Albright writes that "jaws dropped" in the pressroom by her use of what CNN called a "common vulgarity." She knew that her statement "would never in a thousand years have been cleared by the State Department in advance" (205). She found that diplomats from Latin America were upset by her breach of formal language. Venezuela's representative said, "I wouldn't say that word, not even on my farm" (205). But she weathered the storm and was selected to represent the administration at the funeral of the four men in Miami. Albright observes that the "*cojones* quote developed a life of its own" (207). It appeared on bumper stickers in Miami. Advisor Tony Lake told Albright every time he heard the comment "he wanted to cross his legs" (207). Most telling was the reaction by President Clinton, who publicly stated that Albright's comment was "probably the most effective one-liner in the whole administration's foreign policy" (qtd. in Albright 207).

Albright's selection as Secretary of State generated hostility, some coming from those who did not want a woman in charge of U.S. foreign policy or others who claimed she lacked the breadth of experience to serve in such a position. Like many political insiders, Albright confronted significant opposition among many in the Clinton White House. Her rise to the position of Secretary of State began in her own denial of thinking so boldly. She observes that for most of her life she never would have considered having a chance to be named Secretary. "I could picture myself as a behind-the-scenes policy coordinator," she writes, "but not in a post as visible as Secretary of State" (Albright 215). Several prominent friends asked her to consider seeking the post in 1994, when it was assumed that Warren Christopher would resign at some future time. She made her decision and informed Clinton's Chief of Staff, Leon Panetta, that she would be willing to remain as UN ambassador in a second term but she also was interested in being Secretary of State. She realized it was going to be a battle and listed a number of other contenders for the job, including former Senator Sam Nunn. She found that among Washington, D.C., insiders she always was a "second tier" candidate or one with an "outside chance." She discovered the world of gender politics as well:

> Some of the Democratic Party's most influential "wise men" advised me early on not to "campaign" for the job. I thought, *hmmm*. Obviously I wasn't going to manufacture campaign buttons, but I doubted that George Mitchell and Dick Holbrooke were sitting demurely at home waiting for the phone to ring. I was sure they would do everything they could to activate the network of supporters and friends each had developed. (217)

She observes that for men in Washington "reliance on such networks is second nature" (217). Washington women also had networks but they "were primarily social or philanthropic. Men focused on power. Women focused on everything except power" (219). Albright activated her own network. Although much smaller than many male networks, it did include some powerful individuals, mostly women. She was disturbed by the fact that most men supported others and that her support was primarily from women. Albright wanted her selection or rejection to be based on merit and not gender, although many supporters wanted her appointment to be a litmus test for Clinton's support of women. She stumbled when trying to deflect criticism about her lack of intellect. As she told a reporter, "I'm not that smart, [but] I work very hard" (219). Her friends "lectured" her that a man would never make such a disparaging comment. "I wondered," she concludes, "if the men being considered had their own quiet fears or were questioning themselves as I was" (219).

In describing the events surrounding her appointment, Albright saw no reason to separate personal and public dimensions of her life story. As she waited for the phone call from the White House with the final decision, Albright writes that she needed support and asked a friend to stay over night. She loaned her friend "one of my flannel nightgowns so she would not have to go home. In the morning we sat in my living room wearing matching pink terrycloth bathrobes, afraid to take showers because we might miss the call" (223). She and her friend sipped coffee all morning, and Albright concluded that Clinton had made the offer to someone else. When Clinton finally called with the offer, Albright accepted, "hugged" her friend and "sat down for several minutes trying to absorb the fact that [her] life had just been transformed" (223). She called her family, took a bath, had her "hair done, put on a red dress and jacket and a pearl necklace with an eagle pendant and headed for the White House" (223).

Albright found that explaining her life as Secretary of State required references to her family. She reports that the best answer to describing her life rested in a single word: motion. Moreover, she could no longer maintain her many friendships. She broke so many dates for dinner or a show, noting that she "finally stopped trying. I simply did not have time for a private life," she recalls (339). The single exception, she writes, was "my grandchildren, with whom I spent absolutely as much time as I could" (339). Albright also learned an important lesson in the life of a professional woman. "When I was younger, I couldn't understand why older women insisted on talking about their grandchildren," she observes. "Now I understood: it's impossible not to" (339).

One of the problems Albright faced came early in her term as Secretary of State when several newspapers reported that her grandparents were Jewish and had died in the Holocaust. The story itself did not present a problem. Instead the fact that Albright had been raised as Roman Catholic, did not know of her Jewish ancestry, and had no idea that her grandparents died at the hand of the Nazis seemed incredulous to some observers. Many of her critics used this event to question her honesty and suggest her hypocrisy by denying her Jewish heritage. As one reviewer of *Madame Secretary* writes, "her claim never to have heard or suspected that her family died in the Holocaust and her belated public acknowl-

edgment of her Jewish origins are thoroughly unconvincing. But then she was
dealing with real politics" (I. Williams 32).

A major problem that Albright faced as the senior member of the Clinton
cabinet concerned her response to the Monica Lewinsky scandal. In the polar-
ized atmosphere surrounding questions of the president's character, Albright
also found herself under attack for her own ethical conduct in office. While the
questions about Clinton's personal life did not prevent officials from doing their
jobs, she admits that the "uproar was impossible to block out" (Albright 350).
Ironically, Albright found that political leaders from around the world failed to
understand the public debate over the president's private life. They admired
Clinton and he "was enormously popular" with foreign leaders. She hoped for a
positive outcome. "I still wanted to believe that the whole business had been
cooked up to destroy the President and that this would become clear when the
full truth came out" (350).

While dealing with major global conflicts in Asia and Africa in the midst of
the scandal, Albright found herself under attack by some Republicans who
claimed that she was dishonest with the Congress. Seeing "gridlock or peril"
across the world, she found her confidence level down and her goal to be an
activist Secretary slipping away. Moreover, in August and September of 1998,
major newspapers across the United States, including the *New York Times*,
Washington Post, and *Wall Street Journal*, called Albright a "failure" as Secretary in front page stories.

With the attacks upon her foreign policy came personal criticisms as well.
Maureen Dowd of the *New York Times* said that Albright had failed in her "special responsibility as a betrayed woman to denounce the President publicly over
Lewinsky" (qtd. in Albright 352), and a *New Republic* columnist wrote that con-
cealing truth "is one of Albright's lifetime habits" (qtd. in Albright 352). She
heard rumors she was going to resign and "began telling friends that the reason I
look fatter was that I had grown a thicker skin" (Albright 352). Ironically, one of
the public officials who was most supportive of Albright was North Carolina's
very conservative Senator Jesse Helms. He told her she was not a failure, that
she had not lied to him, and "if anyone tries to take your job, they'll have to go
through this [Foreign Affairs] committee" (qtd. in Albright 352).

When Clinton was forced to reveal the details of his sexual relationship
with Lewinsky, the press was especially interested in the reactions of Albright
and Donna Shalala, Secretary of the Department of Health and Human Services.
"We were the two women from the cabinet who had defended him in front of
television cameras the last time the full cabinet had met. . . . As a result, some
women's groups were outraged that we hadn't quit" (Albright 355).

Albright reports she was torn about how she would respond to Clinton when
he spoke of the scandal to the Cabinet. As the senior cabinet member, the Secretary of State would be obliged to speak first after Clinton's apology and explanation. She looked at Clinton and said: "The sad thing is we had all expected
you to be Mike McGwire and hit seventy home runs. It is so rare to have a Democrat reelected and able to serve two terms. You have given us all a great op-

portunity and now we all have to prove ourselves worthy of people's trust through our work" (356). While some cabinet members expressed outrage toward Clinton and others wanted to forgive Clinton's sins in order to be good Christians, Albright took a different path: "I did not think it was the cabinet's role to play pastor. I was angry with the President for risking so much for less than nothing, but I had learned from my own experience not to be surprised when a man lies about sex. . . . The President had not betrayed me; he had betrayed the First Lady and it was up to Hillary, not the cabinet, to deal with that" (357). In discussing her comments to Clinton regarding his marital infidelity, she recalls that she learned the "danger of wandering rhetorically into the alien world of male sports. As Erskine Bowles smilingly reminded me, McGwire's first name is Mark, not Mike" (357).

The Clinton scandal also gave Albright deeper insight in the way other women handle conflict. She observes that although she often met with Hillary Clinton, the First Lady did not discuss the impact of the Lewinsky affair upon her life in the White House. "Given my own experience with Joe," Albright writes, "I thought she might want to share her feelings about the business with Lewinsky, but she never raised the subject and I did not feel it my place to pry" (357). In thinking of her own marital problems, Albright recalls, "when I was upset with Joe, half the city of Washington had known how I felt. My heart was on my sleeve. Hillary's was better protected. She is a person fully in charge of herself and in any case didn't want anyone feeling sorry for her. I could identify with that (357).

Albright experienced an epiphany while dining with Hillary Clinton and Queen Noor of Jordan at the White House. Recently widowed with the death of King Hussein of Jordan, Queen Noor was an American-born wife with small children who was thinking about her future. The three women met and ate the first two courses, "but when it was announced that we had a choice of three desserts, we simultaneously asked for samples of them all—rich chocolate, fruit pie, and heaps of ice cream" (358). The women discussed global politics, people they knew in common, and the question of writing their memoirs. When she returned home Albright reflected on "what had been a remarkable evening" (358). The three women came from disparate backgrounds but had been "given extraordinary opportunities to participate directly in the highest level of world affairs. We were passionate in our beliefs, had experienced severe tests at certain stages in our lives, and were now very much in the public eye" (358). But once again Albright had to acknowledge the role of gender for all three women. "It struck me as well," she concludes, "that we had in common a personal connection related to the men we had married. In different ways and at various times, we had each been left to explore the boundaries of our own inner strength by a husband who had deceived, deserted, or died" (358).

To conclude her book, Albright considers a variety of lessons that she learned in her life. She observes that people are given choices in life, and she learned from her parents that "you have to fight to achieve all you can" with the gifts you have. "At first to me that meant doing well in school," she continues.

"Later it meant being a good wife and mother and so on through all the stages of life up to and including Secretary of State" (512). Her life as wife and mother seemed to have equality with her life as a professor and diplomat. Her final paragraph of the memoir addresses the question of how she would like to be remembered. Mentioning that she tried to make her parents proud, that she served her country with great energy, and that she had taken strong stands to support freedom around the world, her last sentence is revealing: "Perhaps some will also say that I helped teach a generation of older women to stand tall and young women not be afraid to interrupt" (512).

Critical Responses to *Madame Secretary*

Critical reviews of books, films, and movies provide a glimpse into the ways an audience may react to a specific text. Although reviewers are specialized in their training and often have a specific agenda based in part on their status and ideology, they offer feedback that helps explain the success or failure of a given text. As Philip Tompkins observes, reviews are valuable for scholars in that reviewers "reveal their perceptions and value judgments of the art form under analysis. They do, after all, have some effect on other receivers" (438). Most critics who reviewed *Madame Secretary* considered gender an appropriate lens through which to assess the autobiography. Thus, in describing the central themes of Albright's life from the perspective of gender, reviewers implicitly endorse Albright's view that gender is a major subtext of her personal and public life. For example, Susan Page of *USA Today* opens her review by observing that Henry Kissinger "never told us about the difficulty of balancing work and home" (5D). But Albright prepared a "different kind of memoir" according to Page, a book that included "rejection, grief and second thoughts as well as ambition and success—the sort of zigzag life more common to women than men" (5D). Page observes an irony in Albright's narrative that linked her personal and professional life in one event: "What seems undeniably true is that her divorce, however unwarranted, led to [a] much more prominent role as she struggled to recover" (5D).

Other critics used gender as a means of identifying specific problems in the book. Gabriel Schoenfeld, for example, finds *Madame Secretary* a weak addition to the collection of memoirs by former secretaries of state. Schoenfeld charges that the book "reveals a great deal about many things, if also surprisingly little" about means and ends in U.S. foreign policy. Indeed, the first 120 pages of the book take readers on a "candid tour of Albright's childhood, adolescence, dating life, marriage, parenthood, and divorce" (70). Schoenfeld argues that Albright's attention to gender issues weakened the book. Readers expect "something more, some deeper reflections on the purposes of American power" (71) in the life story of a secretary of state. In fact, Schoenfeld writes, Albright took "innumerable diversions" (71) often related to gender issues. For example, Albright's discussion of the Fourth World Congress on Women in

Beijing in 1995 and of Hillary Clinton's role in the event frustrated Schoenfeld. "This UN feminist gabfest receives the same quotient of attention in Albright's pages as the threat posed by Osama bin Laden and al Qaeda," concludes Schoenfeld, "and one gets the unfortunate sense from her recitation that it was a pinnacle of her diplomatic career" (72). Schoenfeld also criticizes Albright for discussing her role as the first female Secretary of State. She "still seems to see herself less as a Margaret Thatcher or a Golda Meir—that is, a woman who made it to the top by dint of experience and sheer mental candlepower—than as a somewhat undeserving beneficiary of affirmative action who must be perpetually on guard for slights" (72). Schoenfeld was troubled by what he called Albright's "journey of self-discovery" (72) in discussing intimate details in the same context as foreign policy. One "cannot help wondering about the connection between such displays of unseriousness and the visible difficulties of the Clinton team" (72). The conclusion is that Albright "has unwittingly written a withering exposé of herself and the administration she served" (72).

In a mixed review of *Madame Secretary* published in the *Washington Post*, Walter Russell Mead observes that the "ultimate audience" for a diplomatic memoir is not the "book-buying public of today" (T04). Instead, Albright is presenting "her case for why the Clinton administration should be rated among the successful presidencies when historians sum up the record" (T04). But instead of a comprehensive account of the administration's foreign policy, Albright "has given us the memorist's equivalent of a tease" (T04). Readers see her private side and she "discreetly lets slip a few facts about her personal and emotional life" (T04). As a result, Albright is "more frank and confessional about her private life than her career" (T04). Mead concludes that readers learn more about her divorce and family issues than the "policy infighting that roiled the Clinton administration" (T04).

In a scholarly journal review of *Madame Secretary*, Tomicah Tilleman of the School of Advanced International Studies at Johns Hopkins University finds both strong and weak elements in the book. Tilleman notes that Albright's "style is more accessible than her predecessors' books, but many will find that her 'policy light' approach skimps on rigour and analysis" (195). If the reader has lowered expectations, the book will be an "engaging account of the Secretary's life," but those searching for an "intellectual framework" to examine Albright's foreign policy will come away "empty handed" (196). As other reviewers note, Albright presented her personal life in the same detail at times as her public life: "Albright's divorce followed her departure from the [Carter] White House. The book's account of the event is as detailed as its description of negotiations surrounding the Middle East peace process" (196). Moreover, with "her marriage over, Albright sought fulfillment by devoting herself to international affairs" (196). She began teaching at Georgetown University, advising leaders in the Democratic Party, and working with European leaders such as Vaclav Havel. Calling the book "honest, personal, and unpretentious," Tilleman asserts that it will draw criticism for its "persistent substitution of anecdotes for original thinking" (196) and its failure to describe a coherent intellectual philosophy behind her decisions.

The most hostile review of *Madame Secretary* was written by Ian Williams, a correspondent for *The Nation* magazine who was troubled by Albright's past. Williams opens by claiming that a "desire for social respectability has always been intense in Albright, a former Catholic who became an Episcopalian after marrying into money, and who long suffered from a curiously convenient amnesia about her Jewish relatives" (32). Williams claims that Albright's prejudices "come through loud and clear" in the memoir (32). "As the child of Czech refugees, she had more justification than most for her reflexive anti-Communism and perhaps even for her Eurocentrism" (32–33). Williams attacked Albright for being "all but indifferent to domestic policy" (35) as a cabinet member, a curious charge given she was in charge of foreign affairs. Williams also questioned Albright's "nominal attachment to feminism, although one cannot help suspecting that this had more to do with self-advancement than with principle" (35).

Although critical reviews of *Madame Secretary* were mixed, the book succeeded in telling Albright's story and joining the canon of autobiographies of major American diplomats. The fact that some reviewers expressed frustration, and even contempt, with Albright's rejection of traditional public and private spheres of discourse affirms the importance of her career as the first female to serve as Secretary of State. Albright claimed that she worked in a gendered political culture and most reviewers were eager to raise the issue in their analysis of her life story.

Analysis of *Madame Secretary*

From the perspective of the narrative paradigm, readers identify with Albright as a person overcoming the challenges of social status, gender, and religion. Narrative fidelity demands that a text offer a narrative that makes sense to readers and corresponds to their own life experiences. While all readers have opinions about immigrants to the United States, the role of women in the world, and the place of religion in one's identity, the point of narrative fidelity concerns whether Albright's own story resonates with audience views of such topics. It appears that Albright is successful at this level because her claim of complete candor in writing the book and her willingness to seamlessly merge personal and public aspects of her life create a synergy that fosters reader connections to the narrative. By allowing readers to see her striving professionally at the same time her marriage is in dissolution and her children are being kept in the dark about their father's affair with another woman, Albright affirms her reader's experiences, personal or shared with others, in which personal crises become part of one's professional experience and evolving identity. A life story that ignores a personal crisis in favor of a recounting of public details asks readers to participate in a narrative that is incomplete. The fact that in his autobiography Ronald Reagan offers a single sentence about his first marriage to Jane Wyman became a common complaint of many book reviewers. They saw this lack of detail and candor as the outcome of a sanitized narrative that lacked a genuine commitment to telling the story of one's life.

The second dimension of the narrative paradigm, the ability of a text to fulfill the needs of narrative probability, rests upon the ability of the story to be coherent and logical for readers. Although *Madame Secretary* follows a fairly straightforward chronological path, it is divided into four sections. The first section focuses on a childhood dominated by her status as a war refugee, a child of an elite family displaced by Nazism and then by communism. The second section tells the story of her immersion in American culture and eventual entry into formal legitimacy through her education at a prominent college and her marriage to a son of an established family. The third section covers her success in education and politics at the same time her marriage is dissolving and her identity is under threat. The fourth section describes her rebirth. In this period her personal doubts and professional goals merge together, and her work as a scholar and diplomat becomes the foundation of her personal life. These four sections of her life story fulfill the requirements of narrative probability because they recount the journey of many women in the 1960s and 1970s as new ways of constructing one's identity as a female emerged. Significantly, the pivotal event of her adult life appears to be her divorce. In the appendix to *Madame Secretary*, Albright provides a six-page chronology of her life, from birth to her completion of work in the Clinton Administration. As with most such lists, the chronology contains a mixture of personal and professional dates, with children's births listed as well as many important appointments, missions, and accomplishments. Most telling, however, is the specificity Albright uses to recall the event: "January 13, 1982, Joe Albright announces he wants a divorce. January 31, 1983, Divorce Final" (Albright 514).

In considering standpoint theory and the function of being in a subordinate group, Albright's autobiography tells the story of a powerful political figure who defined her achievements through gender, status, and power. Although she succeeded in the male-dominated worlds of her life, moving from academe to politics and finally to diplomacy, she regularly embraced her ability to see the world in different ways based on her position as an outsider. Wood lists five "key claims" of feminist standpoint theory; each can be applied to the text in order to explain the rhetorical dimensions of *Madame Secretary*.

First, society is "structured by power relations, which result in unequal social relations for women and men" (Wood, "Feminist Standpoint Theory" 62). The result is that the experiences typically open and closed to men and women "shape what they know and how they understand cultural life" (62). As a woman, every time Albright worked to advance her professional life, she had to consider how success might affect her marriage, her children, and her social life. She knew that she would suffer in terms of her own guilt as well as judgments of people she knew when she sought success in her family and professional life. As a result, the doors that were not easily open to her always demanded considerable reflection and attention, something she did not see in the men in her world who were advancing to the highest echelons of diplomacy and academe.

Second, subordinate groups have a more accurate view of reality than do those of privileged groups. Marginalized groups better understand their location in society as well as the structures that define power; on the other hand, privileged groups "have a vested interest in not seeing oppression and inequity that accompany and, indeed, makes possible their privilege" (62). One result of this perspective is that subordinate group members are more likely to explore "political analyses of oppression" (62) than those in privileged positions. Like many people, Albright was not always cognizant of her status until a specific event forced her to acknowledge her subordinate status. As described throughout the book, the insights she gained empowered her both as a person who could be happy and successful and as a diplomat who sought her own voice in the politics of foreign affairs.

Third, a person who moves from a subordinate group to the privileged group ("the outsider-within") gains "double-consciousness, being at once outside of the dominant group and intimately within that group in ways that allow observation and understanding of that group" (62). Albright reports many personal challenges in her autobiography as a means of stepping back to reflect upon all the ramifications of her decisions and the decisions of those around her. She became attuned to the gender challenges of working in Washington, D.C., and although she, too, became part of the system, she also could see how it functioned from the vantage point of a person outside the power elite. She reflects upon her life and recalls those times she willingly suppressed or even rejected central elements of her identity in order to gain access to privilege. Although in hindsight she did not call herself a hypocrite or a fraud, she is willing to reveal the mistakes she made in personal judgment and in behavior, lessons she gained by her dual status as an insider and outsider.

Fourth, standpoint refers not simply to the experience itself of being marginalized, but to a "critical understanding of location as experience" (62) and the fact that standpoint is shaped by social and political discourse. Albright learned through experiences and relationships that her place in life defined her status and guided how others communicated with her and she, in turn, with them. Like many women married to successful men in the 1950s and 1960s, the so-called "American princes" of the day, it took a divorce and reconsideration of her life, both personal and professional, for Albright to gain the critical understanding of her life as a woman and immigrant to the United States.

Fifth, any "individual can have multiple standpoints that are shaped by membership in groups defined by sex, race-ethnicity, sexual orientation, economic class, etc." (62). Although standpoint theory emerged from a feminist perspective, Wood makes it clear that standpoint is shaped by anyone who holds membership in a marginalized group. Thus, according to some studies African American women have a deeper sensitivity to oppression because they experience it simultaneously in relation to gender, race, and as insiders and as outsiders. In Albright's case, she was young enough as a refugee to the United States that she easily assimilated into mainstream norms and values; yet, she was she old enough to have vivid memories of her European heritage and the challenges it brought to trying to blend in and embrace the norms of a third- or fourth-generation American family. Albright came to value her heritage and its importance for her identity personally and professionally, but at the same time she acknowledged her discomfort because of her ethnic heritage, her family's lower income status, and her own personal appearance as well as being an intelligent and ambitious woman.

Conclusion

Madame Secretary provides significant insight into the evolution of a successful American leader who had to balance the challenges of gender, ethnic status, class, and even religion. Although Albright provides a detailed account of many important events in the recent history of the United States, including the challenge of Middle Eastern politics and NATO's effort to prevent human rights abuses in Kosovo, readers also learn about individual identity and political discourse. In studying historical texts, rhetorical critics must consider the intersection of private and public events in a single narrative. This chapter suggests that the narrative paradigm complements the goals of standpoint theory as a critical tool to generate insights into the rhetorical dimensions of autobiography. Madeleine Albright's book presents a rich work for historians, political scientists, feminists, and rhetorical critics. Each will ask different questions in examining the text, but all will find Albright's life story an important case study of gender, power, and collective memory.

Chapter Nine

Finding the Sensible Center: Christine Todd Whitman's *It's My Party Too* as Activist Autobiography

Kristina Horn Sheeler

Following closely on the heels of the 2004 presidential election, Christine Todd Whitman released *It's My Party Too: The Battle for the Heart of the GOP and the Future of America*. Ostensibly an opinion piece outlining the dire consequences of the hold of the "social fundamentalists" on the Republican Party, Whitman outlines core Republican values in an effort to reinvigorate the "radical moderates" to take back the party. As she claims, "it is time for Republican moderates to assert forcefully and plainly that this is our party too, that we not only have a place, but a voice—and not just a voice, but a vision—a vision that is true to the historic principles of our party and our nation" (Whitman 11–12). *It's My Party Too* explicates Whitman's vision as the reader embarks on a first-person account of life growing up in an active Republican household and the core principles of the party instilled in her as a child. Autobiography serves as the framework through which Whitman provides evidence, reveals ideology, recuperates public image, and advances her activist agenda. This strategy not only gives voice to moderate Republicans, but also allows Whitman to voice her explanations regarding controversial decisions during her time as New Jersey governor and administrator of the Environmental Protection Agency. The autobiographical form functions rhetorically to provide validation for her claims and illustrate the practicality of her version of Republican ideology for solving the country's ills.

This chapter advances the argument noted above by first explaining that *It's My Party Too* demonstrates William L. Howarth's characteristics of oratorical autobiography. As autobiography, then, the form provides valuable rhetorical resources for Whitman to create identification with her readers even as she advances an activist agenda. Whitman, as the embodiment of the lived experiences about which she writes, enacts the "good reasons" on which Republican ideology is premised, contemplates the powerful intersections of the personal and political, and provides a role model for other women seeking political office even in the face of powerful gender stereotypes.

Oratorical Autobiography

It's My Party Too functions as what Howarth describes as an oratorical autobiography. In "Some Principles of Autobiography," he explains that to conceive of autobiography as oratory means that the rhetor (1) defends her faith in and devotion to political doctrine, (2) demonstrates a "strong and principled character" through which the story functions "to confirm the validity of the argument," and (3) presents the vocation as the theme, "the special summons that guided an entire life's work and now its story" (367–71). Extending on Howarth, Martha Solomon explains that oratorical autobiographies center around the importance and meaning of the author's life work more so than other personal narratives. The goal is "to explain both why the author devoted his or her life to a particular type of work and how his or her efforts were important in that vocation" (354). "Belief in a superior force" (Howarth 371)—in Whitman's case the Republican Party and its core principles—works to unify the various fragments of the life as written. *It's My Party Too* explicates Christine Todd Whitman's life work, to date, as an active member of the Republican Party, and specifically as a "moderate" Republican working to reclaim her party from the "social fundamentalists." As the story's protagonist, Whitman's devotion to politics, and particularly what she sees as the goal of politics—making citizens' lives better—resonates because of her strong character.

It's My Party Too serves as a platform demonstrating Whitman's strength of character through her devotion to politics. She begins the first chapter by stating the problem that prompted the writing:

> The people of this county deserve better from their politics and their politicians than they've been getting in recent years. . . . You can be passionate and civil, believe deeply and yet respect the beliefs of others. That has always been my understanding of how our political system should work, and it has always informed the way I have tried to conduct my own political career. (Whitman 27)

A few pages later, Whitman states the problem more pointedly: "They [social fundamentalists] seem to have forgotten that one of America's greatest strengths has always been its ability to respect a broad range of ideas centered on a core set of values—freedom, opportunity, diversity. They also seem to have forgotten that you can respect specific differences while adhering to shared central principles" (73). Whitman repeatedly recounts those "shared central principles" as the reason for her political devotion. Civility, respect for others, freedom, diversity, and opportunity frame the narrative through which Whitman substantiates her commitment to a political life, and such values work to define Whitman's strength of character.

Whitman learned these shared central principles growing up in the Todd household where civil political talk was simply a way of life. Whitman's earliest recollections from childhood are political in nature: "I have been around politics literally for my entire life. . . . My parents, and their parents before them, had been active in the GOP since the early days of the twentieth century. . . . My parents actually met at the 1932 Republican National Convention in Chicago" (31). Her ability to talk politics was probably a result of family dinner conversations. "For as long as I can remember," recalls Whitman, "political discussions were the staple of dinner conversation with my parents" (31–32). However, those conversations were not always one-sided. "I shared my father's fiscal conservatism but leavened it with the social concerns my mother held," writes Whitman (45). In fact, New Jersey's largest newspaper listed Whitman's mother, Eleanor, as a woman who could become New Jersey's first woman governor. Whitman's approach to managing differences may have indeed been one she learned from her parents:

> One thing they [my parents] both also believed deeply, and that they taught me emphatically, was that politics was not just about winning elections; it was also about governing. They insisted that accomplishing good in a democracy requires accommodation and compromise, that politics should be about the art of the possible, a belief that is all too uncommon in our politics today. (33)

For Whitman, "the art of the possible" requires the involvement of as many voices as possible and a skilled leader who can find a way to blend those voices into a chorus that resonates with individual citizens.

Whitman's devotion to the principle that various viewpoints can come together productively guides her political life today. However, interviewers often challenge her, wanting to know why she stays in the party since she is so critical of her beloved GOP. Dana Milbank, writing in the *Washington Post*, goes so far as to critique Whitman's inability to use "her leverage to move the party," saying she poses "no flight risk to the GOP" (A06). Milbank and others who criticize Whitman paint her as ineffectual, too nice, "inconsistent," and even "clueless." They find fault with her refusal to name names when it comes to what is wrong with the party. Whitman responds, "that's too easy . . . It then becomes a spitting contest" (qtd. in Milbank A06). Yet, the autobiographical nature of *It's My Party Too* indicates that leaving isn't an option. As both Howarth and Solomon explain, one of the purposes of oratorical autobiography is to explain the *meaning* of one's devotion, one's faith in that which has been a lifelong calling. Changing parties would undermine such devotion. Instead, Whitman seeks to define and defend her version of Republicanism and how her efforts to locate the productive middle were and are important to advancing the party. In her eyes, the party has simply lost its way.

Christine Todd Whitman has adopted Kenneth Burke's comic frame when it comes to her fellow Republicans. Burke explains that adopting a comic perspective allows one to see another not as evil but as mistaken, and if one is mistaken, she or he can learn from that mistake and move toward corrective action (41, 171). Whitman's view is not without its error-prone characters, namely those "social fundamentalists" who have hijacked the party. But using Whitman's logic, current conditions can change and even the "social fundamentalists" may be able to find their way home once reunited around core Republican values. Furthermore, the comic perspective's primary tool is perspective by incongruity or irony (308–9). While it may appear incongruous for Whitman to call herself a Republican while she openly criticizes the conservative wing of the Republican Party, her version of Republican ideals, as learned growing up and embodied in her political life, comes alive for the reader and demonstrates the evidence in support of her claims. Perspective by incongruity becomes a reality in Whitman's final chapter, "A Time for Radical Moderates." As an allusion to Ronald Reagan's "A Time for Choosing," Whitman pairs together two terms not normally thought to co-exist, "radical" and "moderate." She acknowledges that the term "appears to be an oxymoron," but goes on to explain that "it is time for moderates in the Republican Party to become activists—activists for the sensible center, for reasonable policies based on fundamental Republican principles, which address the challenges America faces at home and in the world" (Whitman 228). She uses the incongruity to reframe what it means to be a Republican and energize those individuals who identify with her frustrations. As she frames the story:

> The basic principles that define Republicanism have not changed. We still believe in limited government, lower taxes, the power of the markets, and a strong national defense. Those basic core beliefs are shared by millions of Americans who, although they may not be comfortable with the rightward shift in the party, are not ready to give up on it. The way to change the party is from within. That is why I stay. (27)

The party she first embraced believed "that government had a responsibility for those who, through no fault of their own, were not able to claim their piece of all that America had to offer" (46). The Republican approach, according to Whitman, is "more respectful of people . . . [but] in a very real sense we've lost our way" (46). Through numerous examples Whitman claims value in Republicanism, or what she now identifies as "radical moderates," and demonstrates that value and worth in her own political actions. In an effort to claim value for her political life and reunite the party, she vows to stay and change it from within.

A large portion of the book recounts the efforts of Whitman's political life and calling through the theme of unity, or what Howarth would characterize as the "belief in a superior force" (371), an electorate and party committed to Republican ideals. Whitman's overall goal claims to "bring the Republican Party, and American politics generally, back toward the productive center" (Whitman

11). And each milestone in her political life presents an opportunity for consensus building. For example, Whitman remembers her Environmental Protection Agency (EPA) appointment fondly, thinking she "had the opportunity to work with Democrats to create an effective administration that could unite rather than divide the country" (14). She recalls the strong commitment that she "truly had a chance to build a consensus on how to move forward to achieve the next generation of environmental progress" (17). However, her efforts were not without their roadblocks.

Even though an undercurrent of disappointment resonates with her narrative of her EPA experiences, the optimism toward consensus remains. In fact, she devotes an entire chapter, "This Land is Our Land," to clarifying her environmental goals. Her vision going into the appointment was always to "build partnerships around shared goals for a better environment" (155). Time and again her perspective by incongruity comes into play: "The pursuit of environmental progress and economic prosperity were not mutually exclusive goals" (163). These apparent opposites demonstrate a "common sense" approach. She explains, "I regularly talked about common sense in environmental policy making, and I made the case clearly and consistently that environmental progress and economic prosperity are not mutually exclusive goals" (191). And she goes on to say, "unless we succeed in shifting the environmental debate away from the extremes and back to the sensible center, we will be unable to meet the challenges we face in a timely and responsible way" (195). Each story returns to the theme of unity and consensus, painting Whitman as a sensible, reasonable political actor who possesses the strength of character to persevere even in the most difficult of circumstances.

Recognizing the difference between winning at all costs and governing requires an ability to find common ground. Whitman warns the Republican Party: "The party must remember that while winning elections is surely important, it is every bit as important to win them in ways that allow you to govern all the people once the ballots are counted" (2). Whitman learned this philosophy from her parents, who "respected each other's views and . . . firmly believed that moderates and conservatives both had contributions to make to the success of the party. They knew that excluding one or the other would be political foolishness" (33). Much of the autobiography, then, illustrates the foolishness of the current partisan divide and, by contrast, the practical wisdom Whitman has found in the center as instilled by her parents.

Recalling the 1956 local election and her mother's job as an election official to ensure that ballots were counted fairly, Whitman remembers the trust she witnessed in the room. "Everyone in the room knew her role was only a formality; they all trusted one another. These people were, after all, friends and neighbors. After witnessing the bitter Florida recount, I marvel that scenes such as that were ever really possible" (40). But Whitman's optimism that those scenes are possible does indeed provide inspiration.

In another example she discusses the speech she delivered as co-chair of the 1996 Republican National Convention, which brought to the forefront Whitman's "abortion problem." A line in a draft version of Whitman's speech read, "for all our differences, whether over the issue of choice or gun control, our Party is united by this goal: electing Bob Dole the President of the United States" (80). Yet, this line had the convention planners up in arms. "This simple declarative statement," recalls Whitman, "was hardly earth-shattering, yet you would think I was calling for state-sponsored infanticide" (80). Refusing to give up, Whitman ad-libbed the line back into the speech when she delivered it, infuriating some of the attendees. She explains her actions as important for the party. "It would be a sad day for the Republican Party if we couldn't even mention the fact that we had differences. . . . I didn't think we should repeat the error the Democrats made in 1992 when they had denied then Pennsylvania governor Bob Casey the opportunity to make a brief speech on abortion at their convention because he was pro-life" (80). Finally, political consultants came out of the woodwork to advise Whitman on how to solve her "abortion problem," urging that she "modif[y] her pro-choice position to make it more acceptable to pro-life voters" (81). Whitman saw their advice as "less than honest" and wasn't about to change her beliefs.

Finding a point in the center doesn't mean giving up your own beliefs; it merely requires focusing on the larger goal despite differences on how to get there. Such an approach comes across as practical rather than extreme, emphasizing common sense and collaboration rather than exclusion or division. Rhetorically, it constructs the political process as one of civil deliberation rather than winning and losing. Whitman's viewpoint is a breath of fresh air in today's divisive climate and her example is instructive in how to advance such a philosophy even though at times it is not successful.

Balance, consensus, and unity around the ideals of the Republican Party that were and are Whitman's life frame Whitman's autobiography as oratory. Through these characteristics, *It's My Party Too* clearly functions to fulfill Howarth's notion of the oratorical autobiography. As Whitman explains, "through most of my public life, despite the challenges, a career in politics has been a good fit for me—it has enabled me to balance the demands of my career with the priorities of my family while allowing me to make a difference" (Whitman 211). In other words, Whitman, as the protagonist of the drama, demonstrates her faith and devotion to political doctrine, her strength of character, and the calling or vocation that has demanded she make a difference. The hallmark of Whitman's political character is indeed her effort at building strong coalitions that respect a variety of viewpoints. The reviewers of her book appear to have caught on to that piece of the story as well. Matt Miller, writing in the *New York Times*, claims: "In passages that will surely bore the pundits but possibly resonate with normal Americans, Whitman repeatedly makes the case for a productive political center" (15). And if Whitman's claims resonate with "normal Americans" as Miller suggests, *It's My Party Too* appears to have capitalized on the rhetorical resources of autobiography as well.

Rhetorical Resources of Autobiography

As autobiography, the central argument of *It's My Party Too* necessitates a narrative form. The narrative paradigm, according to Walter Fisher, views human beings as essentially storytellers. He asserts that stories, in order to demonstrate narrative rationality or "good reasons," must possess narrative probability, a sense of coherence, and narrative fidelity, whether the stories "ring true" with what the audience knows to be true (Fisher 8). "The operative principle of narrative rationality is identification" (9). Martha Solomon extends Fisher's argument to explain that oratorical works written by leaders of a movement "serve as an inspirational model for followers and as a tool for recruiting new members" (355). The details of the life offer "implicit arguments or 'good reasons' for supporting a cause" (355). According to Thomas Benson, autobiography possesses the ability "to summon the power of direct experience" (Series vii).

As sustained narratives, autobiographies offer special rhetorical resources to the author. According to Solomon, autobiographies depict the emergence of the author's beliefs from personal experience "and the ability to demonstrate the feasibility and desirability of enacting the tenets of their doctrine" (355). Whitman most effectively demonstrates this characteristic in the second chapter of *It's My Party Too*, titled "Whatever Happened to the Big Umbrella?" In this chapter, Whitman puts into words why she is a Republican. She starts from the beginning. The notion of umbrella comes from her father. As Whitman recalls, "the most important part of an umbrella is a central stick. Everything else depends on that strong central core, and although each of the ribs that radiates off the central sticks helps give shape to and supports the umbrella's canopy, without that connection to the center, they aren't much use" (Whitman 30). This analogy works its way through the remainder of the book and serves as an object lesson for the practical ideology that has framed Whitman's life. As Whitman explains at the conclusion of this chapter, "it's time for moderates to lead an effort to unfurl the party's big umbrella and make room, once again, for all those who share in the fundamental principles for which the party has long stood, putting an end to the narrow litmus tests that are dividing our party and which could ultimately lead it back into the political wilderness" (70). Though readers may disagree with Republicanism as it is currently configured, who can disagree with the practical explanation of the importance of the center stick to the umbrella or with the critique of the division that currently faces our country? Here autobiography works rhetorically to demonstrate the desirability of working from the center, the hallmark of Whitman's political life.

Secondly, Solomon argues that the nature of autobiographies "enhances the persuasive force of this depiction and enactment for the receptive reader" (355). She also contends that "autobiographies complement and supplement formal arguments by offering sustained, personal examples of a particular ideology enacted in a real life" (355). In Whitman's autobiography, each chapter offers sustained personal examples around a particular theme. Whether it is the rise of the social fundamentalists within the Republican Party and the challenges they pose to moderates like Whitman on the issues of religious faith, abortion, stem

cell research, gay marriage, attracting African Americans to the Party, preserving the environment, or the challenges of being a woman in politics, Whitman
demonstrates her claim as living proof of its enactment.

Furthermore, Whitman herself admits her own shortcomings, an important
characteristic for achieving Fisher's narrative rationality. For example, when
planning her first inaugural as governor in 1993, bands from each of New Jersey's counties were invited. The problem was that "even without thinking about
it, every band they selected came from predominantly white high schools . . .
because the people in charge of selecting the bands went to people they knew"
(Whitman 116). She "had appointed an inaugural event committee with little
diversity" (116). Admitting and learning from mistakes is an important feature
of a political autobiography as it communicates a persona that is human, fallible,
rather than one that is god-like. Such human qualities enhance the believability
of the narrative because they define characters with whom readers can identify.

Autobiographies as rhetorical narratives build identification between the
author and readers in an effort to engage the reader. *It's My Party Too* creates
identification through the use of self-disclosure and humor. In one story, Whitman details how she learned "what a tricky thing a photo op is" (37). Whitman
attended her first Republican National Convention at the young age of nine.
While this fact could work to suggest her privileged political upbringing, Whitman instead recalls a story that was rather embarrassing for her mother, a story
with which many readers might be able to identify on several levels. The 1956
RNC was held in San Francisco and Whitman's mother, Eleanor Todd, was a
convention official, so the young Christie had the run of the convention hall.
Apparently, after a trip to Disneyland, Christie came back to the hall wearing a
favorite souvenir, a hat with a fake dagger through her head. At the same time
her mother was in a press conference as a member of the Arrangements Committee, and Whitman recalls that it was rather boring. "So before too long, some
of the reporters were practically begging me (and my hat) to join my mother in
the front of the room. Without thinking . . . I did. Flashes suddenly started going
off and, needless to say, that was the picture that ran alongside all the stories
about the press conference in the San Francisco papers the next day" (37). The
experience creates identification through the use of humor, and it provides an
opening through which Whitman can reveal through childlike eyes the pageantry
and importance of the political process as she learned it.

As a result, autobiographies work inductively, using the strategy of enactment as proof for the common sense nature of their claims. The rhetor, capitaliz-
ing on identification, depicts herself as a regular woman who struggles, rather
than as a god-like figure larger who is than life. According to Solomon, autobiographies offer an opportunity for "rhetors to demonstrate the impact of an ideology on a life" (363). Whitman's commitment to core Republican values has
influenced her life and personality. Her "enactment of . . . beliefs, narrated in
[her] autobiograph[y], is compelling proof of the healthy influence of" (363)
Republican ideology as she lives it.

Autobiography as Activist Text

Audience resonance must be achieved in texts such as Whitman's that also contain a persuasive agenda. According to Martha Watson, the women activists she studied write autobiographies as "agents for a larger social group that seeks social justice. . . . In short, they become social activists because the scene impels them to act to assure a noble goal" (104–5). Relying on the autobiographical form is a wise rhetorical choice, according to Watson, because "even if the reader lacks sympathy for the particular cause advocated, the author is seen as an admirable figure who endures struggle and hardship for a goal beyond herself. Such sacrifice and dedication can inspire followers to sustained action, resolving that such efforts shall not have been in vain" (105). Whitman's example serves as such inspiration. She is a woman of character seeking to change the system in which she finds herself, not by changing her beliefs, but by asserting those beliefs even in a time when it is not popular to do so.

Whitman advocates changing politics as we know it, and in particular the Republican Party, "from within." "Too often," Whitman writes, "our politics focuses solely on winning an ideological battle without any concern for how the way the victory is achieved might affect the winner's ability to govern. If we can change that dynamic, we will change our politics, and our country, for the better" (Whitman 27). As Whitman records her life, she demonstrates the importance, value, and significance of her cause and implicitly urges the readers' action. Whitman's activist agenda includes "recruiting bright, capable, articulate, Republican minority and women candidates at the local level and . . . grooming them, like it [the Republican Party] does any other candidate, for higher office" (Whitman 232). It includes "fill[ing] the gap that has been left by the current political leadership by taking the lead in building a significant minority presence in the GOP" (233). It includes "reclaim[ing] for the party the issue of fiscal responsibility" (233), becoming "more vocal and insistent . . . in the conduct of America's foreign policy" (235), "actively searching for means to engage the world in ways that are consistent with, and advantageous to, our own national interest" (237), "advocating a renewed effort to build an international coalition of our major allies to bring Iraq into the family of nations" (239), "lead[ing] the way to more positive, issues-oriented campaigns at every level of government" (242), and overall simply "ensuring that the party follows the right path" (243).

Whitman's activist agenda comes across unmistakably, and this book represents only the first step. In the final paragraph of the book, she directs the reader to a web site that holds more information: www.mypartytoo.com. Since the writing of the book, Whitman has formed a political action committee, also called It's My Party Too, and affiliates and chapters in nearly thirty states have emerged to date. The agenda of the book promotes more than a large readership. The timing of Whitman's release, just following the 2004 election, provides ample opportunity to motivate a grassroots political organization in time for the election season of 2008.

Correcting the Political Record

Political autobiographies as activist texts argue for the correction of public perceptions, providing the public with information not necessarily communicated in the prevailing storyline. Estelle Jelinek claims that autobiographies are the author's "effort to rectify what they see as the public's misconception of them, an effort not only to authenticate who they really are but also to prove their worth as human beings" (*Tradition* 186). Watson elaborates on this point, arguing that "for a person deeply involved in a cause . . . writing a life is an accounting for decisions and actions. To adopt Burkean terminology, [autobiographers] depict themselves as agents who act in specific ways (agency) in particular circumstances (scene) to accomplish a clear end (purpose)" (103). Whitman displays herself as a radical moderate Republican woman searching for the "productive middle" in order to help the GOP rediscover its core values and advance a better future for America. Margo Perkins' account of Black women activist autobiographies states that activist autobiographies:

> seek to provide that side of the story silenced or distorted in hegemonic accounts of the period. . . . Activists who write autobiography aim to fill in or recast important information about key events or issues in the struggle that have been elided in the dominant accounts of the period. On another level, writing autobiography also affords activists one means of recuperating their own public image. (70–71)

Whitman takes every opportunity to set the record straight on her decision-making both as governor and as EPA administrator.

Whitman's public image was badly tarnished during her tenure as President George W. Bush's EPA administrator, and the chapter titled "This Land Is Our Land" functions forcefully to right/write the public record. Here Whitman explains her commitment to the environment and the decisions she made while in office. Three decisions in particular revealed that she and the president were at odds when it came to environmental policy: the Kyoto protocol, arsenic levels in drinking water, and the Clear Skies initiative. The decision on arsenic levels in drinking water will serve as just one example of Whitman's efforts to correct the public record.

As Whitman explains the arsenic issue, it was a "last minute" decision by the Clinton administration to lower the acceptable level of arsenic in drinking water from 50 parts per billion to 10, and the water companies had until 2006 to comply. While she had approved the same level in New Jersey while governor, she wanted more time to investigate whether 10 ppb was indeed the most appropriate level nationwide as well as the implications of such a change for water companies and their customers. In other words, she attempted to mediate environmental protection and business interests, and the primary way she did that was through scientific investigation. Her decision comes across as very reasonable in the narrative. She acknowledged that the current 50 ppb was too high, but that EPA staff "had not fully calculated, to my satisfaction, whether meeting the new standard would be affordable for the five thousand small water companies . . . where arsenic occurs naturally in ground water supplies" (Whitman 158). Whitman also explains that she "wanted to avoid what had happened in New River, Arizona, where the local water company shut down because the cost of upgrading its treatment system to meet the 50 ppb standard was too high" (158). Finally, she argues that putting off the measure to assess the relevant costs would not do harm since the measure would not go into effect until 2006. While the autobiographical form provides Whitman the time and space to explicate her decisions, that luxury is not always present to political officials in the moment.

Aware of the political turmoil such a decision might cause, Whitman admits that the announcement would require a thorough explanation detailing why the extra time was necessary, "and we had to emphasize that there was no doubt that we would end up lowering the standard—and I tried" (159). But as Whitman suggests, she "was frankly stunned by the firestorm this decision ignited. Rather than get any credit for a sincere effort to get a new regulation right, the administration's political enemies pounced. [Her] decision was perceived as a golden opportunity to portray the president as an enemy of the environment" (160). One newspaper headline even claimed "EPA to allow more arsenic in water" (160), which was clearly not the case. "I found these attacks absolutely outrageous, well beyond the bounds of typical partisan rhetoric," Whitman maintains. "We weren't forcing anyone to drink arsenic-laced water, we weren't rolling back existing regulations, and we most certainly were not raising the acceptable levels and urging kids to increase their intake of arsenic. Yet the truth was no match for the vitriol we had unleashed" (160). At the end of the story, "after receiving the advice of the National Academy of Sciences and after securing money to develop technology to find more affordable methods of removing arsenic from water supplies . . . we lowered the standard to exactly where it had been proposed, to 10 ppb; and we made it effective in 2006, exactly when it was first proposed" (160). Whitman recounts statements by Al Gore, Bill Clinton, and Dick Gephardt claiming the administration tried to *increase* arsenic levels. What comes across in this narrative is that Whitman acted reasonably and sincerely, trying to find a balance between environmental protection and business interests. She uses the autobiography as an effort to correct the public record on some very controversial decisions during her time in office.

Not only did Whitman have the environmental lobbies and Democrats to deal with, which was no surprise, but also those within the Republican Party forcefully lobbied the president on a variety of issues, from stem cell research and gay marriage to environmental protection. This "party within the party," as Whitman calls them, was a more formidable source of opposition with which she had to contend, and several chapters of the autobiography allow her to set the record straight. An event from her EPA tenure again serves as a useful example. In Whitman's first trip as EPA administrator, she met with the other G8 ministers to solidify the President's campaign commitment to environmental protection. However, before Whitman had even returned from the trip, "the administration abruptly reversed itself in a way that would have serious consequences" (168). As Whitman explained, "I assured my G8 counterparts that the president's campaign commitment to seek a mandatory cap on carbon dioxide emissions was solid and that the administration sincerely agreed that global climate change was a serious problem that demanded attention" (172). She states that she "was pleased that things had started off so well" (172). However, Whitman was later called into the president's office, and she quickly realized that she "was there to be told that he had decided to reverse himself. He knew that his decision was leaving me out on a limb, and he apologized for that," but he believed that the potential U.S. energy crisis made it a bad time to impose additional environmental regulations on utilities. While Whitman explained to the president her balanced solution in which "the president could keep his promise to cap carbon dioxide emissions, without threatening the energy supply . . . the White House didn't see it that way" (175–76). The section then describes the strong effort the social fundamentalists made to secure the President's support for their approach to managing the environment.

Despite their differences of opinion, Whitman insists on President Bush's commitment to the environment. However, she does level harsh criticism that resonates more broadly than just environmental policy:

> The administration's insistence on playing strictly to the base in explaining the president's opposition to ratifying the Kyoto Protocol, coupled with his reversal on the regulation of carbon dioxide, was an early expression of the go-it-alone attitude that so offended our allies in the lead-up to the Iraq war. The roots of our difficulties in forging a strong multinational alliance to fight terrorism go all the way back to how we handled Kyoto as well as other international issues, including our participation in the International Criminal Court and the imposition of steel tariffs. (78–79)

This comment resonates with many Americans who may find fault with current U.S. efforts in Iraq. Further, this example, while it gives voice to Whitman's version of the story, also indicates her displeasure with the decisions of the administration and provides additional evidence of her commitment to balance in spite of the obstacles with which she was faced.

Watson explains that autobiographers "depict themselves as agents who struggle against a scene of injustice and inequality" (103). This depiction materializes in *It's My Party Too* in which Whitman struggles not only with the opposition party, but also against the "social fundamentalists" who have hijacked the Republican Party. Watson goes on to explain that the struggles of autobiographers "are largely for the benefit of others. Without exception, as they write their lives, their efforts have not been fully successful" (104). Whitman must explain why she made the decisions she did and make it clear her lack of success was because of the stubborn social fundamentalists standing in her way. "The tension between the scene—what is—and the purpose—what ought to be—

becomes the explanation for their controversial activities and behaviors. In their depictions they become the agents who struggle to alter the scene" (Watson 104). Whitman's autobiography illustrates her efforts to alter the political scene, to change it for the better, sometimes successfully and sometimes not.

The Personal is Political

Jelinek argues that women's political autobiographies may not necessarily unfold chronologically. As she explains, "disjunctive narratives and discontinuous forms are more adequate for mirroring the fragmentation and multidimensionality of women's lives" (*Tradition* 188). Whitman's *It's My Party Too* is no different. The first chapter articulates Whitman's major claim about taking back the Republican Party from the social fundamentalists. Throughout this chapter, she intersperses stories and anecdotes that illustrate what she knows or has learned through experience. The stories aren't necessarily chronological in nature, but illustrate the intersections between the public and political life. For example, Whitman discusses the speakers at the 2004 Republican National Convention, admitting that it was the best since 1988 "from where she sat" because she "felt at home among" her fellow Republicans (Whitman 8). Two pages later she recalls her early days as President Bush's EPA administrator and the reaction of some Republican congressmen who did not believe a Republican could ever get a favorable editorial in the *New York Times*. She concludes that "from my experience in politics, on most questions the middle ground is the only productive ground" (10). Then a few pages later she recalls her first meeting with Vice President Cheney, her "first job in Washington in 1969," and her boss Donald Rumsfeld (15). The story itself isn't necessarily chronological in nature, but the fragments work together to create a coherent narrative, relying on argument from personal history to illustrate the type of Republican woman who can make it in politics. Hers is a life that can be imitated, not a larger-than-life picture, encouraging others to become active as well. As Perkins argues, "activists' texts repeatedly reveal that there is little separation between the two realms: i.e., what is personal is almost always political and vice versa. The effectiveness of . . . narratives as political intervention relies in part on their skill as storytellers: their ability to map the personal onto the larger political terrain in provocative and engaging ways" (Perkins 100).

The autobiographical form provides many resources for the autobiographer, including the narrative force of making an argument as well as the ability to right/write the political record in the rhetor's own words toward presenting, in Whitman's case, her approach to finding the sensible center as a way to manage political decision-making. Such a sensible approach not only illustrates the intersection between the personal and political life, it opens the door to capitalize on identification as a strategy for advancing the activist agenda of the political autobiography. One additional resource for women's political autobiographies in particular is the important opportunity it creates to discuss the role of women in politics. By way of identification, Whitman's narrative resonates with the stories of other women in positions of leadership and gives voice to a story that has been historically absent from politics.

Women and Politics

While Whitman has faced many challenges, her acute awareness of the additional hurdles women face in the political world demonstrate for the reader how to manage them. For example, after college, in her first political job with the Republican National Committee, she had "one of [her] first exposures to just how far women had to go to be taken seriously in politics" (Whitman 65). She recalls a newsletter put out by the New Jersey State Republican Committee in which her new position at the RNC was discussed. The story read, "'Good luck and good learning to Chris Todd. . . . She's papa bear's pretty bundle of charm, wit, and political savvy'" (65). Whitman recalls that even today the tone of the story angers her.

Whitman devotes an entire chapter to the special challenges she has faced as a woman, titled "A Woman in the Party." The stories range from a lack of respect and stereotypes plaguing women in political roles to special skills she believes women have in politics, to special victories Whitman has achieved for herself and other political women. One important piece of advice has to do with role models, and how desperately young women aspiring to political roles need experienced women to step into a mentoring relationship. Additionally, the chapter underscores one of the important themes of Whitman's consensus building ideology, that of political relationships as the root of political decision-making and leadership.

Stereotypes clearly pervade the perceptions of women in political roles. In 1969, Whitman worked in the Office of Economic Opportunity for Donald Rumsfeld. Bill Bradley, the basketball star and eventual Senator, was to be a summer intern working *for* Whitman. Apparently, that was not communicated effectively to Bradley. Whitman says, "imagine my surprise when, on his first day in the office, he was introduced to me and then promptly asked me to get him a cup of coffee—no doubt because I was a young woman, and I was there. I quickly explained that he was there to work with me; I was not there to work for him. I also told him where he could get his coffee (and resisted the temptation to tell him what he could do with it)" (206). Whitman uses the story to discuss how unusual it was for women to have political jobs at the time, but even decades later the condescending tone still pervades the ways that women are perceived and discussed. Not only do the media write stories about women that reinforce gender stereotypes, but also the Republican Party was not as supportive of Whitman's 1990 senate race as she would have liked. Her nearly four decades of experience in politics allow her a degree of perspective on the role of women in politics, and even though times have changed, the challenges facing women have not. She states emphatically that there are still some conventions in politics that "are designed to marginalize women" (217).

Furthermore, Whitman believes, based on her experience, that "voters still hold women candidates to a different, and in some ways, more rigorous standard than they do their male counterparts, and women voters are tougher on women politicians than they are on most men. These reasons may be why far too few women serve in public office at the state and national level" (202–3). The odds were long, but Whitman somehow managed to succeed in New Jersey, and she attributes her success, in part, to faring better than anyone thought in her early race against Bill Bradley. Had she actually had the financial support of the Republican National Committee, like she was promised, she might have had the resources to mount the ad campaign that any winning candidate needs. Whitman's critique adds another example to the mounting evidence about financial viability that is increasingly necessary for any political candidate. Financial resources also suggest a political network; in other words, the root of any successful campaign is a network of supporters. Political relationships are key to success.

Another secret of Whitman's success lies with her luck in simply growing up "with strong female role models in my mother and grandmother, both of whom carved places for themselves in politics separate from their husbands" (199–200). Whitman provides the following advice:

> A woman (especially one who also takes pride in being a wife and mother) who hopes to pursue a successful political career requires more than inspiration, however; she requires support from her family, and I have had that in abundance. What has made my career in politics possible was my good fortune in having a strong partner with whom to share the demands of political life, my husband, John. While politics provided a good fit for me as I was able to balance the demands of young children with part-time political office holding, having the support of my spouse was key. Had John not been there to attend school functions I had to miss or to drive the kids to various events when I couldn't, none of it would have worked. He not only filled the gaps my career created . . . but he was also my chief cheerleader and supporter, urging me on even when I was ready to call it quits. (200)

She has succeeded because of relationships, and in particular family relationships, including a supportive spouse. One additional challenge political women sometimes face is the lack of someone to fulfill a "first spouse" role. While her husband John may not have given up his busy career to become Whitman's "first gentleman," he did provide the support and stability that anyone in politics requires in order to manage public and private life challenges.

Whitman continually emphasizes throughout *It's My Party Too* the importance of collaboration, consensus, and creative problem-solving in managing political decision-making. She believes that as a woman, she may have an edge in this strategy and that there are indeed "many benefits in politics to being a woman" (218). For example, she believes "women bring a different perspective and a different set of life experiences to their jobs than men. . . . We also tend, I think, to set a different tone" (220). Whitman tells of many compliments she has received by individuals with whom she has worked over the years:

> They were impressed that in my offices, people worked together much more collegially than they did in offices run by men. There was less competition to see who got the credit when things went right and who got the blame when things went wrong. Instead, they saw a greater sense of teamwork, where people sought to work with one another in pursuit of larger goals, rather than pursue their own personal goals at the expense of others. I always felt that my responsibility was to find the best person for a job, set out the agenda and goals, and let them find creative ways to get there. I was never uncomfortable with the fact that I couldn't know, or do, everything. (221)

She also admits that being a woman means that there were different things that "got on the legislative agenda—and agenda setting is one of the most important aspects of governing" (222). Whitman sees her gender as an advantage that can overshadow the very real stereotypes, misperceptions, and obstacles facing women in political roles.

In order for women to capitalize on those potential advantages, there must be more women in politics, and Whitman feels obligated "to bring more women in to the arena" (225). To that end, she mentions the Whitman Series, a mentoring program designed to bring more women into political roles. She also discusses organizations supported by both parties designed to help women overcome some of the institutional barriers to their success in politics, such as the WISH List and EMILY's List.

All in all, *It's My Party Too* serves as an inspiration to women hoping to enter the world of politics. Whitman offers a wealth of experiences from which other women can learn. She emphasizes the importance of relationship building, role models, and mentors in order to achieve political success. And she embodies those values she advocates, relying on networks, collaboration, and building consensus in her political life. Her story resonates not only with Republican women, but also with any woman hoping to make it in politics.

This chapter has argued that Christine Todd Whitman's *It's My Party Too* not only demonstrates William L. Howarth's characteristics of oratorical autobiography but also capitalizes on the rhetorical resources of autobiography in advancing Whitman's activist agenda for politics as we know it. The text as an activist document creates identification with the reader as it illustrates the "good reasons" on which Republican ideology is premised, with Whitman as the embodiment of those lived experiences. Whitman's endeavors serve an important mentoring function for other women aspiring to a political life as she demonstrates how she overcame financial and stereotypical obstacles to achieve political success.

Many have speculated that the publication of her autobiography signals that Christine Todd Whitman's days in politics are not over. The activist theme in the work, in particular the detailed efforts at righting the public record, demonstrates Whitman's great care and thoughtfulness in making decisions and giving a voice to as many people affected by those decisions as possible. In an era when women public figures still receive media coverage and battle public perceptions different from their male counterparts, Whitman has taken her political future into her own hands through the rhetorical resources of the activist autobiography. Through this example, women public figures have yet another means at their disposal for the dissemination of political information, enhancing their political agency and inspiring them to believe that change remains a viable goal.

Conclusion

Never underestimate the importance of what we are doing here. Never hesitate to tell the truth. And never, ever give in or give up.

—Bella Abzug

"The typical autobiography," suggests Wayne Shumaker in *English Autobiography: Its Emergence, Materials, and Forum*, "is a summing up, a review of the whole life or an important segment of it" (103). As evidenced in the preceding chapters, however, the autobiographies of women political leaders contain far more than simply interesting stories or "summations." Instead, the arguments detailed throughout this book suggest these life stories perform several functions. For example, the personal narratives describe the "textual space" in which women operate and to which they must respond (Gilmore 85). The autobiographies examined in this volume reveal that this "textual" or "in-between space" (Mayhead and Marshall 13) blends the personal with the political and vice versa, creating a synergy between these two seemingly oppositional categories of lived experience. As Arlyn Diamond suggests, "the value of autobiography . . . is not the suppression of the subject in the realm of the social, or in abstract lessons, but in the fascinating interplay between the political and personal which forms our lives" (231). This notion becomes even more obvious when one considers that once these women publish their autobiographies they make their "personal dreams and nightmares," beliefs and values, decisions and actions "part of the public discourse" (Sayre, "Proper" 258). As several of these autobiographers argue in their narratives, political dialogues in the twenty-first century must consider the entirety of the human condition.

The events women leaders recount in their personal narratives and the decisions they describe play a significant historical and cultural role: they construct an identity that intersects with the socio-cultural milieu (Barat 165). This identity has the power to shape communities, interest groups, observers, and perhaps even government itself. In their autobiographies, the women represented in this study have woven the threads of their identities into a tapestry, declaring their positions on "sexuality, race, gender, class" as well as "politics, law, science and communities" (Gilmore 224). As Hayden White points out in his treatise on historical narratives, writings such as autobiographies entail choices "with distinct ideological and even specifically political implications" (ix). While much remains to be accomplished, one cannot deny the collective impact the discourses of these political women and others like them have had on U.S. society.

Women leaders achieve offices of power and influence in part because of the diligence with which they advance their political ideologies and the success they achieve in operationalizing those priorities. These ideologies appear not only in official government documents, interviews, or speeches; the personal stories contained in women's political autobiographies, such as those discussed in this book, provide the underpinnings of and arguments about these belief systems. The narratives both embody and explicate the political and rhetorical strategies these leaders employ in their efforts to act on their convictions.

By rising to positions of power not readily or usually extended to females, the authors of these autobiographies serve as powerful symbols to inspire other women to enter the field of politics. Some of these women specifically use their work to encourage, instruct, and empower contemporary and future women leaders. The politicians studied in this volume have produced dynamic, interesting, and instructive stories. As demonstrated in each chapter, these works provide an understanding of the intersection between the personal and political and illustrate triumphs and obstacles each woman encountered as she negotiated the gendered boundaries of politics. The autobiographies serve not only as a recorded history of the past, but also as a clarion call to future generations of women to lead. In answering the question, "Why an American-focused women's anthology now [in 2003]?," feminist writer Robin Morgan replies:

> Because American women are nowhere near finished with *our* revolution, for *ourselves*. Because what happens here is also critical to the entire world. Because like it or not, this is now the sole superpower, and every U.S. policy has global ripple effects. Because the world comes *to* us: approximately one million immigrants arrive in the United States each year; 52 percent from Latin America, 30 percent from Asia, 13 percent from Europe. Because such realizations should inspire not guilt—a paralyzing counterproductive emotion—but *action*. Because *what you and I do matters. How* we do it means understanding what we have (and haven't) done. (italics orig., Morgan xxvii)

In telling their political lives, Barbara Jordan, Patricia Schroeder, Geraldine Ferraro, Elizabeth Dole, Wilma Mankiller, Hillary Rodham Clinton, Madeleine Albright, and Christine Todd Whitman have reiterated their belief that what each person accomplishes in her life matters. Once again they have demonstrated their commitment to women's active leadership, to making a difference for all. Both the autobiographies of these remarkable females and the discussions of their personal narratives highlight the need for and reality of women's involvement in all levels of politics and serve as impetus and inspiration for scholars and activists alike.

Bibliography

Abzug, Bella. "Women's Environment and Development Organisation." Plenary speech, United Nations Development Programme, United Nations Fourth World Conference on Women, Beijing, China, September 12, 1995. United Nations Economics and Social Development. http://www.un.org/esa/.

Agnew, Brad. "Wilma Mankiller: Cherokee." In *The New Warriors: Native American Leaders since 1900*, edited by R. David Edmunds. Lincoln, NE: University of Nebraska Press, 2001.

Alabi, Adetayo. *Telling Our Stories: Continuities and Divergences in Black Autobiographies*. New York: Palgrave Macmillan, 2005.

Albright, Madeleine. *Madame Secretary: A Memoir*. With Bill Woodward. New York: Miramax, 2003.

Anderson, Karrin Vasby, and Kristina Horn Sheeler. *Governing Codes: Gender, Metaphor, and Political Identity*. Lanham, MD: Lexington Books, 2005.

Anderson, Linda. *Women and Autobiography in the Twentieth Century: Remembered Futures*. London: Prentice Hall/Harvester Wheatsheaf, 1997.

Andrews, William L. *African American Autobiography: A Collection of Critical Essays*. Englewood Cliffs, NJ: Prentice Hall, 1993.

———. "African-American Autobiography Criticism: Retrospect and Prospect." In *American Autobiography: Retrospect and Prospect*, edited by Paul John Eakin, 195–215. Wisconsin Studies in American Autobiography. Madison, WI: University of Wisconsin Press, 1991.

———. "Dialogue in Antebellum Afro-American Autobiography." In *Studies in Autobiography*, edited by James Olney, 89–98. New York: Oxford University Press, 1988.

———. Introduction. In *African American Autobiography: A Collection of Critical Essays*, edited by William L. Andrews, 1–7. Englewood Cliffs, NJ: Prentice Hall, 1993.

———. Introduction. In *Sisters of the Spirit: Three Black Women's Autobiographies of the Nineteenth Century*, edited by William L. Andrews, 1–22. Bloomington, IN: Indiana University Press, 1986.

———, ed. *Sisters of the Spirit: Three Black Women's Autobiographies of the Nineteenth Century*. Bloomington, IN: Indiana University Press, 1986.

———. *To Tell a Free Story: The First Century of Afro-American Autobiography, 1760–1865*. Urbana, IL: University of Illinois Press, 1986.

———. "Toward a Poetics of Afro-American Autobiography." In *Afro-American Literary Study in the 1990s*, edited by Houston A. Baker Jr., and Patricia Redmond, 78-91. Chicago: University of Chicago Press, 1989.

Arrington, Ruth M. "Some American Indian Voices: Resources in Intercultural Rhetoric and Interpretation." *The Speech Teacher* 24 (1975): 191–94.

Asante, Molefi Kete. *The Afrocentric Idea*. Rev. and exp. ed. Philadelphia: Temple University Press, 1998.
———. *Afrocentricity*. Rev. ed. Trenton, NJ: Africa World Press, 1988.
———. *See also* Smith, Arthur L.
Auster, Elizabeth. "Hillary Tells Just Enough For Now." *Plain Dealer*, June 22, 2003: G3. LexisNexis Academic. http://www.lexisnexis.com/.
Barat, Erzsebet. "The Discourse of Selfhood: Oral Autobiographies as Narrative Sites For Construction of Identity." In *Representing Lives: Women and Auto/biography*, edited by Alison Donnel and Pauline Polkey, 165–73. London: Macmillan 2000.
Barrington, Judith. *Writing the Memoir: From Truth to Art*. Portland, OR: Eighth Mountain Press, 1997.
Benson, Thomas. "Rhetoric and Autobiography: The Case of Malcolm X." *Quarterly Journal of Speech* 60.1 (1974): 1–13.
———. Series Editor's Preface. In *Lives of Their Own: Rhetorical Dimensions in Autobiographies of Women Activists*, by Martha Watson, vii–viii. Columbia, SC: University of South Carolina Press, 1999.
Bjorklund, Diane. *Interpreting the Self: Two Hundred Years of American Autobiography*. Chicago: University of Chicago Press, 1998.
Black, Allida. "Jordan, Barbara." In *Notable American Women: A Biographical Dictionary Completing the Twentieth Century*, edited by Susan Ware, 327–29. Cambridge, MA: Belknap/Harvard University Press, 2004.
Blackburn, Regina. "In Search of the Black Female Self: African-American Women's Autobiographies and Ethnicity." In *Women's Autobiography: Essays in Criticism*, edited by Estelle C. Jelinek, 133–48. Bloomington, IN: Indiana University Press, 1980.
Blanche, Jerry D., ed. *Native American Reader: Stories, Speeches and Poems*. Juneau, AK: Denali Press, 1990.
Blewett, Neal. "The Personal Writings of Politicians." In *Australian Political Lives: Chronicling Political Careers and Administrative Histories*, edited by Tracey Arklay, Johon Nethercote, and John Wanna. n. p. Canberra, AU: ANU E Press, 2006. ANU E Press. http://epress.anu.edu.au.
Boulware, Marcus H. *The Oratory of Negro Leaders: 1900–1968*. Westport, CT: Negro Universities Press, 1969.
Braden, Waldo W., ed. *Oratory in the New South*. Baton Rouge, LA: Louisiana State University Press, 1979.
Braxton, Joanne M. *Black Women Writing Autobiography: A Tradition Within a Tradition*. Philadelphia: Temple University Press, 1989.
Brée, Germaine. "Autogynography." In *Studies in Autobiography*, edited by James Olney, 171–79. New York: Oxford University Press, 1988.
Breslin, Rosemary, and Joshua Hammer. *Gerry! A Woman Making History*. New York: Pinnacle Books, 1984.
Brignano, Russell C. *Black Americans in Autobiography: An Annotated Bibliography of Autobiographies and Autobiographical Books Written since the Civil War*. Rev. and exp. ed. Durham, NC: Duke University Press, 1984.
Briscoe, Mary Louise. "Political Autobiography." *American Notes & Queries* 16.1 (1977): 6–8. Academic Search Premier. http://web.ebscohost.com.
Brodzki, Bella, and Celeste Schenck, eds. *Life Lines: Theorizing Women's Autobiography*. Ithaca, NY: Cornell University Press, 1988.

Bronikowski, Lynn. "An Eventful Life; Hillary Clinton's Book Not Just About Scandal: It Touches Hearts Too." *Rocky Mountain News*, June 18, 2003: 9D. LexisNexis Academic. http://www.lexisnexis.com/.

Brownley, Martine Watson, and Allison B. Kimmich, eds. *Women and Autobiography.* Wilmington, DE: Scholarly Resources, 1999.

Brumble, H. David III. *American Indian Autobiography.* Berkeley and Los Angeles, CA: University of California Press, 1988.

Bruss, Elizabeth W. *Autobiographical Acts: The Changing Situation of a Literary Genre.* Baltimore, MD: Johns Hopkins University Press, 1976.

Burgchardt, Carl R. "Barbara Charline Jordan (1936–1996): Texas Senator, U.S. Representative." In *American Voices: An Encyclopedia of Contemporary Orators*, edited by Bernard K. Duffy and Richard W. Leeman, 217–24. Westport, CT: Greenwood, 2005.

Burke, Kenneth. *Attitudes Toward History.* 3rd ed. Berkeley and Los Angeles, CA: University of California Press, 1984.

Bush, George W. "Bush Speech on Tribal Sovereignty." Response to Journalist Mark Trahant. Unity Journalists of Color Convention, Washington, D.C., August 6, 2004. "Bushisms: Adventures in George W. Bushspeak," About.com: Political Humor. http://politicalhumor.about.com/.

Cahill, Susan, ed. *Writing Women's Lives: An Anthology of Autobiographical Narratives by Twentieth-Century American Women Writers.* New York: HarperPerennial, 1994.

Calloway-Thomas, Carolyn, and John Louis Lucaites, eds. *Martin Luther King, Jr., and the Sermonic Power of Public Discourse.* Tuscaloosa, AL: University of Alabama Press, 1993.

Campbell, Karlyn Kohrs. "The Rhetoric of Women's Liberation: An Oxymoron." *Quarterly Journal of Speech* 59 (1973): 74–86.

Carpenter, Ronald H. *History as Rhetoric: Style, Narrative, and Persuasion.* Columbia, SC: University of South Carolina Press, 1995.

Clinton, Bill. *My Life.* New York: Knopf, 2004.

Clinton, Hillary Rodham. *Living History.* New York: Simon & Schuster, 2003.

Cockshut, A. O. J. *The Art of Autobiography in 19th and 20th Century England.* New Haven, CT: Yale University Press, 1984.

Cohen, Andrew. "A Work in Progress: Whatever Its Claims, *Living History* Is Not a Tell-All Book. Nor Is It Really a Memoir. Rather, It Is a Contrivance—A Selective Account of Hillary Clinton's First 55 Years. There Are No Secrets or Surprises." *Ottawa Citizen*, June 29, 2003: C5. LexisNexis Academic. http://www.lexisnexis.com/.

Colford, Paul D., and Thomas M. DeFrank. "Hil Book Is One in a Million. Mass Printing Planned." *Daily News*, April 29, 2003: 3. LexisNexis Academic. http//www.lexisnexis.com/.

Collected Black Women's Narratives. The Schomburg Library of Nineteenth-Century Black Women Writers. New York: Oxford University Press, 1988.

Collins, Patricia Hill. "Comment on Hekman's 'Truth and Method: Feminist Standpoint Theory Revisited': Where's the Power?" *Signs: Journal of Women in Culture and Society* 22.2 (1997): 375–81.

———. "Learning from the Outsider Within: The Sociological Significance of Black Feminist Thought." *Social Problems* 33.6 (1986): S14–S32.

Conway, Jill Ker. *When Memory Speaks: Reflections on Autobiography.* New York: Knopf, 1998.

———, ed. *Written by Herself: Autobiographies of American Women: An Anthology.* New York: Vintage Books, 1992.

Culley, Margo, ed. *American Women's Autobiography: Fea(s)ts of Memory*. Madison, WI: University of Wisconsin Press, 1992.

Deloria, Vine, Jr. *Custer Died for Your Sins*. New York: Avon Books, 1969.

———. "Intellectual Self-Determination and Sovereignty: Looking at the Windmills in Our Minds." *Wicazo Sa Review* 13.1 (1998): 25–31.

Diamond, Arlyn. "Choosing Sides, Choosing Lives: Women's Autobiographies of the Civil Rights Movement." In *American Women's Autobiography: Fea(s)ts of Memory*, edited by Margo Culley, 218–31. Madison, WI: University of Wisconsin Press, 1992.

Diamond, Irene, and Gloria Feman Ornestein, eds. *Reweaving the World: The Emergence of Ecofeminism*. San Francisco: Sierra Club, 1990.

Dixon, Lynda D. "The Cherokee Way: A Rhetorical Analysis of Principal Chief Chadwick A. 'Corntassel' Smith's Speech, 'Let Us Build One Fire.'" In *The Rhetoric of Western Thought*, 9th ed., edited by James L. Golden, Goodwin F. Berquist, William E. Coleman, J. Michael Sproule, and Ruth Golden, 433–42. Dubuque, IA: Kendall/Hunt, 2007.

Dole, Elizabeth. "An America We Can Be Speech." In *Elizabeth Hanford Dole: Speaking from the Heart*, by Molly Meijer Wertheimer and Nichola D. Gutgold, 199–205. Praeger Series in Political Communication. Westport, CT: Praeger, 2004.

———. *Hearts Touched with Fire: My 500 Favorite Inspirational Quotations*. New York: Carroll and Graf, 2004.

———. Interview with Elizabeth Dole. By Nichola Gutgold and Molly Wertheimer. July 8, 2003, Washington, D.C.

———. "National Prayer Breakfast Speech." In *Elizabeth Hanford Dole: Speaking from the Heart*, by Molly Meijer Wertheimer and Nichola D. Gutgold, 131–37. Praeger Series in Political Communication. Westport, CT: Praeger, 2004.

———. "Republican National Convention Speech, 1988." In *Elizabeth Hanford Dole: Speaking from the Heart*, by Molly Meijer Wertheimer and Nichola D. Gutgold, 147–50. Praeger Series in Political Communication. Westport, CT: Praeger, 2004.

———. "Republican National Convention Speech, 1996." In *Elizabeth Hanford Dole: Speaking from the Heart*, by Molly Meijer Wertheimer and Nichola D. Gutgold, 183–88. Praeger Series in Political Communication. Westport, CT: Praeger, 2004.

"Dole, Elizabeth Hanford." In *Current Biography Yearbook: 1997*, edited by Elizabeth A. Schick, 145–48. New York: H. W. Wilson, 1997.

Dole, Robert J., and Elizabeth Dole. *The Doles: Unlimited Partners*. With Richard Norton Smith. New York: Simon and Schuster, 1988.

———. *Unlimited Partners: Our American Story*. With Richard Norton Smith and Kerry Tymchuk. New York: Simon and Schuster, 1996.

Doriani, Beth Maclay. "Black Womanhood in Nineteenth-Century America: Subversion and Self-Construction in Two Women's Autobiographies." *American Quarterly* 43.2 (1991): 199–222. JSTOR. http://www.jstor. org/.

Drummond, A. M., and Richard Moody. "Indian Treaties: The First American Dramas." *Quarterly Journal of Speech* 34 (1953): 16–22.

Dyer, Richard. "A Full-Blooded Biography of the Cherokee Chief." *Boston Globe*, December 30, 1993, city edition, living sec.: 47. LexisNexis Academic. http://www.lexisnexis.com/.

Eakin, Paul John, ed. *American Autobiography: Retrospect and Prospect*. Wisconsin Studies in American Autobiography. Madison, WI: University of Wisconsin Press, 1991.

Einhorn, Lois J. *The Native American Oral Tradition: Voices of the Spirit and Soul.* Westport, CT: Praeger, 2000.

Felski, Rita. *Beyond Feminist Aesthetics: Feminist Literature and Social Change.* Cambridge, MA: Harvard University Press, 1989.

Ferraro, Geraldine. *Changing History: Women, Power, and Politics.* Wakefield, RI: Moyer Bell, 1998.

———. *Ferraro: My Story.* With Linda Bird Francke. Toronto: Bantam, 1985.

———. *Ferraro: My Story.* With Marie C. Wilson and Linda Bird Francke. Evanston, IL: Northwestern University Press, 2004.

———. *Framing a Life: A Family Memoir.* With Catherine Whitney. New York: Scribner, 1998.

Fisher, Walter R. "Narration as a Human Communication Paradigm: The Case of Public Moral Argument." *Communication Monographs* 51 (1984): 1–22.

Foner, Philip S., and Robert James Branham, eds. *Lift Every Voice: African American Oratory 1787–1900.* Tuscaloosa, AL: University of Alabama Press, 1998.

Foss, Karen A., and Sonja K. Foss. "The Status of Research on Women and Communication." *Communication Quarterly* 31 (1983): 195–204.

———. *Women Speak.* Prospect Heights, IL: Waveland, 1991.

Foss, Sonja K. *Rhetorical Criticism: Exploration and Practice.* 2nd ed. Prospect Heights, IL: Waveland, 1996.

Foss, Sonja K., Karen A. Foss, and Robert Trapp. *Contemporary Perspectives on Rhetoric.* Prospect Heights, IL: Waveland, 1985.

Foster, Frances Smith. *Witnessing Slavery: The Development of Ante-Bellum Slave Narratives.* 2nd ed. Madison, WI: University of Wisconsin Press, 1979.

Franklin, Vincent P. *Living Our Stories, Telling Our Truths: Autobiography and the Making of the African-American Intellectual Tradition.* New York: Oxford University Press, 1995.

Fresno (CA) Bee. "Barbara Jordan: A Remarkable Life Came to an End in Texas This Week," January 20, 1996, home edition, metro sec.: B4. LexisNexis Academic. http://www.lexisnexis.com/.

Friedman, Susan Stanford. "Women's Autobiographical Selves: Theory and Practice." In *Women, Autobiography, Theory: A Reader,* edited by Sidonie Smith and Julia Watson, 72–82. Wisconsin Studies in American Autobiography. Madison, WI: University of Wisconsin Press, 1998.

Fulton, DoVeanna S. *Speaking Power: Black Feminist Orality in Women's Narratives of Slavery.* Albany, NY: State University of New York Press, 2006.

Gaard, Greta, ed. *Ecofeminism: Women, Animals, and Nature.* Philadelphia: Temple University Press, 1993.

Gale, Maggie B., and Viv Gardner, eds. *Auto/Biography and Identity: Women, Theatre, and Performance.* Manchester, UK: Manchester University Press, 2004.

Gates, Henry Louis, Jr. *Loose Canons: Notes on the Culture Wars.* New York: Oxford University Press, 1992.

———. *The Signifying Monkey: A Theory of African-American Literary Criticism.* New York: Oxford University Press, 1988.

Gelfant, Blanche H. "Speaking Her Own Piece: Emma Goldman and the Discursive Skeins of Autobiography." In *American Autobiography: Retrospect and Prospect,* edited by Paul John Eakin, 235–66. Wisconsin Studies in American Autobiography. Madison, WI: University of Wisconsin Press, 1991.

German, Kathleen. "Figurative Language in Native American Oratory 1609–1912." *The Howard Journal of Communications* 9 (1998): 20–40.

Gilmore, Leigh. *Autobiographics: A Feminist Theory of Women's Self-Representation.* Ithaca, NY: Cornell University Press, 1994.

Golden, James L., and Richard Rieke. "Black Rhetoric." In *African American Rhetoric: A Reader,* edited by Lyndrey A. Niles, 45–70. Dubuque, IA: Kendall/Hunt, 1995.

Goldman, Anne E. "Autobiography, Ethnography, and History: A Model for Reading." In *Women, Autobiography, Theory: A Reader,* edited by Sidonie Smith and Julia Watson, 288–98. Madison, WI: University of Wisconsin Press, 1998.

Gordon, Ann D. "The Political Is the Personal: Two Autobiographies of Woman Suffragists." In *American Women's Autobiography: Fea(s)ts of Memory,* edited by Margo Culley, 111–27. Madison, WI: University of Wisconsin Press, 1992.

Grady, Sandy. "Magnificent Voice Stilled at Last." *Philadelphia Daily News,* January 23, 1996, city edition, Viewpoints: 3B. LexisNexis Academic. http://www.lexisnexis.com/.

Green, Rayna. "Native American Women." *Signs* 6.2 (1980): 248–67.

Gusdorf, Georges. "Conditions and Limits of Autobiography." In *Autobiography: Essays Theoretical and Critical,* edited by James Olney, 28–48. Princeton, NJ: Princeton University Press, 1980.

Gutgold, Nichola D. *Paving the Way for Madam President.* Lexington Studies in Political Communication. Lanham, MD: Lexington Books, 2006.

———. "The Rhetoric of Elizabeth Dole: Managing Rhetorical Roles 1987–1999." PhD diss., Pennsylvania State University, 1999.

Hamilton, Charles V. *The Black Preacher in America.* New York: William Morrow, 1972.

Harlow, Barbara. *Resistance Literature.* New York: Methuen, 1987.

Harrison, Robert D., and Linda K. Harrison. "The Call from the Mountaintop: Call-Response and the Oratory of Martin Luther King, Jr." In *Martin Luther King, Jr., and the Sermonic Power of Public Discourse,* edited by Carolyn Calloway-Thomas and John Louis Lucaites, 162–78. Tuscaloosa, AL: University of Alabama Press, 1993.

Hartman, Mary S., ed. *Talking Leadership: Conversations with Powerful Women.* New Brunswick, NJ: Rutgers University Press, 1999.

Hartsock, Nancy C. M. "The Feminist Standpoint: Developing the Ground for a Specifically Feminist Historical Materialism." In *The Feminist Standpoint Revisited and Other Essays,* by Nancy Hartsock, 105–32. Boulder, CO: Westview Press, 1998.

———. "The Feminist Standpoint Revisited." In *The Feminist Standpoint Revisited and Other Essays,* by Nancy Hartsock, 227–48. Boulder, CO: Westview Press, 1998.

———. *The Feminist Standpoint Revisited and Other Essays.* Boulder, CO: Westview Press, 1998.

———. "Political Change: Two Perspectives on Power." In *The Feminist Standpoint Revisited and Other Essays,* by Nancy Hartsock, 15–31. Boulder, CO: Westview Press, 1998.

Heilbrun, Carolyn G. *Writing a Woman's Life.* New York: Norton, 1988.

Hekman, Susan. "Truth and Method: Feminist Standpoint Theory Revisited." *Signs: Journal of Women in Culture and Society* 22.2 (1997): 341–65.

Hernández-Ávila, Inés. "Relocations Upon Relocations: Home, Language, and Native American Women's Writings." *American Indian Quarterly* 19.4 (1995): 491–507.

Holmes, Barbara A. *A Private Woman in Public Spaces: Barbara Jordan's Speeches on Ethics, Public Religion, and Law.* Harrisburg, PA: Trinity Press International, 2000.

hooks, bell. "Choosing the Margin as a Space of Radical Openness." *Framework: The Journal of Cinema and Media* 36 (1989): 15–23.

Hornsby, Alton, Jr. Review of *Barbara Jordan: A Self Portrait*, by Barbara Jordan and Shelby Hearon. *Journal of Southern History* 46 (1980): 137–38. JSTOR. http://www.jstor.org/.

Howarth, William L. "Some Principles of Autobiography." *New Literary History* 5 (1974): 363–81.

Hunter-Gault, Charlayne. "Independent, Pragmatic, and Self-Centered." Review of *Barbara Jordan: A Self Portrait*, by Barbara Jordan and Shelby Hearon. *Ms.* 7 (February 1979): 43–44.

Imbarrato, Susan Clair. *Declarations of Independency in Eighteenth-Century American Autobiography*. Knoxville, TN: University of Tennessee Press, 1998.

Ingram, Susan. *Zarathustra's Sisters: Women's Autobiography and the Shaping of Cultural History*. Toronto: University of Toronto Press, 2003.

It's My Party Too. It's My Party Too Political Action Committee (PAC). http://www.mypartytoo.com (accessed January 31, 2006).

Ivins, Molly, "She Sounded Like God." *New York Times Magazine*, 29 December 1996: A1. ProQuest Historical Newspapers. http://proquest.umi.com/.

Jackson, Ronald L. II, ed. *African American Communication and Identities: Essential Readings*. Thousand Oaks, CA: Sage, 2004.

———. "Toward an Afrocentric Methodology for the Critical Assessment of Rhetoric." In *African American Rhetoric: A Reader*, edited by Lyndrey A. Niles, 148–57. Dubuque, IA: Kendall/Hunt, 1995.

Jahn, Janeheinz. *Muntu: An Outline of the New African Culture*. Translated by Marjorie Grene. New York: Grove, 1961.

Jamieson, Kathleen Hall. *Beyond the Double Bind: Women and Leadership*. New York: Oxford University Press, 1995.

Jelinek, Estelle C. "Introduction: Women's Autobiography and the Male Tradition." In *Women's Autobiography: Essays in Criticism*, edited by Estelle C. Jelinek, 1–20. Bloomington, IN: Indiana University Press, 1980.

———. *The Tradition of Women's Autobiography: From Antiquity to the Present*. Boston: Twayne, 1986.

———, ed. *Women's Autobiography: Essays in Criticism*. Bloomington, IN: Indiana University Press, 1980.

Johansen, Bruce E., and Donald A. Grinde Jr. *The Encyclopedia of Native American Biography: Six Hundred Life Stories of Important People from Powhatan to Wilma Mankiller*. New York: De Capo Press, 1998.

Johnson, Troy. "The Occupation of Alcatraz Island: Roots of American Indian Activism." *Wicazo Sa Review* 10.2 (1994): 63–79.

Jordan, Barbara. *Barbara C. Jordan: Selected Speeches*. Ed. Sandra Parham. Washington, DC: Howard University Press, 1999.

———. "Ethical Dilemmas of Leadership." In *Barbara C. Jordan: Selected Speeches*, edited by Sandra Parham, 89–93. Washington, DC: Howard University Press, 1999.

———. "Testimony Before the House Judiciary Committee (Watergate)." In *Barbara C. Jordan: Selected Speeches*, edited by Sandra Parham, 105–8. Washington, DC: Howard University Press, 1999.

Jordan, Barbara, and Shelby Hearon. *Barbara Jordan: A Self-Portrait*. Garden City, NY: Doubleday, 1979.

Kakutani, Michiko. "Books of the Times; A 'Zone of Privacy' with Calculated Polish." *New York Times*, June 10, 2003: E1. LexisNexis Academic. http://www.lexisnexis.com/.

————. "It Pays to Be a Ghost." *New York Times.* March 18, 1979: 94. ProQuest Historical Newspapers. http://proquest.umi.com/.

Kann, Mark E. *The Gendering of American Politics: Founding Mothers, Founding Fathers, and Political Patriarchy.* Westport, CT: Praeger, 1999.

Katz, Lee Michael. *My Name Is Geraldine Ferraro.* New York: Signet, 1984.

Kazin, Alfred. "The Self as History: Reflections on Autobiography." In *Telling Lives: The Biographer's Art,* edited by Marc Pachter, 74–89. Washington, DC: New Republic Books/National Portrait Gallery, 1979.

King, Janice L., "Justificatory Rhetoric for a Female Political Candidate: A Case Study of Wilma Mankiller." *Women's Studies in Communication* 13.2 (1990): 21–38.

King, Ynestra. "Healing the Wounds: Feminism, Ecology, and the Nature/Culture Dualism." In *Reweaving the World: The Emergence of Ecofeminism,* edited by Irene Diamond and Gloria Feman Orenstein, 106–21. San Francisco: Sierra Club, 1990.

Knowles-Borishade, Adetokunbo. "Paradigm for Classical African Orature: Instrument for a Scientific Revolution?" *Journal of Black Studies* 21.4 (1991): 488–500. JSTOR. http://www.jstor.org/.

Lake, Randall A. "Between Myth and History: Enacting Time in Native American Protest Rhetoric." *Quarterly Journal of Speech* 77.2 (1991): 123–51.

————. "The Rhetor as Dialectician in 'Last Chance for Survival.'" *Communication Monographs* 53 (1986): 201–20.

Leishman, Katie. "A Very Private Public Person." *McCalls,* April 1988: 131–35.

Leonard, Mary. "Few Confessions. Hillary Rodham Clinton Is Candid about Her Coiffure, but Not Much Else, in Her Memoir, *Living History.*" *Boston Globe,* June 15, 2003: H8. LexisNexis Academic. http://www.lexisnexis.com/.

Lerner, Gerda. "Resistance and Triumph: An Interview with Gerda Lerner." By Joan Fischer. *Wisconsin Academy Review* 48.2 (2002). Wisconsin Academy of Sciences, Arts and Letters. http://www.wisconsinacademy.org.

Lewis, David Rich. "Native Americans and the Environment: A Survey of Twentieth-Century Issues." *American Indian Quarterly* 19.3 (1995): 423–50.

Lind, Michael. "More than a Voice: Barbara Jordan Stirred a Nation Not Just with Words but with Judiciousness." *Pittsburgh Post-Gazette,* January 29, 1996, sooner edition, A17. LexisNexis Academic. http://www.lexisnexis. com/.

Lisa, Laurie. "Mankiller, Wilma." In *Native American Women: A Biographical Dictionary,* edited by Gretchen M. Bataille and Laurie Lisa. New York: Garland Publishing, 1993.

Loftus, Ronald P. *Telling Lives: Women's Self-Writing in Modern Japan.* Honolulu: University of Hawai'i Press, 2004.

Logue, Cal M. "Transcending Coercion: The Communicative Strategies of Black Slaves on Antebellum Plantations. *Quarterly Journal of Speech* 67 (1981): 31–46.

Lowy, Joan. *Pat Schroeder: A Woman of the House.* Albuquerque, NM: University of New Mexico Press, 2003.

Lyons, Scott Richard. "Rhetorical Sovereignty: What Do American Indians Want from Writing?" *College Composition and Communication* 51.3 (2000): 447–68.

Mankiller, Wilma, ed. *every day is a good day: Reflections by Contemporary Indigenous Women.* Golden, CO: Fulcrum Publishing, 2004.

————. "Guest Essay." *Native Peoples: The Journal of the Heard Museum* 8 (1995): 5.

————. "A New Path for the People." In *Native Universe: Voices of Indian America,* edited by Gerald McMaster and Clifford E. Trafzer. Washington, DC: National Museum of the American Indian, Smithsonian Institution, 2004.

————. Personal communication to Emily Plec, February 26, 2007.

———. "Tribal Sovereignty." *Winter Camp Chronicles.* March 21, 1989. http://twoelk2 .tripod.com/Generations/WCCWilmaMankiller.htm.

Mankiller, Wilma, Gwendolyn Mink, Marysa Navarro, Barbara Smith, and Gloria Steinem, eds. *The Reader's Companion to the History of American Women.* Boston: Houghton Mifflin, 1998.

Mankiller, Wilma, and Michael Wallis. *Mankiller: A Chief and Her People.* New York: St. Martin's, 1993.

Marriott, Alice, and Carol K. Rachlin. *American Epic: The Story of the American Indian.* New York: G. P. Putnam's Sons, 1969.

Marshall, Brenda DeVore, and Molly A. Mayhead, eds. and contributors. *Navigating Boundaries: The Rhetoric of Women Governors.* Praeger Series in Political Communication. Westport, CT: Praeger, 2000.

Mason, Diane. "Wilma Mankiller." *St. Petersburg Times,* March 23, 1992, city edition, Tampa Bay and State sec.: 3B. LexisNexis Academic. http://www.lexisnexis.com/ universe/.

Mason, Mary G. "The Other Voice: Autobiographies of Women Writers." In *Autobiography: Essays Theoretical and Critical,* edited by James Olney, 207–35. Princeton, NJ: Princeton University Press, 1980.

Mayhead, Molly A., and Brenda DeVore Marshall. *Women's Political Discourse: A Twenty-First Century Perspective.* Communication, Media, and Politics Series. Lanham, MD: Rowman & Littlefield, 2005.

McClish, Glen and Jacqueline Bacon. "'Telling the Story Her Own Way': The Role of Feminist Standpoint Theory in Rhetorical Studies." *Rhetoric Society Quarterly* 32.2 (2002): 27–55.

McKay, Nellie Y. "The Narrative Self: Race, Politics, and Culture in Black American Women's Autobiography." In *Women, Autobiography, Theory: A Reader,* edited by Sidonie Smith and Julia Watson, 96–107. Madison, WI: University of Wisconsin Press, 1998.

Mead, Walter Russell. "Woman of the World: How a Secretary of State Came to Age on the Global Stage." *Washington Post,* October 26, 2003: T04. http://infoweb .newsbank.com/.

Mendelsohn, James. *Barbara Jordan: Getting Things Done.* Brookfield, CT: Twenty-First Century Books/Millbrook Press, 2000.

Merchant, Carolyn. *The Death of Nature: Women, Ecology and the Scientific Revolution.* San Francisco: HarperCollins, 1980.

———. "Ecofeminism and Feminist Theory." In *Reweaving the World: The Emergence of Ecofeminism,* edited by Irene Diamond and Gloria Feman Orenstein, 100–105. San Francisco: Sierra Club, 1990.

Middleton, Joyce Irene. "'Both Print and Oral' and 'Talking about Race': Transforming Toni Morrison's Language Issues into Teaching Issues." In *African American Rhetoric(s): Interdisciplinary Perspectives,* edited by Elaine B. Richardson and Ronald L. Jackson II, 242–58. Carbondale, IL: Southern Illinois University Press, 2004.

Milbank, Dana. "Whitman's Moderation in Opposition Won't Win Her Fight Within GOP." *Washington Post,* April 2, 2005, final edition: A06.

Miller, Matt. "A Bigger Tent." Review of *It's My Party Too* by Christine Todd Whitman. *New York Times,* February 6, 2005, late edition, sec. 7: 15. http://www.nytimes.com.

Miller, Nancy K. *But Enough about Me: Why We Read Other People's Lives.* New York: Columbia University Press, 2002.

———. *Subject to Change: Reading Feminist Writing*. New York: Columbia University Press, 1988.

Minzesheimer, Bob. "Clinton's Memoir Sets Torrid Pace." *USA Today*, December 26, 2003: 10D. LexisNexis Academic. http://www.lexisnexis.com/.

Morgan, Robin, ed. *Sisterhood Is Forever: The Women's Anthology for a New Millennium*. New York: Washington Square Press, 2003.

Morris, Richard. "Educating Savages." *Quarterly Journal of Speech* 83 (1997): 152–71.

Morris, Richard, and Philip Wander. "Native American Rhetoric: Dancing in the Shadows of the Ghost Dance." *Quarterly Journal of Speech* 76 (1990): 164–91.

Murphy, John. M. "Knowing the President: The Dialogic Evolution of the Campaign History." *Quarterly Journal of Speech* 84 (1998): 23–40.

Murphy, Marjorie N. "Silence, the Word, and Indian Rhetoric." *College Composition and Communication* 21.5 (1970): 356–63.

Nagel, Joane. "American Indian Ethnic Renewal: Politics and the Resurgence of Identity." *American Sociological Review* 60.6 (1995): 947–65.

Neuman, Shirley, ed. *Autobiography and Questions of Gender*. London: Frank Cass, 1991.

Northcott, Kaye. "Without a Doubt." Review of *Barbara Jordan: A Self Portrait*, by Barbara Jordan and Shelby Hearon. *New York Times Book Review*, 18 February 1979: BR3–BR4.

Old Coyote, Barney. "Contemporary American Indian Rhetoric." Address, annual meeting of the Speech Communication Association, New York, 1973. In *Native American Reader: Stories, Speeches and Poems*, edited by Jerry D. Blanche, 86–90. Juneau, AK: Denali Press, 1990.

Old Person, Earl. "Contemporary American Indian Rhetoric—Another View." Address, annual meeting of the Speech Communication Association, New York, 1973. In *Native American Reader: Stories, Speeches and Poems*, edited by Jerry D. Blanche, 91–94. Juneau, AK: Denali Press, 1990.

Olney, James. "Autobiography and the Cultural Moment: A Thematic, Historical, and Bibliographical Introduction." In *Autobiography: Essays Theoretical and Critical*, edited by James Olney, 3–27. Princeton, NJ: Princeton University Press, 1980.

———, ed. *Autobiography: Essays Theoretical and Critical*. Princeton, NJ: Princeton University Press, 1980.

———. *Memory and Narrative: The Weave of Life-Writing*. Chicago: University of Chicago Press, 1998.

———. *Metaphors of Self: The Meaning of Autobiography*. Princeton, NJ: Princeton University Press, 1972.

———, ed. *Studies in Autobiography*. New York: Oxford University Press, 1988.

———. "The Value of Autobiography for Comparative Studies: African vs. Western Autobiography." In *African American Autobiography: A Collection of Critical Essays*, edited by William L. Andrews, 212–23. Englewood Cliffs, NJ: Prentice Hall, 1993.

Ong, Walter J. *Orality and Literacy: The Technologizing of the Word*. London: Methuen, 1982.

Orbe, Michael P. *Constructing Co-Cultural Theory: An Explication of Culture, Power, and Communication*. Thousand Oaks, CA: Sage, 1998.

Pachter, Marc, ed. *Telling Lives: The Biographer's Art*. Washington, DC: New Republic Books/National Portrait Gallery, 1979.

Page, Susan. "'Madame Secretary': It's Albright Unplugged." *USA Today*, September 16, 2003: 5D. Ebscohost. http://ebscohost.com/.

"Patricia Schroeder in Conversation with Ruth B. Mandel and Mary S. Hartman." In *Talking Leadership: Conversations with Powerful Women*, edited by Mary S. Hartman, 217–35. New Brunswick, NJ: Rutgers University Press, 1999.

Perdue, Theda. *Cherokee Women: Gender and Culture Change 1700–1835*. Lincoln, NE: University of Nebraska Press, 1998.

Perkins, Margo V. *Autobiography as Activism: Three Black Women of the Sixties*. Jackson, MS: University Press of Mississippi, 2000.

Personal Narratives Group. *Interpreting Women's Lives*. Bloomington, IN: Indiana University, 1989.

Philipsen, Gerry. "Navajo World View and Culture Patterns of Speech: A Case Study in Ethnorhetoric." *Speech Monographs* 2 (1972): 132–39.

Plumwood, Val. *Feminism and the Mastery of Nature*. New York: Routledge, 1993.

Pope, Victoria, and Jerelyn Eddings. "An Iron Fist in a Velvet Glove." *U.S. News & World Report*, August 1996: 26+. EbscoHost. http://web.ebscohost. com/.

Popkin, Jeremy D. "Historians on the Autobiographical Frontier." *American Historical Review* 104.3 (1999): 725–48. JSTOR. http://jstor.org.

———. *History, Historians, and Autobiography*. Chicago: University of Chicago Press, 2005.

"Reading Senator Clinton." *New York Times*, June 11, 2003: 30. LexisNexis Academic. http://www.lexisnexis.com/.

Reaves, Michael Crawford. "Wilma Mankiller (1945–)." In *Significant Contemporary American Feminists: A Biographical Sourcebook*, edited by Jennifer Scanlon. Westport, CT: Greenwood, 1999.

Richardson, Elaine B., and Ronald L. Jackson II, eds. *African American Rhetoric(s): Interdisciplinary Perspectives*. Carbondale, IL: Southern Illinois University Press, 2004.

Rodriguez, Barbara. *Autobiographical Inscriptions: Form, Personhood, and the American Woman Writer of Color*. New York: Oxford University Press, 1999.

Rogers, Mary Beth. *Barbara Jordan: American Hero*. New York: Bantam Books, 1998.

Rosen, Ruth. "Hillary's Legacy as First Lady." *San Francisco Chronicle*, August 7, 2003: A21. LexisNexis Academic. http://www.lexisnexis.com/.

Rosenblatt, Roger. "Black Autobiography: Life as the Death Weapon." In *Autobiography: Essays Theoretical and Critical*, edited by James Olney, 169–80. Princeton, NJ: Princeton University Press, 1980.

Royster, Jacqueline Jones. Foreword. In *African American Rhetoric(s): Interdisciplinary Perspectives*, edited by Elaine B. Richardson and Ronald L. Jackson II. Carbondale, IL: Southern Illinois University Press, 2004.

———. *Traces of a Stream: Literary and Social Change Among African American Women*. Pittsburgh: University of Pittsburgh Press, 2000.

Sandstrom, Karen. "Hillary Offers Facts But Little Insight; The Woman Behind the Story Remains Distant." *Plain Dealer*, June 15, 2003: J13. LexisNexis Academic. http://www.lexisnexis.com/.

Sattler, Richard A. "Women's Status Among the Muskogee and Cherokee." In *Women and Power in Native North America*, edited by Laura F. Klein and Lillian A. Ackerman. Norman, OK: University of Oklahoma Press, 1995.

Sayre, Robert F. "Autobiography and the Making of America." In *Autobiography: Essays Theoretical and Critical*, edited by James Olney, 146–68. Princeton, NJ: Princeton University Press, 1980.

———. "The Proper Study: Autobiographies in American Studies." *American Quarterly* 29.3 (1977): 241–62.

Schenck, William. Review of *Barbara Jordan: A Self Portrait,* by Barbara Jordan and Shelby Hearon. *Library Journal* 104 (January 15, 1979): 178.

Schoenfeld, Gabriel. "Altered State: Review of *Madame Secretary: A Memoir* by Madeleine Albright. *Commentary,* January 2004: 69–72. http://infotrace.galegroup.com/.

Scholten, Pat Creech. "Exploitation of Ethos: Sarah Winnemucca and Bright Eyes on the Lecture Tour." *Western Journal of Speech Communication* 41.4 (1977): 233–44.

Schroeder, Pat. *Champion of the Great American Family.* With Andrea Camp and Robyn Lipner. New York: Random House, 1989.

———. "Running for Our Lives: Electoral Politics." In *Sisterhood Is Forever: The Woman's Anthology for a New Millennium,* edited by Robin Morgan, 28–42. New York: Washington Square Press, 2003.

———. *24 Years of House Work . . . and the Place Is Still a Mess: My Life in Politics.* Kansas City, MO: Andrews McMeel, 1998.

"Schroeder, Patricia." *Current Biography.* New York: H.W. Wilson, 1978. Biographies Plus Illustrated. vnweb.hwwilson.web.com.

Shaw, Lorna L. "Orature: A New Perspective in the Study of Human Communication." In *African American Rhetoric: A Reader,* edited by Lyndrey A. Niles, 117–21. Dubuque, IA: Kendall/Hunt, 1995.

Shelby, Annette. "The Southern Lady Becomes an Advocate." In *Oratory in the New South,* edited by. Waldo W. Braden, 204–36. Baton Rouge, LA: Louisiana State University Press, 1979.

Shumaker, Wayne. *English Autobiography: Its Emergence, Materials, and Forum.* Berkeley, CA: Berkeley University Press, 1954.

Smith, Arthur L., ed. *Language, Communication, and Rhetoric in Black America.* New York: Harper & Row, 1972.

———. "Markings of an African Concept of Rhetoric." In *Language, Communication, and Rhetoric in Black America,* edited by Arthur L. Smith, 363–74. New York: Harper & Row, 1972.

———. *See also* Asante, Molefi Kete.

Smith, Sidonie. "The Autobiographical Manifesto: Identities, Temporalities, Politics." In *Autobiography and Questions of Gender,* edited by Shirley Neuman, 186–212. London: Frank Cass, 1991.

———. "Construing Truth in Lying Mouths: Truthtelling in Women's Autobiography." In *Women and Autobiography,* edited by Martine Watson Brownley and Allison B. Kimmich, 33–52. Wilmington, DE: Scholarly Resources, 1999.

———. *A Poetics of Women's Autobiography: Marginality and the Fictions of Self-Representation.* Bloomington, IN: Indiana University Press, 1987.

———. *Where I'm Bound: Patterns of Slavery and Freedom in Black American Autobiography.* Contributions in American Studies 16. Westport, CT: Greenwood, 1974.

Smith, Sidonie, and Julia Watson, eds. *Before They Could Vote: American Women's Autobiographical Writing, 1819–1919.* Women's Studies in Autobiography. Madison, WI: University of Wisconsin Press, 2006.

———, eds. *Getting a Life: Everyday Uses of Autobiography.* Minneapolis: University of Minnesota Press, 1996.

———. Introduction. In *Getting a Life: Everyday Uses of Autobiography,* edited by Sidonie Smith and Julia Watson, 1–24. Minneapolis: University of Minnesota Press, 1996.

———. *Reading Autobiography: A Guide for Interpreting Life Narratives.* Minneapolis: University of Minnesota Press, 2001.

———, eds. *Women, Autobiography, Theory: A Reader*. Wisconsin Studies in American Autobiography. Madison, WI: University of Wisconsin Press, 1998.

Smitherman, Geneva. *Talkin and Testifyin: The Language of Black America*. Boston: Houghton Mifflin, 1977.

———. *Talkin That Talk: Language, Culture, and Education in African America*. London: Routledge, 1999.

Solomon, Martha. "Autobiographies as Rhetorical Narratives: Elizabeth Cady Stanton and Anna Howard Shaw as 'New Women.'" *Communication Studies* 42 (1991): 354–70.

———. *See also* Watson, Martha.

Sommer, Doris. "Not Just a Personal Story: Women's Testimonies and the Plural Self." In *Life Lines: Theorizing Women's Autobiography*, edited by Bella Brodzki and Celeste Schenck. Ithaca, NY: Cornell University Press, 1988.

Sorber, Edna C. "Indian Eloquence as American Public Address." *The Indian Historian* 5 (1972): 40–46.

Spacks, Patricia Meyer. "Selves in Hiding." In *Women's Autobiography: Essays in Criticism*, edited by Estelle C. Jelinek, 112–32. Bloomington, IN: Indiana University Press, 1980.

Spengemann, William C. *The Forms of Autobiography: Episodes in the History of a Literary Genre*. New Haven, CT: Yale University Press, 1980.

Spretnak, Charlene. "Ecofeminism: Our Roots and Flowering." *Reweaving the World: The Emergence of Ecofeminism,* edited by Irene Diamond and Gloria Feman Orenstein, 3–14. San Francisco: Sierra Club, 1990.

Stanton, Domna C. "Autogynography: Is the Subject Different?" In *The Female Autograpy: Theory and Practice of Autobiography from the Tenth to the Twentieth Century*, edited by Domna C. Stanton, 3–20. Chicago: University of Chicago Press, 1984.

Stengel, Richard. "Liddy Makes Perfect," *Time*, 1 July 1996: 30–37.

Stepto, Robert B. *From Behind the Veil: A Study of Afro-American Narrative*. 2nd ed. Urbana, IL: University of Illinois Press, 1991.

Stone, Albert E. *Autobiographical Occasions and Original Acts: Versions of American Identity from Henry Adams to Nate Shaw*. Philadelphia: University of Pennsylvania Press, 1982.

———. "Modern American Autobiography: Texts and Transactions." In *American Autobiography: Retrospect and Prospect*, edited by Paul John Eakin, 95–120. Wisconsin Studies in American Autobiography. Madison, WI: University of Wisconsin Press, 1991.

Stover, Johnnie M. *Rhetoric and Resistance in Black Women's Autobiography*. Gainesville, FL: University Press of Florida, 2003.

Strickland, Rennard, and William M. Strickland. "Beyond the Trail of Tears: One Hundred Fifty Years of Cherokee Survival." In *Cherokee Removal: Before and After*, edited by William A. Anderson. Athens, GA: University of Georgia Press, 1991.

Strickland, William M. "The Rhetoric of Removal and the Trail of Tears: Cherokee Speaking Against Jackson's Indian Removal Policy, 1828–1832." *Southern Speech Communication Journal* 47 (1982): 292–309.

Thompson, Robert Farris. *African Art in Motion: Icon and Act*. Los Angeles: University of California Press, 1974.

Tilleman, Tomicah. "Review of *Madame Secretary*." *SAIS Review* 24.1 (2004): 195–97.

Tompkins, Philip. "The Rhetorical Criticism of Non-Oratorical Works. *Quarterly Journal of Speech* 55.4 (1969): 431–39.

Tuchman, Barbara W. "Biography as a Prism of History." In *Telling Lives: The Biographer's Art*, edited by Marc Pachter. 133–47. Washington, DC: New Republic Books/National Portrait Gallery, 1979.

Turner, Sarah E. "'Spider Woman's Granddaughter': Autobiographical Writings by Native American Women." *MELUS* 22.4 (1997): 109–32.

"2000 Campaign, The." *Newsweek*, 18 January 1999: 4.

Tymchuk, Kerry. Interview with Kerry Tymchuk. By Nichola Gutgold. September 11, 2000, Beaverton, Oregon.

Wagner-Martin, Linda. *Telling Women's Lives: The New Biography*. New Brunswick, NJ: Rutgers University Press, 1994.

Walker, Tom. "Review: Hillary's Memoir Riveting. Book Far More Than Just Titillating Tidbits." *Denver Post*, June 12, 2003: F1. LexisNexis Academic. http://www.lexisnexis.com/.

Warren, Karen. *Ecofeminist Philosophy: A Western Perspective On What It Is and Why It Matters*. New York: Rowman and Littlefield, 2000.

Waters, Kate. Review of *Barbara Jordan: A Self-Portrait*, by Barbara Jordan and Shelby Hearon. *School Library Journal* 26 (October 1979): 166.

Watson, Martha. *Lives of Their Own: Rhetorical Dimensions in Autobiographies of Women Activists*. With James Kimble. Columbia, SC: University of South Carolina Press, 1999.

———. *See also* Solomon, Martha.

Wertheimer, Molly, and Nichola D. Gutgold. *Elizabeth Hanford Dole: Speaking from the Heart*. Praeger Series in Political Communication. Greenwich, CT: Praeger, 2004.

White, Hayden V. *The Content of the Form: Narrative Discourse and Historical Representation*. Baltimore. MD: Johns Hopkins University Press, 1987.

Whitman, Christine Todd. *It's My Party Too: The Battle for the Heart of the GOP and the Future of America*. New York: Penguin Press, 2005.

Williams, Ian. "A Faithful Servant." *The Nation*, 23 February 2004: 32–36. http://infotrace.galegroup.com/.

Williams, Kimmika L. H. "Ties that Bind: A Comparative Analysis of Zora Neale Hurston's and Geneva Smitherman's Work." In *African American Rhetoric(s): Interdisciplinary Perspectives*, edited by. Elaine B. Richardson and Ronald L. Jackson II, 86–107. Carbondale, IL: Southern Illinois University Press, 2004.

Wilson, Darryl. "Wilma Pearl Mankiller." In *Notable Native Americans*, edited by Sharon Malinowski. New York: Gale Research, 1995.

Wilson, Marie C. *Closing the Leadership Gap: Why Women Can and Must Help Run the World*. New York: Viking, 2004.

Wong, Hertha D. Sweet. "First-Person Plural: Subjectivity and Community in Native American Women's Autobigoraphy." In *Women, Autobiography, Theory: A Reader*, edited by Sidonie Smith and Julia Watson, 96–107. Madison, WI: University of Wisconsin Press, 1998.

———. *Sending My Heart Back Across the Years: Tradition and Innovation in Native American Autobiography*. New York: Oxford University Press, 1992.

Wood, Julia. *Communication Theories in Action: An Introduction*. 3rd ed. Belmont, CA: Wadsworth, 2004.

———. "Feminist Standpoint Theory and Muted Group Theory: Commonalities and Divergences." *Women and Language* 28.2 (2005); 61–64.

———. *Gendered Lives: Communication, Gender, and Culture*, 4th ed. Belmont, CA: Wadsworth Thomson Learning, 2001.

Zaeske, Susan. "The 'Promiscuous Audience' Controversy and the Emergence of the Early Women's Rights Movements." *Quarterly Journal of Speech* 81 (1995): 191–207.
Zehren, Charles V. "Convention '96/More than Just a Supportive Spouse." *Newsday*, August 15, 1996: A06.

Index

Jordan, Barbara, x, 2, 3, 14, 15–18, 28–53, 55, 186; at Boston University, 36-37, 38, 40, 45, 46; in Congress, 15, 17, 34, 37–39, 40, 44, 49, 50, 51; education of, 35, 42–43, 44–45; and family, 16, 29, 31, 33–34, 36, 41, 42, 43, 45, 46; keynote addresses of, 15, 32, 39, 51; and marriage, 34; physical incapacity, 17, 32; and privacy, 31–32, 33, 34, 51; and religion, 41; in Texas Senate, 15, 36, 38, 47, 48, 49; and Watergate, 32, 37, 38, 49; voice of, 15, 16, 17, 29, 30, 31, 50, 52, 53
Jordan, Ben, 43

Kempe, Margery, 8
Kimmich, Allison, 3
Kissinger, Henry, 147, 160
kitchen table(s), 144; campaign organized around, 55; issues, 4, 144; media, 61
Knauer, Virginia, 98
Knowles-Borishade, Adetokunbo, 27
Koppel, Ted, 78, 81, 82

Lerner, Gerda, 7, 70
Lewinsky, Monica, 131, 140, 158, 159
liberal feminism, 123, 132, 134, 138, 139, 145n2
Lyndon B. Johnson School of Public Affairs, 17, 51
Lyons, Scott Richard, 118, 126
lyrical code, 27

Mankiller, Wilma, x, 2, 4, 13, 109–29, 186; achievements of, 115; as candidate, 114; as Chief of the Cherokee Nation, 109, 11, 114, 115, 125, 128n7; childhood of, 111–12; as Community Development Director, 113; and kidney disease, 114, 115, 116; and lymphoma, 116; winner of Presidential Medal of Freedom, 116
marginalized groups, 52, 150, 164
Mason, Mary, 8
McKay, Nellie, 21, 23
Meir, Golda, 161
Methodism, 132, 134, 139–41
Mondale, Vice President Walter, 98

Morgan, Robin, 69
Murphy, John M., 133
Muskie, Senator Edmund, 154

narrative paradigm, 147, 150, 162, 163, 165
National Labor Relations Board, 61
National Women's Political Caucus, 61
Native American(s), 110, 115, 118, 124, 126
Native American rhetoric, 4, 110, 116, 118
Native American women, 122, 124, 127
nature, 110, 112, 118, 121, 122, 123, 127
network(s), 156, 157, 181, 182; old girls', 97
Nixon, President Richard, 64, 98
nommo, 26, 27, 28, 31, 51
North, Oliver, 68

Olney, James, 7, 9, 12, 22
oppression, 25, 44, 58, 76, 89, 92, 123, 164; experience of, 57; resistance to, 21; of women, 87
oratorical autobiography, 11, 167–68, 169, 172, 182
orature, 25
Orbe, Mark, 57
outsider(s), 150, 151, 152, 163, 164
outsider-within, 57, 58, 69, 70, 164

Packwood, Senator Bob, 66
Pan-African culture, 20
Panetta, Leon, 156
Patten, Arlyne, 43
Patten, John Ed (Grandpa), 30, 31, 35, 42, 43, 44, 52
Pelosi, Congresswoman Nancy, ix, x, 71
Perkins, Margo, 176, 179
personal life, 29, 33, 35, 160
Pinochet, General Augusto, 68
Planned Parenthood, 61
Popkin, Jeremy, 12
power, 5, 16, 23, 26, 27, 50, 52, 66, 69, 99, 101, 120, 123, 126, 145, 148, 149, 157, 163, 165, 185; American, 160; brokers, 66, 67; of community,

About the Contributors

Karrin Vasby Anderson is associate professor of Speech Communication at Colorado State University, where she teaches courses in political communication, U.S. public address, and public speaking. She received her Ph.D. from Indianan University (Bloomington). Her research on gender and contemporary U.S. political culture has been published in journals such as *Communication and Critical/Cultural Studies, Rhetoric & Public Affairs,* and *Women's Studies in Communication,* and in anthologies such as *American Voices: An Encyclopedia of Contemporary Orators* and *Inventing a Voice: The Rhetoric of American First Ladies of the Twentieth Century.* Professor Anderson is the recipient of the 2003 Feminist Scholarship Award from the Organization for Research on Women and Communication, and co-recipient (with Kristina Horn Sheeler) of the 2005 Carrie Chapman Catt Prize for Research on Women in Politics. Her first book (co-authored with Sheeler), entitled *Governing Codes: Gender, Metaphor, and Political Identity,* was a short-list candidate for the Doris Graber Award, sponsored by the American Political Science Association. Anderson and Sheeler currently are completing their second book together on gender and the U.S. presidency.

Catherine A. Dobris is an associate professor and the Director of Graduate Studies in the Department of Communication Studies at Indiana University, Indianapolis. She also is an adjunct professor in the Department of English and in Women's Studies. She received her Ph.D. from Indiana University (Bloomington). Professor Dobris teaches courses in contemporary rhetorical theory and criticism and in women's studies. Currently, she is involved in a long-term project with Dr. Kim White-Mills, also of Indiana University, Indianapolis, utilizing a feminist perspective to understand how the rhetoric of childcare influences contemporary parenting practices. Additional research interests include examinations of the intersections of gender, class, race, culture, and ethnicity in rhetorical contexts.

Nichola D. Gutgold is associate professor of Speech Communication at Penn State University, Lehigh Valley, where she coordinates the communication across the curriculum initiative. She received her Ph.D. from Penn State University. Professor Gutgold received the 2004 Penn State Advising Award for the Lehigh Valley Campus, the 2002 Lehigh Valley Campus Teaching Excellence Award, and the 1997 Student Appreciation and Recognition Award. She is author of *Paving the Way for Madam President* (Lexington Books 2006), and co-author, with Molly Meijer Wertheimer, of *Elizabeth Hanford Dole: Speaking from the Heart* (Praeger Press 2004). Her other publishing credits include book chapters and journal articles in *Communication Teacher, Women and Language, The Speech Communication Association of PA Annual, Successful Professor, The Review of Communication, Iowa Communication Journal,* and the *South Dakota Journal of Speech and Theatre* as well as a feature in Brydon and Scott's 2005 public speaking text *Between One and Many: The Art and Science of Public Speaking.*

Brenda DeVore Marshall is professor and chair of Theatre and Communication Arts at Linfield College in McMinnville, Oregon. She received her Ph.D. from Southern Illinois University—Carbondale. Her research interests include women's political rhetoric and the rhetorical nature of the arts. With Dr. Molly Mayhead, she co-edited and contributed to *Navigating Boundaries: The Rhetoric of Women Governors* (Praeger 2000) and co-authored *Women's Political Discourse: A Twenty-First Century Perspective* (Rowman and Littlefield 2005). Professor Marshall teaches courses across the communication discipline, including rhetorical theory and criticism, women's political rhetoric, U.S. public address, intercultural, interpersonal, gendered and public communication as well as feminist theory in the college's Gender Studies Program. The recipient of Linfield's Edith Green Distinguished Professor and Samuel Graf Faculty Achievement awards, she participates actively in faculty governance, including service as chair of the Faculty Executive Council, Title IX officer, and faculty trustee. She enjoys gardening, reading, and walking along the Oregon coast with her husband, scenic designer Tyrone Marshall.

Molly A. Mayhead is professor of Communication Studies at Western Oregon University in Monmouth. She received her Ph.D. from Penn State University. Her research interests include Supreme Court rhetoric, women's political discourse, and First Amendment issues. She collaborated with Dr. Brenda DeVore Marshall to write and edit *Navigating Boundaries: The Rhetoric of Women Governors,* published by Praeger in 2000 and to author *Women's Political Discourse: A Twenty-First Century Perspective,* published by Rowman and Littlefield in 2005. Professor Mayhead teaches courses in argumentation, public speaking, rhetorical criticism, freedom of speech, and the rhetoric of the women's movement. She is very active in the faculty union where she serves as chief grievance officer. She lives on a five-acre farm with her husband, renowned presidential scholar Ed Dover.

Emily Plec is an associate professor of Communication Studies at Western Oregon University. She received her Ph.D. from the University of Utah. Her teaching and research areas include rhetoric, intercultural communication, media studies, and environmental communication. A commitment to social justice informs her perspective on communication. She loves dogs, hiking, cheese, backgammon, chocolate, and Pinot Noir. Professor Plec has authored and co-authored several articles, reviews, and book chapters appearing in *The Howard Journal of Communications, The Environmental Communication Yearbook, Communication Teacher, The Journal of the Northwest Communication Association, Studies in Frank Waters, Rhetoric and Public Affairs, The Southern Communication Journal, The American Journal of Semiotics,* and *New Approaches to Rhetoric.*

Kristina Horn Sheeler is an assistant professor of Communication Studies at Indiana University Purdue University Indianapolis (IUPUI). She received her Ph.D. from Indiana University (Bloomington). She teaches undergraduate and graduate courses in persuasion, gender, political communication, and public communication. Professor Sheeler also teaches courses in gender and communication and public communication internationally at South East European University in Tetovo, Macedonia, and has published with co-author Biljana Sazdanovska "Macedonian and US Students' Perceptions of Gender and the Opportunity for Change" in the *SEEU Review.* With co-author Karrin Vasby Anderson, Professor Sheeler has published *Governing Codes: Gender, Metaphor, and Political Identity.* She has published in *Women's Studies in Communication* as well as book chapters in *Navigating Boundaries: The Rhetoric of Women Governors* edited by Brenda DeVore Marshall and Molly A. Mayhead, *American Voices: An Encyclopedia of Contemporary Orators* edited by Bernard Duffy and Richard Leeman, and *The Executive Branch of State Government: People, Process, and Politics* edited by Margaret R. Ferguson.

C. Brant Short is a native of Idaho and received his B.A. in History and M.A. in Speech Communication from Idaho State University. He received his Ph.D. from Indiana University in Speech Communication and has taught at Southwest Texas University, Idaho State University, and Northern Arizona University, where he is professor of Speech Communication. Professor Short has published essays in numerous journals, including *Presidential Studies Quarterly, Journal of Religion and Popular Culture, Western Journal of Communication,* and *Communication Studies* as well as chapters in many books and conference proceedings. He is author of *Ronald Reagan the Public Lands: America's Conservation Debate, 1979–1984* (1989) and editor of two sets of conference proceedings. In 2000–2001, he was the Bradley Senior Fellow at the Montana Historical Society and is working on a biography of Senator Lee Metcalf as well as a book, with Dayle Hardy-Short, on the social construction of wildfire in the American West.